UNSEEN FORCES

A GUIDE FOR THE TRULY ATTENTIVE

UNSEEN FORCES

A GUIDE FOR THE TRULY ATTENTIVE

The search for a new approach to observing
and interpreting the world of physical phenomena

edited by
J. DOUGLAS KENYON

FROM THE ATLANTIS RISING® MAGAZINE LIBRARY

Published in 2016 by Atlantis Rising®
Distributed to the trade by Red Wheel/Weiser, LLC
65 Parker St., Unit 7 • Newburyport, MA 01950-4600
www.redwheelweiser.com

ISBN: 978-0-9906904-5-0

Library of Congress Cataloging Data available on request

Cover and text design by Kathryn Sky-Peck
Photos and Illustrations © *Atlantis Rising Magazine*

PRINTED IN THE UNITED STATES OF AMERICA
MG
10 9 8 7 6 5 4 3 2 1

CONTENTS

Part Three:
Ancient High Technology

Part Four:
Egypt the Unknown

PART FIVE:
ENDANGERED PLANET

PART SIX:
NATURAL ORDER REVEALED

PART SEVEN:
CHALLENGING THE CONVENTIONAL WISDOM

WHO IS PAYING ATTENTION?

BY J. DOUGLAS KENYON

In case you may have missed it, in the last few years a virtual revolution has occurred in the way we think about some of the greatest mysteries in history and science. This book provides some astonishing evidence about a variety of such mysteries, and—we venture to guess—you will find many of them very hard to ignore. However, while you may realize that you need to pay attention, it might surprise you to learn that many of our most trusted institutions are *not* paying attention—at least not in a meaningful way.

Not too long ago we were watching a rerun of the History Channel's report on "Japan's Underwater Pyramids" (*History's Mysteries*). The episode focused on an investigation of recent discoveries near Okinawa, which some believe to be artifacts from a lost civilization and others think are natural formations. The program offered interviews with alternative science stars like Graham Hancock, Robert Schoch, and John Anthony West. It is, of course, great fun to watch the mainstream media wrestle with the shocking possibility that the standard historical paradigm—which says, for one thing, civilization is only about 5,000 years old—might have some holes. We certainly do that in the pages of this book. But lest anyone get the idea that the History Channel and similar outlets have finally begun to see the light, we say, "Not so fast."

The truth, as we see it, is that while the History Channel, and others, have awakened to the audience-building possibilities in programs like *Ancient Aliens*, they yet persist in many shallow distortions of crucial detail, and only the most avid students of the subject can hope to assemble anything like a reliable picture of the state of current research.

One of the comments offered by the History Channel was a reference to the "Bimini Road"—the underwater structure found in the Bahamas in the 1960s by the late Manson Valentine. The Bimini Road, they asserted, had been declared ordinary beach-rock and nothing more—in other words, debunked. On the contrary, the Bimini Road, and other nearby sites, primarily at Andros Island, have now been clearly shown to be prehistoric port facilities, and the so-called research used to discredit the original discovery has, itself, been completely discredited (all of this has been thoroughly reported by archaeologist Dr. Gregory Little and others in the pages of our magazine *Atlantis Rising*). But you are not likely to learn much about it from the History Channel and other mass outlets.

The Bimini Road reference seems more illustrative of the "big lie" phenomenon, long understood by propagandists of all sorts: If a falsehood, or distortion, is told often and loudly enough it will eventually come to be accepted as truth. At that point, undoing the damage could require something more like a revolution. The situation seems particularly difficult in an age when simply getting people to pay attention is difficult, to say the least.

American journalist and syndicated columnist Ellen Goodman recently quoted "former Microsoft techie" Linda Stone that ours is an era of "continuous partial attention." Says Goodman, "At the extreme end are teenagers messaging while talking on the cell phone, downloading music, and doing homework. But adults too live with all systems go, interrupted and distracted, scanning everything, multi-technological-tasking everywhere."

In such a time, Goodman thinks that only the printed word as it might appear in a personal note can truly command an individual's full attention. Such communication, she thinks, may become the ultimate aphrodisiac. Imagine what a sonnet could do.

In an age of increasing polarization, the difficulty of presenting a balanced point of view on sensitive issues is much like walking a tightrope. Though we intend to challenge the entrenched positions of many vested interests, it is not our intention to be identified with their entrenched opposition, because we see problems with the other side as well.

Meanwhile, the scientific establishment, which, we are told, is committed to the pursuit of facts without regard to consequences, draws its authority from a badly corrupted peer review system. Yet simultaneously, important alternative research is virtually excluded from the process.

In the religious domain, as controversy over Dan Brown's novel, and movie, *The Da Vinci Code*, and its sequels, has evolved, many defenders of orthodox Christianity have bitterly rejected what they call bogus history and angrily insisted that the origins of Christianity are just what we have been told, and indeed not the version suggested by *The Da Vinci Code,* with its goddess gospel, paganism, secret societies, and so forth. On the other hand, many who subscribe to what might be termed new age spirituality feel that Brown is actually misrepresenting and distorting a message which deserves to be more fairly and completely told.

In times when the unfortunate cartoon depiction of a prophet can provoke terrorist events around the world, when some believe our elected leaders are out to destroy us, and others argue that nature herself is in the employ of dark forces, one may be forgiven for thinking that reason has been driven into exile and rage itself rules.

Still, as has been said, "It is better to light one candle than to curse the darkness." It is also worth remembering Rudyard Kipling's famous advice: to keep our heads, though all about may be losing theirs.

The "process," after all, we continue to believe, is nature's way of correcting long-standing imbalances and its active unfoldment remains more a cause for hope than alarm.

These days, many of us are learning to take a new look at the role of the "observer" in the world of physical phenomena. Even the popular media has been reminding us that the so-called objective world may not be so objective after all—that the subjective reality may be, indeed, the supreme reality. As in the science fiction thriller *The Matrix,* we suspect we are living in a dream, albeit one from which it is very difficult to awaken.

PART ONE

SCIENCE AT THE EDGE

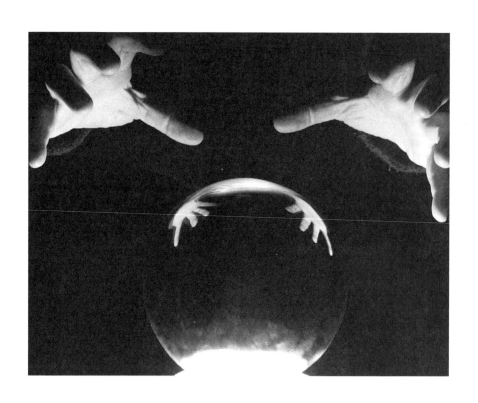

1

CAN WE SEE THE FUTURE?

Scientists, Citing New Research, Say the Answer Is Yes

BY JOHN KETTLER

According to his interview on the Orion Books web site, Dr. Danny Penman has "a degree in Applied Biology and a Ph.D. in Biochemistry from the University of Liverpool," plus a "diploma in Newspaper Journalism from City University in London."

He writes for both the magazine *New Scientist* and the British paper *Daily Mail*. In a piece for the *Mail*, the self-described "hard-bitten skeptic" recently detailed a psi encounter that shattered his own belief in a world confined solely to 3D-space, the rational and the material. It all happened when he met a down-to-earth middle class British woman known as Psychic Sally (Sally Morgan) after being sent by the *Daily Mail* to test her. What happened there forms the first part of this story. First, though, some thoughts on skepticism.

There are skeptics, and there are "skeptics." Here's the difference. A proper skeptic accepts nothing on faith and demands convincing evidence derived from repeated observation and experiment before being willing to change his or her current views, in this case scientific, on a given matter. Once convinced, a true skeptic will then alter the scientific theory to conform to the observed results, even if doing so contradicts a long held, even cherished, theory or model of how things are. Not so for the "skeptic," for whom no amount of proof will ever suffice.

A "skeptic" is someone altogether different than the kind of person just described, in that the "skeptic" *pretends* to be open to new ideas, new scientific principles, and so forth. The truth, though, is that he is someone who has *a priori* ruled out anything and everything that is not of 3D-space, rationalism, and materialism.

If you doubt this then refer to at least the earlier editions of *Real Magic*, by P. E. I. Bonewits (1989). There you'll find the chapter, written by Paul Kurtz, founder of that most high profile home of the "skeptics," CSICOP (Committee for the Scientific Investigation of Claims of the Paranormal). Though the name fairly exudes open-mindedness, the organization, according to some, is anything but that and is prepared, it has been alleged, to use very rough tactics indeed, including, in order to defeat its enemies, the invocation of the very forces it so strenuously denies.

In "Sabotage of a Psychic Experiment" (*http://psymag.tripod.com/issue_1/1_sabotage.htm*) the writers of the October 27, 2001, issue of the online *Psychic Magazine* describe how, after bluster and intimidation had failed to derail a meticulously crafted, rigorous psychic spoon bending demonstration in Uri Geller's home—a demonstration with prominent scientists in attendance as observers—stage magician and professional debunker James Randi, per his own emails, reportedly asked his followers to concentrate negative energy on the specific part of Uri Geller's home where the demonstration was to be held, at precisely the time at which the demonstration was to occur.

The spoon bending demonstration failed utterly but still, it raises disturbing questions about CSICOP and its tactics. What business does an avowed rationalist materialist—arguably CSICOP's best-known member—have in organizing what anyone with even rudimentary occult knowledge would consider to be a black magic attack, let alone one targeted not just at the experiment or the experimenter, but everyone in that part of the house or who might have entered it for hours to follow? The answer was obvious to the writers—money. Geller's demonstration was intended to win the Million Dollar Challenge offered by Randi. Had Geller succeeded, not only would it have cost Randi the prize, but it would've destroyed his credibility and the very basis of his wealth, which is gained from peddling his books, multimedia, and live appearances all over the world. Black magic to protect rational materialism? How ironic. How hypocritical, too.

Of course, this is the same group that threw Velikovsky to the wolves at the special AAAS (American Association for the Advancement of Science) meeting in 1976 ostensibly to review his theories, but, in fact, to ambush him. They would also have us believe that the intelligence officer at Roswell Army Air Force Base, then Major Jesse Marcel, in the only nuclear strike formation in the world (the 509th Composite Group) was such an incompetent boob that he not only didn't know a radiosonde and its radar reflectors when he saw them, but ascribed to them utterly impossible material properties, and would have us believe that the Roswell Crash story of 1947 is really all about parachute equipped dummies thrown out of Skyhook balloons in the 1950s.

For a remarkable discussion of "skeptics" and a discussion of what makes them tick, read retired lawyer of the Supreme Court of New South Wales and the High Court of Australia turned afterlife researcher Victor Zammit's articles (*www.victorzammit.com/skeptics*). Zammit names names, cites other unanswered challenges, describes totally rigged tests set up by the "skeptics"—structured to not only be unwinnable, but which are in fact judged by the "skeptics" themselves.

Nor does Zammit ignore the vexed issue in psi research of the "experimenter effect." He does this by considering what Michael Cremo calls the "knowledge filter," and then goes on to the impact that "out there" ideas have on the "skeptics"—not just in terms of threats to their deeply entrenched belief systems, but to a host of considerations utterly disqualifying them from any possibility of being unbiased observers and empiricists.

DR. PENMAN'S WORLD GOES TILT!

Fortunately for us, Dr. Penman is a proper skeptic who can and will change beliefs and theories to conform with the evidence.

Just as well, seeing as how he suffered a reality tunnel collapse and wound up unexpectedly exploring a gigantic metaphorical cavern system. The story, "Psychic Versus Skeptic," ran in the *Daily Mail* and is available online (*www.newsmonster.co.uk*).

Penman describes how "Psychic Sally" produced one bombshell item after another with no attempt whatsoever to draw him out with leading questions that would permit ambiguous answers later. Mincing no words, she told him "You're going to Greece." He'd decided a few day prior to go on holiday in Crete. When shown a picture of Penman's girlfriend, Sally told him that the girlfriend would be moving to either Oxford or Bristol. As it happens, the month prior, she'd accepted a position as college lecturer in Bristol. Where things went way out, though, was when he was told details of an utterly private family feud—no public records of any kind—concerning a clash of wills over whether his mother got to keep her own name or would adopt her husband's upon marriage. Moreover, he got to have a chat with his dead grandfather (specifically identified with the family name that *wasn't* the same as his birth certificate), and also with his dead mother, who approved of and advised him regarding his current girlfriend and warned him to avoid the previous one.

At this point, Penman had a very strong reaction—fear. As he put it, "I suddenly remembered all of my 'sins' and expected instant divine retribution." He rallied, though, and reverted to his normal empiricist mode: "Despite this, I decided to accept a paranormal explanation for Sally's powers only after ruling out all conventional ones."

Penman carefully checked all available records and quickly concluded that while there was some material available which a determined and lucky searcher might unearth, most of what he was told had no source whatsoever available to Sally. Thus, she'd either plucked it from his mind or had gotten it through psychic and/or mediumistic means.

The plucking possibility, which especially concerned him, was covert hypnotism. To see whether she'd laid the whammy on him as part of her method, he sent in two "undercover" testers wearing wires. In neither case did he find even a whiff of hypnotism. What he and his total of three covert testers did find is that Psychic Sally produced "at least some amazing insights that defied rational explanation." She didn't get everything right, but she did come up with surprising items: such as the (previously unknown to the client) location and nature of a girl's brutal murder; a description of not just one person's house, but the name and story of the ghost haunting it; another person's respiratory issues (annual throat problem); as well as such things like warning of excessive care-giving, to alcoholics and emerging introvertedness in one person's son.

ASSESSING THE EXPERIENCES

Rather than simply falling back on his scientifically trained cynicism, Dr. Penman is not only open to the possibility that Sally is what she claims to be, but argues that (wait for it) "there are possible explanations from within the world [of] science." He goes on to say: "Strange as it may seem, in scientific principle at least, time can theoretically flow forwards and backwards." Thus, Sally could be remembering events yet to occur on our time branch. If this is unclear, then please watch the *Back to the Future* films.

Penman is also open to the possibility of life after death, reasoning that "our minds may reside in energy fields generated by our brains," thus creating the possibility of an imprint being created on that energy matrix, an imprint detectable and readable by those with special gifts or extensive training.

When it comes to what to do with this scientifically inconvenient and awkward set of phenomena, Dr. Penman rises to the challenge.

"Above all, the fact that we cannot understand how psychics such as Sally operate does not mean they are not genuine...I have come to the conclusion that only the foolish mock that which they cannot comprehend." This, then, is the man whose own remarkable experiences inform his RedOrbitNEWS article "Many Scientists are Convinced that Man Can See the Future" (*www.redorbit.com/modules/news*).

Back to the Future poster

THE APPARENT SCIENTIFIC BASIS FOR SEEING THE FUTURE

No, your eyes aren't deceiving you. A rigorous, repeatable experiment has been devised and run enough times, by enough credible scientific researchers, to show that most people can foresee the future to at least a limited degree.

You'd think that if someone randomly showed you images of various sorts of extremes, there'd be no way for you to anticipate what was coming next, let alone react to it in advance, but that's exactly what the work by Dean Radin found. Some will know Radin for his work on identifying negentropic (antirandom) changes in response to large scale societal trauma (9/11, Di's death, and so forth) to the networked True Random Number Generators, which make up the Global Consciousness Project. Time and again, and at way beyond random chance, people being tested somehow correctly not only anticipated the upcoming image, but reacted to it before it ever appeared.

This so intrigued the Nobel Prize winning chemist Dr. Karry Mullis that he offered up himself as test subject. Mullis characterized the experience as "spooky" because he could see "about three seconds into the future." When a Nobel laureate speaks on scientific matters, this tends to get the attention of fellow scientists—at "little" establishments such as the University of Edinburgh and Cornell. Related discoveries were not long in appearing.

Researchers discovered that gamblers reacted to the cards they got before seeing them, that people afraid of certain animals had fear reactions before seeing as much as a single image. Others found evidence in the stories of precognitive events by people who decided not to fly on the planes hijacked on 9/11, soldiers who knew they would come through unscathed when they had no such rational expectation, the more well-known cases of soldiers who knew before a mission or battle that their time was up the next day, even the little girl who dreamed that her Aberfan school was gone (116 students and 5 teachers killed the next day by a huge coal waste avalanche) and that everything was black.

Professor Dick Bierman, a psychologist at the University of Amsterdam, took Radin's simple experiment into realms where facial expressions and external actions were of no concern whatsoever. He carefully monitored not just brain activity, but what parts of the brain were excited, and in what order, right before the images were shown. In 20 expensive, complicated trials, conducted over a period of weeks, he confirmed Radin's work and that of others to such a level that he bluntly stated "We're satisfied that people can sense the future before it happens" and thereupon shifted his investigational focus to determining "what kind of person is particularly good at it."

According to Nobel laureate, Cambridge physicist Dr. Brian Josephson, "So far, the evidence seems compelling. What seems to be happening is that information is coming from the future."

This article first appeared in *Atlantis Rising* #71 (September/October 2008).

UNSEEN FORCES

2

UNDERWATER BASES
AND ALIEN CIVILIZATION

*Is the Answer to the UFO Enigma to Be
Found Deep Beneath the Sea?*

BY DAVID H. CHILDRESS

Ivan T. Sanderson was born in 1911. Before he died in 1973, he wrote over 18 books on the UFO phenomenon. A trained biologist, Sanderson was, nevertheless, fascinated by the unexplained and wrote on many exotic topics, such as mystery animals (including Bigfoot and the Yeti), lost civilizations, UFOs, and "Ooparts," or "Out-of-Place-Artifacts."

In *Invisible Residents*, first published in 1970, he put forward the curious theory that "OINTS"—Other Intelligences—live under the oceans. This underwater, parallel civilization, he proposed, may be twice as old as *Homo sapiens* and may have "developed what we call space flight." In the book, Sanderson argued that the OINTS are behind many UFO or USO (Unidentified Submarine Object) sightings as well as the mysterious disappearances of aircraft and ships in the Bermuda Triangle.

In the years since his book was first published, Sanderson's ideas have been largely dismissed as crackpot ravings, though Hollywood has managed to capitalize on some of them and make several movies along lines suggested by him, including *Cocoon, The Abyss,* and others.

Sanderson's original book is long out of print, but the original theory remains, in whole and in part. In whole, it is the rather fanciful notion that an underwater humanoid civilization—with advanced technology, no less—is inhabiting the deep oceans of our watery planet. In part, he is giving evidence, and attempting to explain, the often bizarre UFO–USO sightings that involve metallic craft exiting or entering large bodies of water, typically the ocean (though in some cases rivers and lakes).

Sanderson subtitled his original book: "A Disquisition upon Certain Matters Maritime, and the Possibility of Intelligent Life under the Waters of This Earth." However, the most important part of his investigation on this subject seems to be the enduring enigma of the UFO phenomena itself and the very real possibility that some UFOs are able to travel underwater, and the related possibility that some theoretical "UFO Bases" are actually underwater, rather than underground or in space as advanced by the typical "Moon as a Space Base" theory.

Indeed, how fascinating a theory for the serious UFO investigator is the suggestion that bases for these craft may well actually be underwater? What better place to have an impenetrable base than deep within the oceans of the planet? Yet, if UFOs, or at least some of them, are coming from beneath the oceans or lakes of our planet, does it necessarily mean that there is another civilization besides our own that is responsible? In fact, could it be that since WWII a number of underwater UFO bases have been constructed on the planet by the very human governments of our planet? We know that many of our governments, on nearly every continent in the world, have constructed submarine bases that are hidden in oceanside cliffs or even entirely underwater. Could some of these underwater bases house UFO-type craft that are capable of moving through the water and through the air as well? Some evidence may be pointing in this direction. On the other hand, as Sanderson and others have conjectured, extraterrestrials may also be using our oceans for space bases. The enigma endures.

Statistically, UFOs are most commonly seen around (1) military bases, (2) electrical power lines, and (3) bodies of fresh water. UFOs coming out of the earth's oceans are, generally, in a category unto themselves.

UFOs don't necessarily have to come out of the water to be around water. A number of UFOs have been noted hovering over bodies of water and apparently lowering a tube down to the water and "sucking it up." These so-called "thirsty UFOs" may be using water to power their craft, may simply need to replenish the on-board water supply much as a commercial jetliner, or, it has been speculated, may be taking water to UFO bases on the Moon.

One famous encounter occurred three years after *Invisible Residents* was published. On May 22, 1973, Japanese student Masaaki Kudou had taken a summer job as a security guard at Tomakomai, on the Japanese island of Hokkaido, at a timber yard near the sea. After a routine patrol around the site that clear, starry night he parked his patrol car, turned off its lights and looked over the lumberyard and the bay beyond.

What seemed at first to be a shooting star coming down toward the bay, suddenly stopped in its tracks, vanished, reappeared, and began to gyrate slowly down over the bay. It stopped about 70 feet above the water and then lowered a transparent tube toward the water with a soft sound (described as "*min-min-min*").

UFO lowers transparent tube to water (computer art by Darklanser)

When the tube reached the water, it began to glow. The tube was withdrawn, and the UFO moved to hover over Kudou's car. Everything around the car was lit up like day. Kudou was afraid the UFO would attack or even kill him.

Leaning over to watch through his windshield, Kudou saw that the UFO was perfectly smooth and glowing white, with windows around it. He could see the shape of humanoid figures through the windows. More brightly lit UFOs and a large, brown cylinder now joined the first. The spheres maneuvered and vanished into the cylinder, which then sped north. Kudou, who felt as if he had been bound hand and foot, regained his senses. His car radio was making static and he had a severe headache. The entire event lasted about 12 minutes. "Experts," as usual, were baffled, especially that high-tech "aliens" would need to slurp up sea water in a Japanese bay. Why do aliens, or their craft, need something so plentiful as water? Could their craft actually be powered by water?

Another thirsty UFO popped up on September 30, 1980 at the White Acres Ranch, near Rosedale, Victoria, Australia. The White Acres Ranch is a cattle station of about 600 acres with several large water tanks. On that night, George Blackwell, a station hand and caretaker, awoke about 1 a.m. to the sound of the farm's cattle going wild. He could hear a "strange screeching whistling" as well, and got up to investigate. The Moon was out on that night and there was no wind at all.

Blackwell saw a domed object about 15 feet tall and 25 feet broad with white top and blue and orange lights. For a while it hovered over a water tank made of concrete about 450 yards from the house. It then came to rest on the ground 20 yards further on. Blackwell drove a motorcycle to within 50 feet of the craft. There was no effect on his motorcycle, but the whistling from the UFO suddenly rose to deafening heights, and suddenly there was a loud bang and the craft lifted off. At the same time, a blast of hot air nearly knocked Blackwell over. The UFO dropped some debris as it flew away eastward at the low altitude of only about 100 feet.

Blackwell examined the site early the next day and found a ring of blackened grass, flattened in a counterclockwise direction. Inside the ring was green grass, but the flowers had disappeared. In a line to the east was a trail of debris which comprised some small rocks, weeds, and cow dung.

For days afterward Blackwell suffered headaches and nausea, and his watch refused to work normally. Most importantly, Blackwell had discovered the water tank that the UFO had been hovering over had been completely emptied of the 10,000 gallons of water that it had originally held!

UFOs sucking up water—for whatever purpose—is just one aspect of our tale. It is the UFOs that actually dive in and out of water that are of critical interest here. In the last 30 years, new sightings have occurred and new information on old sightings has come forth through the Freedom of Information Acts in the U.S., Britain, and Australia.

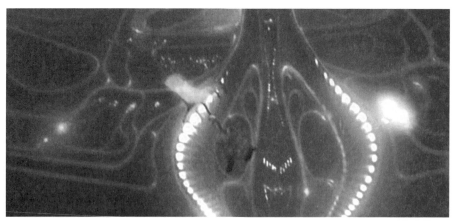

In the 1989 movie "The Abyss" actor Ed Harris is shown the wonders of an alien city at the bottom of the deep ocean (© 20th Century Fox)

UNSEEN FORCES

The government of Australia released 600 pages of UFO-related documents to UFO Research Association of North Adelaide in 2003. Debbie Payne of the Association reported on their findings in *Nexus* magazine (vol. 12, no. 1, Dec. 2004). Payne said that the Australian military had reported a number of UFOs around the top-secret Woomera rocket range in the vast desert of south central Australia, including a flying disc seen during the launch of a test rocket in April 1967.

Many years earlier at Woomera, on October 27, 1952, a dark cigar-shaped object with two portholes was seen to fly rapidly across a clear sky by four witnesses, two of them army officers. Payne suggests that the Woomera facility in Australia, which covers an area the size of England, is the equivalent of Nevada's Area 51 and may be involved in the manufacture of highly advanced aircraft that observers would call UFOs.

Do some of these UFOs—extraterrestrial or man-made—have the ability to go underwater as well, as Sanderson asks us? Payne in her article mentions that UFOs are commonly seen coming out of the water in the Milne Bay area of Papua New Guinea. Says Payne, "Milne Bay is on the easternmost tip of Papua, bordered by the Solomon Sea and the Coral Sea. The surrounding islands and seas were rife with reports of all kinds of weird and wonderful sightings. I believe there may well be an underwater base in this area, because of the number of sightings over such a great period of time and also because the survey map indicates the ocean is very deep in this area. The sea beds around these islands are littered with underwater caverns."

The long-time British UFO researcher Jenny Randles reports in the February 2005 issue of *Fortean Times* that the British government has continued to deny any involvement with the famous 1979 "Pennine Mystery Light Case" as she calls it. Randles reports that during a 48-hour period during February 22–24, 1979, a low-flying military exercise took place over the UK, and several major UFO encounters were reported, possibly related to the military activity. These included three landings in the area known as the Pennine Mountains which run down the center of northern England.

Randles tells the very interesting story of a security guard on the Central Pier in nearby Blackpool who saw a roaring orange UFO moving low across the Irish Sea at 2:45 a.m. on the night of the UFO flap. Half an hour later that night the same security guard saw something else that stunned him. "Climbing up from the cold waters of the sea was a spiraling mass of white lights that swirled upwards like a corkscrew and vanished quickly into the dark sky."

These curious incidents, during officially announced military maneuvers, raise the question of whether the British, and naturally, the Americans, have underwater military bases—bases that are capable of launching, shall we say, UFOs?

The American researcher Richard Sauder has used the Freedom of Information Act to obtain thousands of documents on underground and underwater military bases. In his books *Underground Bases: What Is the Government Trying to Hide?* (1995) and the sequel, *Underwater and Underground Bases* (2001), Sauder details an astonishing amount of technology and activity.

Sauder documents current tunneling technology, and discloses actual designs for underground and underwater military bases. On the subject of underwater bases he shows how flat-topped seamounts, or guyots, whose mesa-like tops may be several hundred feet below the surface, may serve as underwater bases that include airlocks for submarines that enter an oxygen-rich, rock-cut harbor inside the subsurface mountains. Other underwater installations are located near coastlines, and the tunneling under the sea floor can begin at a coastal military base, which is on dry land. Either way, Sauder concludes that underwater bases have been built by various governments around the world—and they are top secret! Also, he suspects that some sort of craft that is both a USO and a UFO can be launched from these underwater bases. Articles on UFOs–USOs appear frequently in newspapers and magazines around the world. On March 28, 2005, the *India Daily* ran a story entitled "Reverse Engineering ET Deep Underwater Craft." Quoting the article (which contains some deviations from usual American-English usage): "Oceanographers and Naval engineers are investigating certain phenomena that show evidence of the presence of extra-terrestrial deep underwater crafts—the floating versions of UFOs. These [craft] are capable of sharp and efficient maneuvering, [have] the implacable stealth to avoid detection, can hover in the deepest parts of the oceans, and are capable of going deep into the tectonic plate levels under the ocean."

The article went on to say that "scientists and engineers are finding solid evidences that these [craft] are present in [significant] numbers under our oceans though undetected and invisible in regular human eyes.

. . . There are not many sightings of these craft as very few people really dive into the depths of the ocean, which is really unexplored. A computer model has recently revealed the possible propulsion systems. The same anti-gravity principles apply though the model becomes much more complex due to buoyancy and other aquatic issues.

"Some divers in different parts of the world have reported sightings of strange underwater objects that propagate on [their] own but there is no real evidence that these are really extra-terrestrial craft. Some believe, there are countries [which] have the knowledge of these craft and are trying to reverse engineer their next generation submarines and underwater craft from these."

The article concluded, "The biggest problem of reverse-engineering these underwater craft is their stealth. As such deep underwater parts of the oceans [are] seldom explored. The super stealth around these vehicles makes them [even more] difficult [to detect]. According to some UFO researchers, these extra-terrestrial craft are busy changing the under-ocean landscapes. The underwater accidents of submarines due to collision with unknown underwater ridges and mountains have increased steadily over the last five years. The navies of many countries have reported these accidents regularly."

It seems startling to consider that UFOs may be real nuts-and-bolts craft using some form of electro-antigravity—hence the bright lights associated with most of them—which allows them dive into the water at any time and presumably dock in underwater installations that have been built, possibly, all over the world!

How intriguing a hypothesis, used in a number of Hollywood movies, that the ultimate docking stations for some of the UFOs seen constantly around the world are deep within our oceans. These underwater docking bases, it appears, may have been built by humans in our distant past (and are still operational to this day), or built by extraterrestrials, or by the current post-war governments of Earth—or even a combination of the three!

This first appeared as an article in *Atlantis Rising* #55 (January/February 2006), as an edited excerpt from the author's introduction to Sanderson's book *Invisible Residents*, recently reprinted by Adventures Unlimited Press, and offered here by permission.

3

WAS I.D. AN E.T.?

*One of the Most Important Questions in the Hot Debate
Over Human Origins Deserves a Closer Look*

BY ZECHARIA SITCHIN

In March 1925, the Tennessee legislature outlawed the teaching of any doctrine denying the divine creation of man as taught by the Bible. In July of that same year, John T. Scopes, a high school teacher, was brought to trial for teaching evolution, in violation of the state law. The ensuing Scopes Trial (or, derisively, the "Monkey Trial") drew worldwide attention to the seemingly irreconcilable conflict between creationism (the old fashioned belief in the biblical account) and evolution (based on Darwin's findings of natural selection).

John Scopes was found guilty and was fined $100; the Tennessee law was repealed in 1967; but the debate has not ended: Is man, *Homo sapiens*, solely the product of a long process of natural selection ("evolution"), or the result of a divine decision, a deliberate act by a Creator ("creationism")?

The evolutionists cannot fathom how the other side can ignore the overwhelming evidence for life's beginnings billions of years ago and claim that it is all the result of six days of creation; the creationists, pointing out that a complex watch required a watchmaker, cannot see how the sudden appearance of *Homo sapiens* as the most complex life form can deny the hand of God.

ENTER "INTELLIGENT DESIGN"

In the past several years, the debate has manifested itself again, with greater vigor, not only in the so-called Bible belt states, but also in such unexpected places as the Michigan House of Representatives and the Pennsylvania education system. One of the more recent instances is Ohio, where the arena is the state's Board of Education.

The hand of God animates Adam. ("The Creation" by Michelangelo)

Reports of these developments in the liberal media do not hide a degree of alarm at these developments—not so much because they continue to occur, but because the attack on Darwinian teachings now come from "creationism in disguise," and "a good disguise" at that (*Time Magazine*). The disguise is called "Intelligent Design" ("I.D." for short). Its proponents, by and large, do not take a position on how life got here; they just deny that natural selection (that is, evolution) alone could have brought us about. Somewhere along the way, they hold, there had to be an Intelligent Designer.

What alarms the media and the scientific community is the fact that the proponents of ID are not Bible-waving old ladies but intellectuals and academics from varied disciplines in science, philosophy, and theology. Their concerted attack on evolutionism has been called by the established scientific community "a wedge strategy to restore Creationism in disguise" (*Science* magazine).

IDENTIFYING THE INTELLIGENT DESIGNER

The proponents of the new version of creationism, one must conclude from a study of their writings and arguments, find it easier to make a case for intelligent design than to answer the question: If so, who was the Intelligent Designer?

While many scientific critics of I.D. hold that the neo-creationists are conservative Christians upset about the displacement of God from school

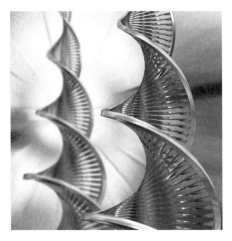

DNA (artist's conception)

curricula, "the fact is that many leaders of the new movement prefer to skirt the question, or even allow an abstract "God" to be embedded in the very beginning of the universe: "No one really knows how the universe got built with DNA that can replicate itself" (in the words of William Dembski, a professor of mathematics).

A NEW YORK TIMES PUZZLER

In its issue of April 8, 2001, *The New York Times*, in a page one article by James Glanz, informed its readers that in spite of some wins by evolutionists in Kansas, Michigan, and Pennsylvania, they "find themselves arrayed not against traditional creationism, with its roots in biblical literalism, but against a more sophisticated idea: the Intelligent Design theory."

But who, if so, was the Intelligent Designer? As I was reading the article on that Sunday morning, I was delighted to learn that:

"The designer may be much like the biblical God, proponents say, but they are open to other explanations, such as the proposition that life was seeded by a meteorite from elsewhere in the cosmos, or the new age philosophy that the universe is suffused with a mysterious but inanimate life force."

That proponents of I.D. consider the bringing of life to Earth by a meteorite as one explanation, I felt, was close enough to my Sumerian explanation that the Seed of Life (what we now call DNA) was imparted to Earth by the invading planet Nibiru during the collision ("Celestial Battle") some four billion years ago.

But it turned out from examining the newspaper's website and earlier editions, that the New York City edition that I was reading excised an intriguing and key sentence from the original article. Here is what the paragraph had read in its original version, with the omitted phrase italicized:

"This designer may be much like the biblical God, proponents say, but they are open to other explanations, such as the proposition that life was seeded by a meteorite from elsewhere in the cosmos, *possibly involving extraterrestrial intelligence*, or the new age philosophy that the universe is suffused with a mysterious but inanimate life force."

"An Advanced Civilization from Another World"

As my readers know, what I have said in my books went beyond the common origin of Life (=DNA) on Earth and elsewhere in the universe. I showed that according to the Sumerian texts (on which the biblical account of Genesis was based), evolution took its course both on Nibiru and on earth. Beginning much earlier on Nibiru, it produced the advanced Anunnaki on Nibiru, but only early hominids on Earth when the Anunnaki had come here some 450,000 years ago. Then, I wrote, the Anunnaki engaged in genetic engineering to upgrade the hominids to *Homo sapiens* (to be in their likeness and after their image, as the Bible says).

While I was still wondering how the extraterrestrial angle was excised from the *Times* article in April 2001, I was delighted to read thus in its editorial on March 17, 2002. Headlined "Darwinian Struggle in Ohio," the editorial explained:

"Adherents of intelligent design carefully shun any mention of God in their proposals. They simply argue that humans, animals, and plants are far too diverse and complex to be explained by evolution and natural selection, so there must have been an intelligent designer behind it all. Whether that designer is God, *an advanced civilization from another world*, or some other creative force, is not specified."

The emphasis of that astounding statement is mine.

Back to Enki?

This is quite an advance in acknowledging the Sumerian data—from the general possibility of an involvement by "extraterrestrial intelligence" in cosmic life to an Intelligent Designer from "an advanced civilization from another world."

It is progress spanning the tale of the collision that spread the seed of life to the genetic engineering by the Lord Enki.

Have the editorial writers of the *New York Times* read my book, *The Lost Book of Enki?*

This article first appeared in *Atlantis Rising* #62 (March/April 2007).

4

Energy from the Vacuum

Could the Power We Need Be All Around Us?

BY LEN KASTEN

"All EM (electromagnetic) systems are powered by energy extracted from the vacuum. They are not powered by the mechanical energy we input to the shaft of a generator, or by the chemical energy in a battery."—Thomas E. Bearden

THE THEORY THAT so-called "empty space" is actually a vibrant ocean of energy makes perfect sense and seems self-evident to some of us.

There really is no other explanation for how billions of stars contain the power to continuously put out prodigious amounts of heat and light for, what appears to be, indefinite periods of time. In the face of this, to argue that the universe is just a vacuum of dead nothingness is almost as senseless as contending that the Earth is flat even though the Sun rises and sets every day. And yet, the worldwide scientific community, men and women of high intelligence and tremendous cumulative knowledge, refuses to acknowledge that this could be so. Even when it is clearly demonstrated, as it was by Dr. T. Henry Moray, they assume it to be some sort of trickery or fraud, and they return to stale scientific dogma.

In the early 1920s, Moray, who was a boyhood admirer of Nikola Tesla, built a free-energy device, weighing about 60 pounds with no apparent power input, that produced 50,000 watts of electricity for several hours. Moray, from Salt Lake City, obtained his doctorate in Electrical Engineering from the University of Uppsala in Sweden in 1918. By the 1930s, Moray had perfected his invention and was able to demonstrate, in test after test, that the device delivered high voltage electrical power simply by tapping ambient energy.

In a well-documented and photographed demonstration, Moray's Radiant Energy Device powered thirty-five 100–watt light bulbs and a 1200–watt iron. Moray's highly publicized demonstrations to scientists, engineers, and government representatives convinced them all that Moray had succeeded in tapping an invisible, universal sea of energy. The Radiant Energy Device utilized 29 transistor-like, cold vacuum tube "valves," or one-way gates, that trapped the energy and accumulated it until it reached a high wattage. Despite all of the publicity surrounding this device, the U.S. Patent Office never granted him a patent. Moray met with constant opposition. He was frequently threatened; his laboratory was broken into and robbed; and he was actually shot at in the streets and in his own office. He eventually installed bullet-proof glass in his automobile, and he kept a loaded gun in plain view on his desk when meeting with strangers.

Dr. T. Henry Moray

SPACE-TIME

One of the theoretical keys to the understanding of the Radiant Energy Device was the work of Hermann Minkowski, a brilliant German mathematician. It was Minkowski who, in 1907, created the mathematical framework that brought space and time together and evolved the concept of space-time. Minkowski was inspired by Einstein's 1905 Theory of Special Relativity and realized that Special Relativity required an entirely new definition of the relationship between space and time. He was able to prove mathematically that time is a fourth dimension of space, and he hypothesized a four-dimensional space-time continuum. This revolutionized Galileo's flat view of space-time in which only simultaneous events were on the same plane in space-time, and substituted a space-time, non-Euclidian cone in which event timing is relative to the observer while the speed of light remains a constant. Einstein then, in 1908, using Minkowski's framework, developed the Theory of General Relativity, which is now universally accepted, and has become the foundation of modern physics. The Einstein-Minkowski framework of space-time supersedes the

Lightning in the hand.

Galilean concept of Absolute Time. Time now becomes relative, and time and space become interdependent; and it becomes possible to convert one to the other. As the fourth dimension of space, time has its own axis in a Minkowski Diagram.

The Einstein-Minkowski space-time theory was largely built upon the Maxwell Equations. This set of four equations developed by James Clerk Maxwell in 1865 comprised mathematical formulations of the behavior of electromagnetic waves in a vacuum. Maxwell was the first to include light waves and photons in the electromagnetic spectrum, and he proved mathematically that all electromagnetic radiation moved at the speed of light. Thus, this constant became an integral component of Einstein's famous formulation, $E=mc^2$, where c is the speed of light.

About Maxwell, Einstein said, "The precise formulation of the time-space laws was the work of Maxwell. Imagine his feelings when the differential equations he had formulated proved to him that electromagnetic fields spread in the form of polarized waves, and at the speed of light! To few men in the world has such an experience been vouchsafed . . . it took physicists some decades to grasp the full significance of Maxwell's discovery, so bold was the leap that his genius forced upon the conceptions of his fellow-workers" (*Science*, May 24, 1940). It should be noted here that both Maxwell and Minkowski were mathematical theoreticians and made their proofs strictly with pure mathematics. It was up to Einstein to translate their results to the realm of physics. Einstein's formulas have been demonstrated in the real world many times, although nowhere as dramatically as in the development of atomic energy.

THE TIME DOMAIN

Dr. Moray achieved his results, more or less, by trial and error and wasn't really knowledgeable about the Minkowski–Maxwell–Einstein theoretical developments. But, he eventually came to virtually the same conclusions. In his book, *The Sea of Energy in Which the Earth Floats* (2012), he concludes that the free energy from the cosmos comes in waves or oscillations, and he was able to tune his device to harmonize with these oscillations and that was the secret of capturing the energy. "Every oscillation," he says, "whether large or small, is completed during the same interval of time. These oscillations all prove the same great fact, that they are governed by the same cycle of time, completed during the same interval of time. Waves of energy have a regular beat note, coming and going as the waves of the sea, but in a very definite mathematical order [Maxwell's?]—coming to the Earth from every direction with a definite rhythm." For energy waves to be propagated through a vacuum rhythmically implies that they are going through some sort of medium where time is the dominant factor, since space is known to be totally devoid of mass.

Moray called it "the luminiferous medium of the universe." The rhythmic oscillations would suggest that the energy from the vacuum is actually coming from what is called the "time domain." Then it is transduced to the spatial dimension through Moray's device and therefore able to do physical work. Thus, the space-time theories of Maxwell, Minkowski, and Einstein would appear to be validated.

ROGUE SCIENTISTS

Since the late 1940s, the related research and development in this country was largely taken over by military-industrial organizations and remains secret, as with the Manhattan Project. It became what Paul LaViolette refers to as "classified physics." So it has been left to what might be called "rogue scientists"—outside the scientific establishment and not able to benefit from the tremendous resources of big budget corporate-university R&D and colleague fellowship—to bring these theories down to earth and before the public. These are the scientist pioneers we must now rely on to make this "Buck Rogers" R&D of practical use in civilian applications.

Probably the most prominent of these researchers is Thomas E. Bearden, whose theoretical work builds on Minkowski–Maxwell–Einstein as well as "outside the box" thinkers such as Dr. Moray. Bearden is a retired Army Lt. Colonel. His Curriculum Vitae on his website says that he is "a theoretical conceptualist active in the study of scalar electromagnetics, advanced electrodynamics, unified field theory, KGB energetics weapons and phenomena, free energy systems, electromagnetic healing via the unified field action of extended Sachs-Evans electrodynamics, and human development. [He is] particularly known for his work establishing a theory of overunity electrical power systems, scalar electromagnetic weapons, energetics weapons, and the use of time-as-energy in both power systems and the mind-body interaction." Bearden is also the Director of the Association of Distinguished American Scientists. This organization claims to be attempting to unify "the major disciplines of science, namely classical EM (CEM), general relativity (GR), and quantum mechanics (QM)."

Bearden came to scientific and public attention in 1980 with the publication of his first book, *The Excalibur Briefing* (1978). This was a brilliant, ground-breaking work that basically explains most paranormal phenomena in terms of a new physics based on a scientific exploration of the virtual state, or in Einsteinian terms, the time domain of space-time.

In this book, Bearden shows how interactions between the two dimensions account for what appear to be miraculous manifestations. In Part One, Bearden takes on such diverse phenomena as remote viewing, the Crystal Skull, mental metal bending, thought photography, psychotronics, UFOs, men-in-black, dowsing, Kirlian photography, foo fighters, and cattle mutilations! Then, in Part Two, he gives the theoretical foundations of all these phenomena in terms of the virtual state, or what he called "hyperspace," a term then in vogue because it was used in "Star Wars."

It could be said that in this book, Bearden succeeded in conceptualizing the miraculous by removing all the layers of mystery. Since it appeared at roughly the same time as *Psychic Discoveries Behind the Iron Curtain* by Ostrander and Schroeder (1970), the two books, taken together, could be viewed as a revolutionary revelation of a new science explaining the invisible powerhouse of energy behind previously inexplicable phenomena. Consequently, the early 1980s became a turning point in the public understanding of what could be called "the science of magic."

E=TC2

For 20 years after *The Excalibur Briefing*, Bearden continued to refine his research, experimentation, and theorization. Then, in 2004, he released the most comprehensive and detailed exposition of his concepts in his 977-page magnum opus, *Energy from the Vacuum* (2004). In this book, Bearden theorizes a new model of thermodynamic interaction in which time becomes a factor. He says that the time dimension, on the fourth Minkowski axis, has the same energy density as mass. Then he enunciates a radically new concept, comparable to Einstein's famous formula. He says, "Multiplying an amount of time t (in seconds) by c2 gives the decompressed spatial energy E that the time t will transduce into. In short, E = tc2 also." This idea that the energy potential from the time domain is identical to the energy that can be derived from the conversion of mass (by E = mc2) is revolutionary. It means that energy releases comparable to atomic explosions can be achieved simply by transducing time, if we knew how.

Bearden says that according to Special Relativity, there is an inverse relationship between mass-energy and time-energy. In his words, "When the mass-energy increases (for example, as a function of velocity), time "dilates" or "decreases" . . . . If mass (3D-space) gains some 3D-spatial energy, then time loses some time-energy. Since time is spatial EM energy compacted by c2, then the relativistic energy changes in the time domain are enormously greater than the corresponding relativistic changes in spatial energy in the photon." That is, by his formula, E=tc2, a negligible amount of time energy transduces to a massive amount of spatial energy by a factor of c2. So the energy given off by any star has been transduced from a tiny reservoir of invisible energy, where the visible energy equals the invisible energy times 186,000 ft./sec.squared! Bearden says that this is a constant, ongoing process in the universe. Time continually dilates, or moves backward, in order to produce spatial energy.

Bearden claims that this process can be engineered on demand by the use of a simple oscillating electric dipole. The negative pole of the dipole attracts the EM energy from the time domain and supplies the energy that is then transmitted to the positive pole. The EM energy is sent back to the vacuum from the positive pole, thus circulating between 3D-space and 4D-space. Bearden explains it this way: "Once the dipole is established, it will extract and transduce EM energy from the vacuum and pour it out in all directions at the speed of light, without ceasing. . . . Real observable EM energy extracted and transduced from the vacuum's virtual energy is precisely what the 'broken symmetry of the opposite charges' on the ends of the dipole means."

Bearden and his colleagues have developed an experimental device utilizing these principles called the Motionless Electromagnetic Generator, or MEG, which is an overunity device; that is, it puts out more energy than it takes in. It has no moving parts. The MEG was granted

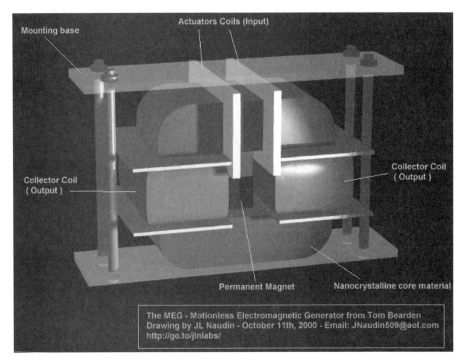

Motionless Electromagnetic Generator

a U.S. patent on March 26, 2002. According to Bearden's website, they have recently achieved a 100:1 ratio of energy-out to energy-in. They are now engaged in a cooperative research project with a friendly foreign nation to develop and market commercial power systems for that nation, based on the MEG. There is no way to know how this device compares with Moray's Radiant Energy Device because Moray took the secret of the valve to his grave. When his son John recently sought to retrieve Moray's patent application papers from the U.S. Patent Office, he found that the folder jackets were still there, but they were empty. The specifications papers themselves were gone.

TIME ENGINEERING

In a paper titled, "Vision 2000: The New Science Now Emerging for the New Millennium," written in 2000 for a conference, Bearden discusses the fact that the original 20 Maxwell Equations were reduced by Oliver Heaviside in the 1890s to just four, excluding what is called "the nondiverged energy flow" in the vacuum, and leaving only vector-based energy, commonly used in modern electronics. Bearden claims that when these excluded formulas are restored, it becomes possible to engineer the time domain.

In the paper he says, "Time-as-energy eventually becomes engineerable, as easily as is spatial energy now. We are always dealing with space-time and with space-time curvature. Any spatial energy flow must be accompanied with a change in energy flow in the time domain, *a priori*." This is accomplished by capturing and directing the longitudinal EM waves that proliferate in the vacuum when space-time becomes curved. These waves do not exist in 3D-space, where only transverse electromagnetic waves are utilized. The potential uses for such controlled usage of longitudinal EM waves boggles the mind. Bearden says, "…matter is a vast superhighway for longitudinal EM waves—the ultimate transparency. An astounding thing emerges: These new causal robotic systems of the future will travel right through the 'superhighway interior' of EM fields and waves and potentials, and thus right through enormous amounts of matter. They can travel through a beam of light, a radio signal, a radar beam, etc. They can communicate with us and be controlled by longitudinal EM waves. They can reside in any EM field, potential, or wave in a human body, a piece of wood, a piece of copper, the ionosphere, or the sun. By mid-century we will be using such robotic systems to explore the interior of the earth, other planets, the interior of the sun, asteroids, space junk, etc."

Development of these space-time EM technologies will revolutionize life on Earth. Bearden says, "Even the poorest developing nation can afford the self-powering electrical power systems that will result in the immediate future. Then the resulting progress of those struggling societies will be rapid indeed, with cheap clean energy available at their disposal. Infrastructures can be built very quickly. Strong attention can be focused on clean drinking water, medical treatment, plentiful food, and other health problems, and on education of the masses. In short, the developing nations can be placed on a very fast lane to the development and financial uplifting of their peoples."

This article first appeared in *Atlantis Rising* #81 (May/June 2010).

5

NIKOLA TESLA & THE GOD PARTICLE

In the Quest for the Elusive "Higgs Boson"
Einstein Was Not Alone

BY MARC J. SEIFER, PH.D.

It was in 1976 while I was in the midst of following another story at the New York Public Library when I found Tesla's name for the first time. It was alleged, in a book on avatars, that Tesla had been born on another planet. He had landed in the mountains of Yugoslavia in 1856 to bring to us humans the induction motor, fluorescent and neon lights, wireless communication, remote control, robotics, and our entire electrical power system. What immediately struck me was that, had this man done all this, surely I would have heard his name before, but I had not.

I then read the O'Neill biography on Tesla and got his book of patents. From this material I was able to ascertain that Tesla was indeed the real McCoy, that is, the fundamental inventor behind all these high-tech creations! He thus became the subject of my doctoral dissertation. I wanted to find out how such an important individual could have been dropped from the history books, and this work was morphed into my 2001 biography *Wizard: The Life & Times of Nikola Tesla*, a book now in its 14th printing, translated into four languages, with over 70,000 copies in print. Tesla is no longer an obscure individual.

However, what has remained obscure are some of his still esoteric inventions and discoveries. For instance, his supposed electric car that derives it's power by means of wireless energy, his discovery of cosmic rays that travel at speeds in excess of 50 times the speed of light, a cosmic ray machine that derives an unlimited amount of power from the atmosphere, a 300-page paper on his bladeless turbine that no one has been able to locate, more information about his top-secret particle beam weapon, and the full implications of his very-well-hidden dynamic theory of gravity.

The writing of the Tesla biography, which took 14 years of daily work, involved travel to every known major Tesla archive from New York and

Massachusetts, to Washington DC; Berkeley California to Belgrade Serbia; attendance and participation as a lecturer at a dozen or more international Tesla conferences held in Colorado Springs; at the site of his Wardenclyffe tower on Long Island, New York; Croatia; Serbia; Tempe, Arizona; Toronto, Canada; and Niagara Falls covering the years 1984–2009. And in all that time, having attended all those conferences, and in meeting all the world's great Tesla experts, no one, as far as I knew, had truly understood Tesla's dynamic theory of gravity, nor its implications.

It has only been in the last several years, since the writing of *Transcending the Speed of Light* (2008), that I have come to fully appreciate Tesla's theory. My source starts with a single statement Tesla made to the well-known New York reporter, Joseph Alsop, at the age of 78, when the inventor was "led to the inescapable conclusion that such bodies as the Sun are taking on mass much more rapidly than they are dissipating it by the dissipation of energy in heat and light" ("Beam to Kill at 200 miles, Tesla claims," Joseph Alsop, *New York Times,* July 11, 1934). Even though I included this quote in *Wizard,* I did not fully understand what Tesla was trying to say. It took nearly another decade to figure it out.

At first, it seems absurd that a body as hot as the Sun would be absorbing more energy than it was radiating, and the only reason I originally gave it any credence was because Tesla said it. However, the more I thought about it, the more it becomes obvious. Of course stars are absorbing more energy than they are radiating. Otherwise, they would burn out in rather rapid fashion.

I hadn't yet, however, linked this statement to the idea of "gravity," or more to the point, to Tesla's never-revealed dynamic theory of gravity.

The next hint had to do with Tesla's criticisms of Einstein's theory of relativity, which he published in a series of articles in the mid-1930s. Tesla's main criticism had to do with Einstein's idea of the curvature of space:

"On a body as large as the sun, it would be impossible to project a disturbance of this kind [for example, radio broadcasts] to any considerable distance except along the surface. It might be inferred that I am alluding to the curvature of space supposed to exist according to the teachings of relativity, but nothing could be further from my mind. I hold that space cannot be curved, for the simple reason that it can have no properties.... To say that in the presence of large bodies space becomes curved is equivalent to stating that something can act upon nothing. I, for one, refuse to subscribe to such a view" (Nikola Tesla, "Pioneer Radio Engineer Gives Views on Power," New York *Herald Tribune*, September 11, 1932).

This turns out to be a very complex process, but like any great idea, it begins with a simple fundamental premise.

As the title of my book suggests, there has to be something wrong with Einstein's theory of relativity, because I am hypothesizing that something can travel faster than the speed of light, and that would violate relativity. Let's start with classical physics. As a youngster, one of my favorite science authors was George Gamow, who happens to be one of the founders of quantum physics. In his watershed book *30 Years that Shook Physics* (1966), which recounts what was happening within his field as he lived it, Gamow says something startling: he tells the reader that, in the 1920s, in the process of measuring the rate of electron spin, Goudsmit and Uhlenbeck discovered that the rate was 1.37 times the speed of light!

As Gamow tells us, this did not violate any principle in quantum physics; what it violated was Einstein's theory of relativity. Thus the physicists of the day had a problem, because relativity had become their new baby. However, what was not well known were two things about Einstein's views and his theory:

1. Einstein did not do away with the all pervasive ether. If photons, or light particles, traveled more like bullets than waves, say from the Sun to the Earth, then they would not have to go through a medium. Einstein emphasized this particle-like aspect of the photon, but he also knew it also operated like a wave. This resulted in the wrong supposition that Einstein had abandoned ether theory. In fact, he had not; he simply said that by its nature, it could not be detected. As Walter Isaacson points out in his new Einstein biography (2007, p. 318), Einstein wrote to Hendrik Lorentz in explicit terms that the ether did, indeed, exist; and in 1920, he gave a speech on the ether at Leiden University.

2. Roland Clark points out in his earlier Einstein biography (1971, p. 78) that Einstein himself said that if the ether could be detected, then relativity must be wrong.

So, clearly, Einstein had a vested interest in keeping the ether non-detectable. But at the same time, Einstein, in the last 30+ years of his life, was committed to what he called Grand Unification, the ability to unite all four forces of the universe into one overriding force or mathematical inter-related paradigm. The four forces are as follows:

- Strong nuclear force, the binding force for the nucleus (holds the nucleus together)

- Weak nuclear force holds neutrons together (binds protons with electrons within the nucleus)

- Electromagnetism binds atoms and molecules together (the sharing of photons by elementary particles)

- Gravity holds planetary systems together (results in giving matter its mass)

Physicists have, to date, combined the first three, but gravity remains the stickler. It is not an overstatement to say that Einstein spent the bulk of his adult career trying to combine gravity with electromagnetism, but he was never able to accomplish this; so, to this day, Grand Unification still remains the unachieved Holy Grail.

Going back to Goudsmit's and Uhlenbeck's discovery, Paul Adrian Dirac figured out a way around the problem. As explained by Gamow, Dirac decided to use the imaginary number i, or the square root of negative one, to stand for the tachyonic orthorotational

Albert Einstein in 1921

speed of the electron. By using this imaginary number, relativity would not be violated. Relativity could now be combined with quantum physics. So, through this mathematical maneuver, all problems between the two theories were overridden and Dirac was awarded a Nobel Prize for his efforts.

So, as I see it, electrons do indeed spin faster than the speed of light, but if we (that is, the physicists) use an imaginary number, this little fact is neatly side-stepped and Einstein's theory can remain sacrosanct.

Tesla, however, never abandoned the ether. Neither, we have seen, did Einstein (or Lorentz), but nobody writes about it; and the ether has remained the elephant in the room for more than a century.

Enter theoretical physicist Peter Higgs. Born in 1929 and educated at Cambridge, now a theoretical physicist at the University of Edinburg, Higgs speculated that there was an all-pervasive field, now called the Higgs field, that permeates all of space and gives matter its mass. This field is made up of Higgs bosons, which would be small particles that bind this field to matter.

Sounds a lot like ether to me. In point of fact, if you dig hard enough, it becomes quite evident that what Higgs did was reformulate, rename, or rephrase the ether in a term that was palatable to mainstream physicists; but make no mistake, what he is talking about is ether, plain and simple. This Higgs boson, or binding particle, has also been dubbed the God particle, the particle that gives matter its mass. This is the particle that physicists are now looking for with their super-collider at Bern on the Swiss/French border. However, you can bet, they are not looking for a particle or form of energy that is operating in a tachyonic realm, that is, in speeds in excess of the speed of light.

Tesla and an artist's conception of the God Particle

Now, lets return to Tesla and his quote above. Starting with the first sentence about directing a disturbance around the surface of a large body, what Tesla is actually talking about here is two related concepts. The first is the ground connection in radio transmission. The second is why there is the need for the ground connection. In point of fact, what Tesla had neatly done, ultimately throughout his entire life, was carefully obscure the reason why radio broadcasts follow the curvature of the Earth (follow the ground connection). The answer has to do with the single sentence he revealed to Alsop in 1934; namely that the Sun was absorbing more energy than it was radiating.

This, in a nutshell, is Tesla's dynamic theory of gravity. All matter is constantly absorbing ether all the time at the tachyonic speed of 1.37 times the speed of light. This is the world of ether. By its nature, the ether exists in a realm that transcends the speed of light.

So, what then is gravity according to this theory? Gravity is simply the absorption of ether by, for instance, the Earth. The reason we fall back to the Earth when we jump up is not because of some mysterious disconnected force called gravity; we fall back to the Earth because we are in the way of the influx of ether. That is what gravity is. It is absorption of ether by the elementary particles. It is the elusive Higgs boson, or God particle, the force/process that gives matter its mass. And it happens in a continuous fashion all the time.

That is why radio broadcasts follow the curvature of the earth. As the wave propagates, it is pushed down to the Earth by gravity, if you will, by this constant influx of ether. So, according to this theory, the reason light particles bend around stars and planetary bodies is not because space is curved, but because these photons are being affected by this constant influx. This theory further speculates that photons are not really massless; their mass would be equivalent to Planck's constant, a tiny factor which Planck had to add to all his calculations to make them work out. If photons have energy, and if energy and mass are equivalent, then by definition, photons must have mass.

Now, to solve Einstein's dream. His goal, we remember, was to combine gravity with electromagnetism. The reason he couldn't do it was because to do so would involve resurrecting a detectable ether; and if that were the case, then, as Einstein himself stated, his theory of relativity would be wrong. Gravity is the influx of ether by the elementary particles. It is the process that gives matter its mass, the so-called God particle. This process occurs at 1.37 times the speed of light. As each elementary particle absorbs ether, two things happen—(1) the process allows or helps the particle to continue spinning and, (2) simultaneously, the energy is converted into electromagnetism. Ether comes in, causes electrons and other elementary particles to spin, and in that process, atoms retain their integrity and convert the constant influx into the electromagnetism, that is, Grand Unification.

This article first appeared in *Atlantis Rising* #83 (September/October 2010).

PART TWO

PERSPECTIVES OF GENIUS

Tolstoy portrait by Nikolayevich, 1884

6

TOLSTOY AND THE PARANORMAL

*Did the Great Writer's Well Known Objections
Contain a Subtext?*

BY JOHN CHAMBERS

"At a round table under a lamp the countess and Alexei Alexandrovich sat talking about something in low voices. A short, lean man with womanish hips and knock-kneed legs, very pale, handsome, with beautiful, shining eyes and long hair falling over the collar of his frock coat, stood at the other end, studying the portraits on the wall…

" 'Monsieur Landau!' The countess addressed the man with a softness and carefulness that struck Oblonsky. And she introduced them.

"Landau hastily turned, approached and, smiling, placed his inert, sweaty hand into the extended hand of Stepan Arkadyich and immediately went back and began looking at the portraits. The countess and Alexei Alexandrovich exchanged meaningful looks."

We have just met Jules Landau, the medium who plays a small but important role in *Anna Karenina* (1878), the immortal novel of personal conflict and high-society adultery in late 19th century Russia, written by Count Leo Tolstoy, who also wrote *War and Peace* and who is considered by many to be the greatest novelist of all time. Alexei Alexandrovich is Anna Karenina's estranged husband who has come to the séance to ask the spirit world if he should allow Anna to have custody of their son. Stepan Arkadyich Oblonsky is Anna's brother, present at the séance because he happens to be in St. Petersburg at the time. Absent from the séance, but looming over the scene because of their passionate and tragic presence throughout the novel, are the beautiful Anna and her lover Count Alexei Vronski, the latter a handsome and charming, but ultimately frivolous and irresponsible, career officer in the army.

In the next scene, Landau falls asleep and does channel a message to Alexei Karenina. The spirits apparently tell Karenina that he shouldn't

THE CLASSIC NOVEL. THE TIMELELESS LOVE STORY

IN A WORLD OF
POWER AND PRIVILEGE,
ONE WOMAN DARED
TO FOLLOW HER HEART.

SOPHIE MARCEAU

ANNA KARENINA

Anna Karenina movie poster

give up custody of their son to Anna. The estranged husband acts on this advice and this is apparently the final straw for the deeply guilt-ridden and almost paranoid Anna, who soon commits suicide by throwing herself under the wheels of a train.

Does this mean Leo Tolstoy believed the dead survive and communicate useful messages to us? Perhaps not. Anna Karenina begins with the Biblical injunction, "Vengeance is mine, I will repay, saith the Lord," and Tolstoy, who had grown fond of his heroine in the course of writing Anna Karenina, may not have believed that God could really be vengeful in this way, and meant the role of Landau to be highly ambiguous at best (Landau is thought to be based on the famous medium D. D. Home, who often conducted seances in Russia and was twice married to Russian women. Tolstoy attended a Home seance in Paris in 1857).

But even this highly ambiguous portrait of a medium is a perplexing departure for Tolstoy, who all his life vehemently denied that there could be a supernatural realm, that life was as crowded with paranormal events as an omni movie theater is with movies. Born on a large country estate financed by his mother's money, Leo Tolstoy (1828–1910) entered Kazan University in 1844 to study oriental languages, dropped out, then squandered huge sums of money gambling. In 1847 he returned to the ancestral estate, Yasnaya Polyana ("Clear Fields"), which he would administer all his life, mastering such skills as horse-breeding, bee-keeping and crop-management. He fought in the Crimean War (1853–1856), distinguishing himself for bravery at the Battle of Sevastopol. The publication of his acclaimed trilogy of semi-autobiographical novels *Childhood, Boyhood,* and *Youth* made him famous at 30. Between 1857 and 1861 he twice visited Germany, France, and England to study educational methods, using this knowledge to open a school for peasant children at Yasnaya Polyana; eventually he wrote and published a Primer for the school. In 1862 he married the beautiful and intelligent Sonya Behrs; the two had 15 children, seven of whom survived. From 1864 to 1878, he wrote *War and Peace* and *Anna Karenina*, at the same time producing numerous other short stories and novellas.

Beginning in 1878, Tolstoy underwent a protracted spiritual crisis. He denounced his two great novels as egotistical and pointless, mere "aristocratic art." He invented his own brand of Christianity, the gospel of which, according to one critic, was "devoid of irrationality, deprived of metaphysical and mystical vision, despoiled of metaphors and symbols, mutilated of its miracles, and sometimes of its parables as well." He told the Russian Orthodox Church (which formally excommunicated him in 1901) that to consider Jesus to be a God and to pray to him was "the greatest blasphemy." He declared that the essence of Christ's ministry was solely to teach men "not to commit stupidities." He became a pacifist and vegetarian, dressing in peasants' clothes and working with the peasants in the fields. Through all this he not only wrote a spiritual autobiography (*My Confession*) and numerous essays on religion and philosophy, but also numerous short stories, one novel (*Resurrection*) and three very long plays. All of Tolstoy's post-1878 writing, while sharply didactic in tone, is considered to be of the highest literary merit. Yale critic Harold Bloom considers Tolstoy's final short story, "Hadji Murat," written when the author was nearly 80, to be the greatest short story ever. At the time of his death at 82, Tolstoy's religious views had influenced many radical religious sects around the world and inspired many distinguished activist-thinkers including Mahatma Gandhi, Boris Pasternak, and Martin Luther King, Jr.

Despite his astounding accomplishments, Tolstoy was always a tormented man. Lurking behind his contemptuous dismissal of the paranormal was an immense despair at what seemed to be the ultimate meaninglessness of life. The critic George Steiner (*Tolstoy or Dostoevsky*, 1959) writes that Tolstoy "suffered from a despair of reason at the thought that men's lives were doomed through illness or violence or the ravenings of time to irremediable extinction. . . . His relentless veracity compelled him to recognize that there is no definitive proof for the immortality of the soul or the survival of any consciousness whatsoever . . . Tolstoy was harassed to the edge of self-destruction by the apparent absurdity of human existence."

Steiner says that "Out of this desperate meditation there grew a consoling myth . . . Tolstoy came to deny the reality of death. He wrote in

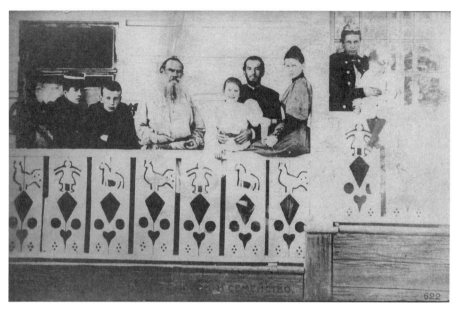

Tolstoy and family

his Diary for December 1895 that man is 'never born and never dies and always is.'" Steiner quotes Tolstoy as later writing that the kingdom of God "must be established here and now, on this Earth and in this, the only real life that is accorded us . . . there is no evidence for the existence of another world and . . . the kingdom of God must be built by mortal hands." Any communication from an afterworld would vitiate man's efforts and there was no such communication.

Another intense preoccupation of Tolstoy's was of the absolute distinction between the spiritual healthfulness of rural life and the corrupting nature of urban life. George Steiner writes, "Tolstoy saw experience morally and aesthetically divided. There is the life of the city with its social injustices, its artificial sexual conventions, its cruel display of wealth, and its power to alienate man from the essential patterns of physical vitality. On the other hand, there is life in the fields and forests with its alliance of mind and body, its acceptance of sexuality as hallowed and creative, and its instinct for the chain of being which relates the phases of the Moon to the phases of conception and which associates the coming of the seed-time with the resurrection of the soul."

In an early scene in *Anna Karenina*, Konstantin Levin, one of the book's main protagonists, who represents the vibrant and morally healthful spirit of the countryside, argues with Vronsky about spiritualism. The setting is a high-society party. Levin rejects table-tapping channeling, which was as popular in the 1870s among the aristocracy of Russia as it had been in the 1850s among the aristocracy of France. Levin declares, "When electricity was found, it was merely the discovery of a phenomenon, and it was not known where it came from or what it could do, and centuries passed before people thought of using it. The spiritualists, on the other hand, began by saying that tables write to them and spirits come to them, and only afterwards started saying it was an unknown force."

Vronsky, representing an aristocracy with too much money, time, and privilege on its hands to be forced to take full responsibility for its actions, replies, on the other hand, "Yes, but the spiritualists say: now we don't know what this force is, but the force exists, and these are the conditions under which it acts. Let the scientists find out what constitutes this force. No, I don't see why it can't be a new force, if it…"

Levin interrupts, "Because, with electricity, each time you rub resin against wool, a certain phenomenon manifests itself, while here it's not each time, and therefore it's not a natural phenomenon."

In placing the arguments against spiritualism in the mouth of the virtuous and country-dwelling Levin, and those for spiritualism in the mouth of the decadent and city-dwelling Vronsky, Tolstoy shows us where his true sentiments lie.

Tolstoy's apparently virulent hatred of spiritualism persisted all his life. In 1889–90, he wrote a four-act, anti-channeling comedy, "The Fruits of Enlightenment." It was first of all meant for his family, who performed it at home at Christmas with friends. But it was also intended for the public. Soon staged in Moscow, it has been fairly regularly performed ever since, the most recent U.S. performance being in Russian, in August 2005, under the direction of seasoned Moscow director Sergey Kokovkin, at the Russian Theatre Summer School in Middlebury, Vermont.

The action of "The Fruits of Enlightenment" takes place in the home of the upper-class Zvezdintsev family—mother, father, son and daughter. Tolstoy portrays all four as arrogant, idle, and frivolous. Friends and hangers-on circulate through the house, intent only on participating in the seances the Zvezdintsevs regularly host.

Playwrite Anton Chekov with Tolstoy

Tolstoy has two purposes in "The Fruits of Enlightenment": the first is to savagely skewer the spiritualist beliefs of his time, the second is to show that the shrewd, hardworking peasants and servants in the household are superior to the misguided, condescending Zvezdintsevs and their friends. The participants have long, boring, pseudo-scientific discussions before the séances on the nature of channeling. But Tolstoy stages the séances in such a way as to show that the servants themselves fake the effects, the servant girl Tanya, for example, hiding under the couch unbeknownst to the participants and sliding it along the floor "at the behest of the spirits." Tolstoy makes it perfectly clear that he believes spiritualism is either a form of self-deception in which both medium and séance-goers participate, or an outright fraud perpetrated by professionals—and, in the case of the Zvezdintsevs, by the servants.

Still: in reflecting on Tolstoy's work, there is just the suspicion that it was only Tolstoy the rational man—however powerful and penetrating his powers of analysis might have been—and not entirely Tolstoy the consummate artist who railed all his life against the possibility that there were inexplicable phenomena peeking through from other levels of reality. There is not only, in *Anna Karenina*, the puzzling if ambiguous role of the medium Jules Landau; there is also, in the same book, the disturbing, occult motif—often remarked on by reader and critic—of the horrific, shared, premonitory nightmare of Anna and Vronsky. Henri Troyat tells the story (*Tolstoy: A Biography*, 1967):

"A still more awesome menace is Anna's famous dream, in which a little muzhik in rags appears, bending over an iron plate and mumbling incomprehensible words in French, 'and she sensed that he was performing some strange ritual over her with this piece of iron, and awoke drenched in cold sweat.' She had this nightmare several times. Vronsky himself was affected by it through a kind of telepathy and the moment Anna throws herself under the wheels of the train, she sees, in a flash, 'a little man, muttering to himself and tapping on the iron above her.' "

Did the great seer Tolstoy know more in his heart than his mind would suffer him to accept?

This article first appeared in *Atlantis Rising* #54 (November/December 2005).

7

THE BATTLE OVER LIGHT

Goethe's Challenge to Newton

BY JOHN CHAMBERS

In his *Doctrine of Colors* (1810), Johann Wolfgang von Goethe (1749–1832) writes, "In the second part [of this book] we occupy ourselves with the exposé of the Newtonian theory which has so far obstructed with force and prestige a free view of color phenomena we fight against a hypothesis that, although it is no longer found useful, still retains a traditional respect among men. . . . We encounter this eighth wonder of the world as an ancient relic that is already abandoned and threatens to collapse, and so we begin right away, without further ado, to reduce it, beginning with the roof, to let the Sun shine at long last into the old rats' and owls' nest and reveal to the eyes of the surprised wanderer how labyrinthine and disconnected the building style was, how narrow and needy, accidental and artificial, deliberately contrived and wretchedly patched up."

Goethe was unquestionably Germany's greatest poet, author of the incomparable verse drama *Faust* (part I, 1808, part II, 1832). But what right does a poet have, even a great one, to deconstruct the carefully demonstrated theory of Sir Isaac Newton (1642–1727) that sunlight is a mixture of light of all colors?

The answer is: perhaps some right, if the poet is Johann Wolfgang von Goethe, the 143 volumes of whose collected works include not only poetry, plays, novels, autobiography, criticism, and correspondence but also treatises on mineralogy, botany, anatomy, and optics. Goethe was a phenomenon, hardly a man: "Every new work by Germany's greatest poet and writer was read as soon as it appeared and was totally unpredictable," writes philosopher Walter Kaufmann. He was also strange: "His wisdom abides, but it seems to come from some solar system other than our own," declares Yale scholar Harold Bloom.

Scion of a wealthy and loving upper-middle-class Frankfurt family, Johann Wolfgang von Goethe early displayed a virtuosity with language

Johann Wolfgang von Goethe in "The Roman Campagna" (1786, Städelsches Kunstinstitut, Frankfurt)

that mesmerized all who listened. He studied law at the University of Leipzig and graduated, but ultimately practiced little. Vigorous, brilliant, seductive, original, witty, insightful, prodigiously industrious, and extremely attractive to women, Goethe soon became a primary force in the German literary movements of Sentimentalism and Sturm und Drang (Storm and Stress), producing scores of gallant love poems and, at 22, a successful five-act drama, "Götz von Berlichingen" (1771).

At 24, Goethe created a sensation with his best-selling novel *The Sorrows of Young Werther* (1774), which tells the story of a profoundly self-absorbed man who falls in love with a woman who is already engaged, grows more in love with her as he finds he cannot have her, exiles himself for awhile—and then, returning to a final refusal, blows his brains out with a revolver belonging to the husband of his now-married beloved. *Werther* struck a chord in pre-Romantic Europe; there ensued a spate of copycat suicides by those believing themselves in Werther's predicament. According to one source there were 24 such suicides in Germany in 1774 alone. The fatal fad didn't die out until the end of the century.

Faust (F.W. Murnau, 1926)

In Catholic–Lutheran Germany of the 18th century, suicide was a mortal sin, and even its portrayal in literature was considered sinful. The daring and rebellious Goethe couldn't have written *Werther* were he not moving light-years beyond conventional Christianity. By age 20, he had decided that imitating Christ was pointless and one ought to find the best in oneself and imitate that. By his early 30s, Goethe was speaking of Christianity with derision, declaring in 1782 that "I for my part could not be persuaded by an audible voice from heaven that a woman has given birth without a man or that a dead man has risen again; on the contrary I regard these as blasphemies against the great God and His revelation in Nature."

The poet/novelist/playwright had been something of a pantheist very early on, believing that God inhabited a Nature made benevolent by His presence. This belief was shattered forever in June 1777 when his beloved sister Cornelia, only 26, died four weeks after giving birth to her second daughter. Ever afterward Goethe carried with him, in the words of his biographer Nicholas Boyle, "a tragic awareness of the possibility that a human being may have to face an ineluctably wretched destiny and that neither Earth nor heaven may offer any response to the cry of the heart for love."

But if God was inscrutable, perhaps even non-existent, Goethe would always believe that huge powers resided within the human being, and in 1775 this already wholly autonomous individual, open to anything, had taken an administrative post in the Duchy of Saxony-Weimar not far from Leipzig. On and off for the rest of his life Goethe spent time every week in the splendid 300-room, 22-staircase, Versailles look-alike palace of the Duke Carl August, fulfilling there a dazzling variety of tasks that included at one point being acting Prime Minister of Weimar for two months. During all these years, Goethe never stopped writing poetry and prose, but he would soon discover that his administrative functions took a toll of his spiritual energies. This was one reason why the poet/privy counselor turned his attention to the physical sciences; he found a balm to the soul in the silent communion with nature that these studies offered.

Was Goethe deeply interested in the occult? In all his works there is only the rare reference to the paranormal. In *Poetry and Truth* (1811–1822), Goethe tells us that, returning from a visit to his first love, Friederike Brion, one night when he was 21, "I was riding, on horseback, over the path to Drusenheim, when. . . not with the eyes of the body but of the spirit, I saw myself on horseback coming toward me on the same path. I was dressed in a suit I had never worn before, pale grey and with some gold. As soon as I had shaken myself out of this reverie, the vision vanished. It is strange, however, that I found myself, eight years later, once again on the same road, returning from Friederike and wearing, not by design but by chance, just this sort of suit." His associate Johann Peter Eckermann quotes Goethe as saying that premonitions occur in dreams because we can sometimes "extend the feelers of our soul beyond the limits of our body," adding that such dreams were not mere "presentiments" but actual "insight into the immediate future."

On balance, though, Goethe had far more disdain than respect for the staples of esoterica, including in particular secret societies that purported to harbor the wisdom of the ages. Inducted into the Masons in 1780, Goethe quickly advanced through the usual grades and joined the order within the order, the Illuminists, in 1783. Soon, though, he was writing, "They say you can best get to know a man when he is at play . . . and I too have found that in the little world of the brethren all is as it is in the great one. . . . I was already saying this in the forecourt, and now I have reached the ark of the covenant I have nothing to add. To the wise all things are wise, to the fool foolish." In 1790 he wrote a comedy, "The Grand Kophta," that harshly satirized the Masons; in it he portrayed, strictly as a swindler, the real-life figure of Count Cagliostro, a Rasputin-like Italian who, claiming to be thousands of years old, wealthy, and possessed of the highest occult gifts of a Mason, was then touring the courts of Europe conducting séances, making prophecies, bilking noblemen, and in general cutting a high-visibility swathe as genius/con-man/benefactor of mankind. In Palermo in 1787, Goethe visited the household of Cagliostro's mother and discovered that the "Count" was the ne'er-do-well son of a poverty-stricken family and that he had borrowed money from his mother and then disappeared. Returned to Weimar, Goethe repaid the debt anonymously (the family thought the money was from Cagliostro). The experience deepened his disgust for all pretenders to any secret knowledge of an occult world.

At that time Goethe was well into his scientific studies, which included mineralogy, botany, anatomy, and optics, and it's likely that the strangeness of the alternative lines of scientific speculation that he developed in these areas contributed greatly to the notion that he was deeply into the occult. Goethe in his researches was astonishingly original. Seeking to discover a primal pattern in rock which in its manifest development accounted for all the shapes of rock, the poet ended up believing that crystallization was the organizing principle behind the entire mineral world. Goethe was sure he discerned in human beings an "intermaxillary bone" in the upper jaw that established an organic relationship between man and animal and would enable him to find the underlying unity, visible to the informed eye, behind the multiplicity of animal forms in the natural world. The poet/scientist scoured vegetation for the "primal plant" (*Urpflanze*), hoping to find in nature the basic pattern—one in which plant form was probably reduced to a repeated sequence of elements such as sprout, leaf, and growth point—which lay behind the complex variety of the vegetable world.

In all of this (none of which stood up to rigorous scientific examination despite Goethe's lifelong persistence in advancing his views) the poet-scientist was not seeking some archetypal plant or mineral or animal which, in accordance with the beliefs of Plato, dwelt in a world of ideal forms which were more real than the world of things. Goethe thought there was no such world of ideal forms and that only the here-and-now on Earth existed in all his endeavors. The poet/scientist sought first the ideal "Ur"—shapes that might actually exist on earth, then the ideas of the primal patterns he thought would encompass every variety of form in the plant, the animal, and the mineral world.

Goethe was thus very far from being a hermeticist or cabbalist, someone who believes that the entire physical universe is infused in every atom and in equal portion with living mind or soul. The poet believed that nature was dumb, and would have said with William Blake that "where man is not, Nature is barren." Increasingly, Goethe suspected that when we see soul in nature or in "the beyond," we are merely projecting our own hopes and fears onto zones that are likely empty of God and soul.

Goethe vigorously rejected the notion that nature has an essence, a soul, something independent of what we grasp with our five senses. Man is a part of nature, and he also rejected the notion that man himself has an essence, believing, in the words of Walter Kaufmann, that "man is his

Goethe's "Chromatic Circle," an illustration from *Doctrine of Colors*

deeds." Goethe wrote in the *Doctrine of Colors*, "We really try in vain to express the essence of a thing. We become aware of effects, and a complete history of these effects would seem to comprehend the essence of the thing. We exert ourselves in vain to describe the character of a human being but assemble his actions, his deeds, and a picture of his character will confront us."

This was at the heart of Goethe's profound disagreement with Newton; light itself, declared the poet, has no essence. There was nothing behind or beyond white light as we perceive it which could contain the beingness of colors. "Colors," decreed the poet, "are the deeds of light." Goethe was deeply affronted by the implication of Newton's theory of light that we cannot accept the reality of what is presented to us through our senses even if our vision is a purified one. Writes Kaufman, "Goethe's immense lucidity [in expressing his ideas] is inseparable from his habit of seeing things instead of relying on pure concepts alone . . . Goethe always could find words for what he saw and felt. He mistrusted words that were not backed up by any experience. And he had no need of mathematical certainty."

The great attraction behind Goethe's (utterly unproven) assertions about light is that they seem to imply that there is a third alternative between accepting the evidence of the senses and accepting the truth of an unseen (if experimentally verifiable) world of equations. But there may be another, powerful, reason why Goethe stuck so tenaciously, to the end of his days, to his theory of "chromatics." Nicholas Boyle writes in *Goethe: The Poet and the Age: Volume I: The Poetry of Desire*:

"A recent exegesis, of great brilliance, has shown that the underlying structure of Goethe's unwearying argument for a new chromatics is that of a defense of Arianism—the heretical belief that Christ was not divine—against the tyrannical sophistries of the established Trinitarian Christology. Light is tortured, indeed crucified, with the instruments of the scientists, who, like a churchful of theologians parroting inherited dogmas, endeavor to split up the pure simplicity of divinity into seven colors or three persons or some other magical number in which they would rather put their trust then in what their eyes and their reason tell them. It may have been within a couple of months of his moment of conversion [to his new theory of light] that Goethe began to make the comparison of light suffering at the hands of Newton and his followers with Christ suffering at the hands of the orthodox."

The irony is that Newton himself was an Arian and did not believe that ultimately the crucifixion of Christ had any significance. This was not public knowledge in Newton's time, nor was it in Goethe's but, probably, had the poet known, he would not have ceased trying to find some felt and human reality behind the ever steadily ossifying technology of the modern world.

This article first appeared in *Atlantis Rising* #56 (March/April 2006).

8

DOSTOEVSKY & SPIRITUALISM

Did the Author of Crime & Punishment *Have Personal Knowledge of Another World?*

BY JOHN CHAMBERS

In *The Brothers Karamazov,* the masterpiece of the towering 19th century Russian novelist and short-story writer Fyodor Dostoevsky, Ivan Karamazov tells the story of an atheist who didn't believe in life after death and who, after he died, was sentenced by God to walk a billion miles in penance. Colin Wilson summarizes the story in *The Occult* (1971), "The atheist lay on the road and refused to move for a million years; however, he eventually dragged himself to his feet and unwillingly walked the billion miles. And when he was finally admitted to heaven, he immediately declared that it would have been worth walking ten times as far just for five minutes of heaven."

Dostoevsky himself experienced visions of heaven that were almost as ecstatic. They came to him in the form of "ecstatic auras"—sudden discharges of electrochemical energy that signal the start of an epileptic fit. One such ecstatic aura (Dostoevsky had hundreds of them in his lifetime) came to him the night between Easter Sunday and Easter Monday; he described it in his secret diary as follows:

"I felt . . . that heaven had come down to Earth and absorbed me. I really perceived God and was imbued with Him. Yes, God exists . . . I cried. And I can recall no more. . . .

"I do not know whether that blessedness lasts seconds, hours or minutes, yet, take my word, I would not exchange it for all the joys which life can give."

More than one hundred years earlier, on April 5 and 6, 1743—strangely enough, also an Easter weekend—another world-famous writer, and one of an even more spectacularly mystical bent than Dostoevsky, confided to his secret diary a description of the ecstatic aura he had just experienced.

Fyodor Dostoevsky

This was Emanuel Swedenborg (1688–1772), the Swedish seer, psychic and scientist who claimed there was direct mystical communication between our world and the spiritual realm and who affirmed Christ as the true God. Medical researchers Elizabeth Foote-Smith and Timothy J. Smith write that "fortunately, Swedenborg kept a record of his dreams (which was not intended for publication) during the critical years from 1743 to 1744, and for 20 years he kept his Spiritual Diary, consisting of five volumes. . . . Based on his own testimony, Swedenborg had multiple symptoms of temporal lobe epilepsy, including a characteristic aura, falling, loss of consciousness, convulsions, visual and auditory hallucinations, and trance states." Swedenborg described his pre-epileptic seizure somewhat as Dostoevsky described his, "Had also in my mind and my body a kind of consciousness of an indescribable bliss, so that if it had been in a higher degree, the body would have been as it were dissolved in mere bliss. This was the night between Easter Sunday and Easter Monday, also the whole of Easter Monday."

Swedenborg's visions of heaven, dictated to him by the angels and gathered in the course of numerous astral voyages, fill numerous volumes and were taken with the utmost seriousness during the 19th century by authors and thinkers such as Blake, Emerson, Coleridge, Carlyle, Henry James Sr., Tennyson, the Brownings, Oliver Wendell Holmes, Thoreau, Goethe, and many others. Could Swedenborg's admittedly unorthodox descriptions of a higher reality really have been merely the product of maverick and uncontrolled electrochemical charges rampaging through his brain (according to the literature, ecstatic auras are characterized by "intense elation and ineffable all-pervading bliss, a feeling that the secrets of the universe [are] about to be revealed")? Or, if Swedenborg's visions were really visions, or only in part electrochemical, does that then mean that the epileptic fits of Fyodor Dostoevsky also provided the

Russian writer with a gateway through which he could glimpse, like Blake, "an immense world of delight, clos'd by your senses five"?

And do Dostoevsky's swift but ecstatic visions of other realms peek out here and there in his novels and short stories?

But first of all: Just who was Fyodor Dostoevsky?

He was a man whose life was almost terrifying in its steady progression of shattering events and unheard-of personal woes. All of these made him stronger; they also drove him daily to distraction.

Emanuel Swedenborg

Dostoevsky's father was an impoverished doctor in a Moscow charity hospital who tyrannized his little family. When Fyodor was 15, his father was murdered by three of his serfs, in circumstances that still remain obscure. Dostoevsky hated his father, and felt vaguely responsible for his death. The theme of patricide runs through much of his writing.

Far worse awaited. He attended military engineering college—which he hated—graduated, fulfilled his duties, then threw himself into his great love: literature. He scored an early success with his first novel, *Poor Folk*. But he became attracted to radical politics and frequented a secret society promoting the socialism of Saint-Simon and Fourier. In 1848, he was arrested with friends and found guilty of disseminating anti-government literature.

His sentence was severe—eight years of hard labor in Siberia (later commuted to four by Tsar Nicolas I)—but, in the words of Vladimir Nabokov, "a monstrously cruel procedure was followed before the actual sentence was read to the condemned men." He and his friends were sentenced to death and brought to the place of execution before a firing squad. They were tied to posts. Dostoevsky and his companions thought they had only minutes left to live. Then an official stepped forward and commuted the sentence to penal servitude. Nabokov writes that after this horrendous experience of sham execution "one of the men went mad. A deep scar was left in Dostoevsky's soul by the experience of that day."

Dostoevsky spent the next four years condemned to hard labor in Siberia. In 1854, he was forced to serve in the army in Semipalatinsk, an Asiatic hellhole. In 1858, he married and returned to St. Petersburg, beginning a life of incessant activity as a novelist, journalist, and editor. His first wife died and he married his stenographer. Throughout the 1860s to the 1880s, he published his great novels *The Humiliated and Wronged* (1861), *Notes from the Underground* (1864), *Crime and Punishment* (1866), *The Idiot* (1868), *The Possessed* (1871), *A Raw Youth* [or, *The Adolescent*] (1875), *The Diary of a Writer* (1876-80), and *The Brothers Karamazov* (1880).

He had fame now, but not much fortune. Imprisonment had broken his health; ever afterward he was subject to epileptic fits. He was addicted to gambling, periodically losing every cent he owned. The great writer fought with everyone. "Over and above all this," writes Marc Slonim, were "his ecstatic flights, his carnal temptations, and the rambling of his tormented soul in search of God, harmony, and truth." He died at age 60.

Given such a life, it is hardly surprising that Dostoevsky's novels are populated with tormented, desperate, driven, and divided souls. Still, the light of the spirit—for good and for ill—flickers spasmodically in these tattered people. They know they have free will, and they cannot bear the knowledge. George Steiner writes, "They stand at the outermost limits of freedom; their next step must lead either to God or to the pit of hell." The natures of Dostoevsky's protagonists are torn; it is as if their souls are partially atomized, as if they live in an incessant, mild, epileptic state that leaves them at every moment open to God—and to the devil. Steiner writes that "Dostoevsky's multiple vision of the soul allowed for the likelihood of occasional fragmentation . . . 'ghosts' could be manifestations of the human spirit when the spirit acts as pure energy, divorcing itself from the coherence of reason or faith in order to sharpen the dialogue between different facets of consciousness. . . . What counts is the intensity and quality of the experience, the shaping impact of the apparition upon our understanding . . . Dostoevsky surrounded his personages with a zone of occult energies; forces are attracted towards them and grow luminous in their vicinity, and corresponding energies erupt from within and take palpable form. . . . Correspondingly, he drew no firm barrier between the world of ordinary sense-perception and other, potential worlds." Steiner quotes Merezhkovsky: " 'To Dostoevsky, the plurality of worlds was a manifest truth.' "

For all that, Dostoevsky did not believe in spiritualism. For him, spiritualism was a form of "isolation" that trivialized religion through mysticism, when what was needed was more faith in true orthodoxy. Perhaps channeled "spirits" existed, but proof of their existence proved only that the spirits existed; it did not prove that God existed. The spirits were, finally, trivial and irrelevant. In 1875, the great Russian chemist D. I. Mendeleev (1834–1907), best known as the formulator of the periodic table of chemical elements, set up a commission in St. Petersburg to investigate the claims of spiritualism. Dostoevsky waged war against spiritualism in his newspaper columns while also waging war against Mendeleev's methods, which he found high-handed and manipulative. The commission's final report roundly rejected spiritualism as anything but a conscious or unconscious fraud, effectively quashing its popularity for decades.

Still, Dostoevsky was fascinated by the imagery of spiritualism—was he fascinated by more than that?—and that imagery sometimes peeps through in his works. Professor Ilya Vinitsky of the University of Pennsylvania has found strong evidence of Swedenborg's influence in Dostoevsky's 1873 short story "Bobok." The anti-hero, the "bobok," is an alcoholic literary man named Ivan Ivanovich who attends the funeral of a distant relative and then, as Professor Vinitsky writes, "remains in the cemetery, where he unexpectedly 'overhears' the cynical, frivolous conversations of the dead. He discovers from these exchanges that human consciousness goes on for some time after the death of the physical body, lasting until total decomposition." The deceased persons end up communicating only with the single, unpleasant, gurgling, onomatopoeia word *bobok*. Then, says Dr. Vinitsky, "the dead, realizing their complete freedom from earthly conditions, decide to entertain themselves by telling tales of their existence 'on the top floor'—that is, during their lives. But Ivan Ivanovich suddenly sneezes, and the dead fall silent (more, as the narrator suggests, from their reluctance to share such an important secret with a living man than from embarrassment or fear of police)."

Professor Vinitsky believes this short story is a semi-satirical representation of the afterlife as described by Emanuel Swedenborg in his *On Heaven, the World of Spirits and on Hell, as They Were Seen and Heard by Swedenborg* (1758). Swedenborg asserts that "after death the human soul goes through several stages of purification of its internal content (good or evil) and as a result finds its deserved eternal reward: paradise or hell." The first two states of man after death take place in the grave and last "for some several days, for others months or even an entire year." In this "second state," man's "exterior" disappears—putrefaction sets in—and the spirits of the dead become "visibly just what they had been in themselves while in the world, what they then did and said secretly being now made manifest, for they are now restrained by no outward considerations, and therefore what they have said and done secretly, they now say and endeavor to do openly, having no longer any fear of loss of reputation, such as they had when they were alive."

There is evidence in Dostoevsky's other works both great and small of the influence of Swedenborg. In the short story "The Dream of a Ridiculous Man," the much-belittled narrator astral-travels to another world, which is actually an alternative and Edenic Earth. Swedenborgianism also influenced Dostoevsky's vision of evil in *Crime and Punishment*. According to the Nobel Prize-winning poet Czeslaw Milosz, Svidrigailov's dreadful image of an eternity in a bathhouse infested with spiders resembles some visions of hell described by Swedenborg.

The influence of Swedenborg is seen most powerfully, however—when it is playing over the contorted, visionary faces of so many of Dostoevsky's characters—in the wonderful depiction of Father Zosima in *The Brothers Karamazov*. The discourses of Zosima contain clear Swedenborgian teaching about the spiritual world, particularly that hell is always a voluntary spiritual state.

But in creating the character of Zosima, Dostoevsky does far more than find a spokesman for Swedenborg. In all his works, Dostoevsky's abiding and tormenting concern is with whether God exists. In his portrayal of Zosima—the utterly good man, and the beloved mentor of the one "good" Karamazov brother, the priest Alyosha—he seems to be telling us that his answer is: "Yes."

This article first appeared in *Atlantis Rising* #55 (January/February 2006).

9

H. G. WELLS
AND NEAR-DEATH EXPERIENCE

*Did The Great Science-fiction Writer Know More About
Such Things Than He Would Let On?*

BY JOHN CHAMBERS

"She was not clear whether it was night or day nor where she was; she made a second effort, wincing and groaning, and turned over and got in a sitting position and looked about her. . . . She seemed to be in a strange world, a soundless, ruinous world, a world of heaped broken things. And it was lit—and somehow this seemed more familiar to her mind than any other fact about her—by a flickering, purplish-crimson light."

This isn't a description by a Japanese survivor of the atomic bomb exploding over Hiroshima in August 1945, though it sounds like one.

Rather, it's a description, by a French soldier, of a German atomic bomb exploding over the Eiffel Tower in Paris in the late 20th century.

The description appears in *The Last War: A World Set Free*, a novel published by founder of science-fiction H. G. Wells in 1913. In *The Last War,* Wells also provides a detailed description of an artificially induced chain reaction, calling this process a "disease of matter." Not until the early 1930s did any scientist think such a thing might be possible.

In *The War in the Air*, a novel published in 1908, the English novelist/social prophet had again proven equally prescient. The novel describes a surprise air attack on Manhattan. Wells sets forth the disposition of the enemy powers as it actually would be during the Second World War: the Japanese rule the Pacific, while the Germans conquer Europe under the leadership of a charismatic fanatic who is half Napoleon, half "Nietzsche's Overman revealed."

The farther in time we get from H. G. Wells (1866–1945), the more uncannily prophetic he seems. Certainly not all his imaginings have come

H. G. Wells

true. There has been no invasion from Mars (*The War of the Worlds*, 1898), nor have there been any feats of time travel (*The Time Machine*, 1894–95) that we know of. But scattered here and there throughout Wells' many novels, short stories, and essays are astonishingly apt descriptions, not only of events that would come to pass, but of speculative ideas that would catch fire only many decades later.

In the short story "The Man Who Could Work Miracles" (1898), the actions of the eponymous narrator dramatize the notion, first popularized by medium Jane Roberts' in her Seth books of the 1970s, that "our thoughts create reality." They also make real the concept, vividly fleshed out in the *Back to the Future* movie trilogy of the 1980s, that if we were to travel back to the past we would change the present and the future. The hero of "The Man Who Could Work Miracles" discovers he can make anything happen and create any object simply by wishing it so. He begins with minor feats like materializing a rose. He soon becomes involved in righting social injustices. Eventually he gets so carried away that he doesn't want the day to end and inadvertently wishes that the Earth would stop rotating on its axis. He gets his wish—and momentum tears everything movable off our planet's surface, carrying the debris forward in a cataclysm of destruction. The narrator hastily wishes himself back to the time in the past before he had acquired these magical powers, also wishing that he not acquired them, and that he forget he ever had. All this happens, and as the story ends the Earth is moving forward on its calm and customary path.

How was Wells able to be so amazingly accurate in so many of his predictions?

The startling answer may be that he actually had seen the future.

Herbert George Wells was born into a working-class family in Bromley, Kent, so poor it seemed unlikely Wells would ever even qualify for college. At age 14 he was apprenticed to a draper; he despised this and broke away, attending night school and becoming a teacher's assistant at The Holt Academy in Wrexham, Wales. Eventually, Wells would receive a scholarship to study biology, attend lectures in London, and in 1888 acquire a college degree in science, thus paving the way for a brilliant career as a writer. But it was while he was at Holt, in 1886, just before his twenty-first birthday, that something may have happened to the future writer that changed, more radically than any sojourn at a college, the entire future course of his life.

Wells tells us in his *Experiment in Autobiography* (1934) that he was playing football with some students early on in his stay at Holt when one of them threw him roughly to the ground. Wells managed to get up, but felt very ill and had a terrible pain in his side. He staggered off the field and somehow made it back to his room. He writes:

"In the house I was violently sick. I went to lie down. Then I was moved to urinate and found myself staring at a chamber pot half full of scarlet blood. That was the most dismaying moment in my life. I did not know what to do. I lay down again and waited for someone to come." Wells seems to have lost consciousness for the next few hours. "Nothing very much was done about me that evening, but in the night I was crawling along the bedroom on all fours, delirious, seeking water to drink. The next day a doctor was brought from Wrexham. He discovered that my left kidney had been crushed."

No one expected H. G. Wells to live. But the future author, languishing in bed for many days, finally began to recover. He returned to work, but started coughing blood again. Tuberculosis was diagnosed. This disease, and its complications, was to dog him for the rest of his life.

H. G. Wells Time Travel Stamp

During the first days of his illness—when he almost died—did Wells have a near-death experience that revealed the future to him?

Nowhere in all of his voluminous writings does he tell us that anything of the sort happened. But Wells wrote two short stories that seem to describe near-death experiences, the second in startling detail.

In *The Truth in the Light: An Investigation of Over 300 Near-Death Experiences* (1995), authors Dr. Peter and Elizabeth Fenwick polled several hundred near-death experiencers (NDErs) to find out what happened after they got beyond the experiences of the white light and the glowing tunnel.

H. G. Wells, *Things to Come* cover

One quarter of the responders said they had been "left standing at the entrance [to the afterworld], but prevented from going in by some kind of barrier, a point of no return." Sometimes the barrier was psychological; other times it was physical, such as the "low green trellis fence," reported in one case, or the "wrought-iron gate—a tall church window-shaped gate," reported in another.

The other-worldly entities on the other side of the barrier often appeared in groups of three. One responder encountered three "young Indian men . . . young Indian princes, or rajas"; another stood before "three old Chinese men who all had long white beards and who also wore white robes." Often only the middle entity faced the experiencer directly.

The Fenwicks found that the well-known NDE "life review" often contained tantalizing glimpses of the experiencer's future. One interviewee, arriving at a church, observed "two large trestles, each with a book resting on them." A spirit guide flicked through the pages, which were blank, then stated, "This will be your life if you go back." The empty pages suddenly filled up. Though conflicted by what he saw, the responder decided he had no choice but to return to life.

In 1995, the same year that the Fenwicks published their research report, near-death experiencer Dannion Brinkley published his *Saved by the Light*. Brinkley described how, when horrifically struck by lightning and technically "dead" for 28 minutes, he found himself in a crystalline "cathedral of knowledge" where "beings of light" granted him 117 glimpses of possible future events. Brinkley later reported that, by early 1998, 95 of these events had come true.

A century earlier, in 1896—ten years after his brush with death and at the beginning of his career as a fiction writer—Wells wrote the short story "Under the Knife" in which the patient-narrator, slipping out of his body during surgery, careens around the physical universe undergoing what sounds very much like a near-death experience.

In 1906, Wells wrote a short story, "The Door in the Wall," which, while not mentioning death till the end, contains many of the critical details of a near-death experience as they were to be set forth in works like *The Truth in the Light* and *Saved by the Light* close to a century later. These details would not be known until the last decade of the 20th century, when medical science had advanced to the point where victims could sometimes remain "dead" for periods of as long as a half-hour before they were resuscitated.

As Wells' "The Door in the Wall" begins, the narrator, Wallace, then aged 5 or 6, finds himself standing in front of a mysterious green door. He wants to go in, but feels "either it was unwise or it was wrong of him." Yielding to the temptation and entering, he finds himself in a gorgeous garden with "something in the very air of it that exhilarated . . . something in the sight of it that made all its color clean and perfect and subtly luminous."

The boy proceeds down a wide path and meets three beings: two panthers who now escort him, and a "tall, fair girl" who he meets at the end of the path and who picks him up and kisses him. The girl leads him to a "spacious, cool palace" where he experiences a timeless interlude of events and game-playing, every detail of which he will forget. A second triad of beings appears: "two dear playfellows who were most with me," and "a somber dark woman, with a grave, pale face and dreamy eyes . . . who carried a book, and [led me] into a gallery above a hall." The woman opens the book and, the narrator tells us, "in the living pages of that book I saw myself . . . in it were all the things that had happened to me since ever I was born."

This apparent classic NDE life review becomes vaster: "Then, I turned the pages over, skipping this and that, to see more of this book and more, and so at last I came to myself hovering and hesitating outside the green door in the long white wall, and felt again the conflict and the fear." The boy begins to turn this final page and is stopped by the woman. They struggle; the woman yields; the boy no sooner sees the page when he finds himself no longer in the enchanted garden but in "a long gray street in West Kensington, weeping aloud . . . because I could not return to my dear playfellows who had called after me, 'Come back to us! Come back to us soon!'"

The boy has returned to grim reality, and all through his life he will long to return to the enchanted garden. He chances upon the green door three more times. Each time he does not enter, feeling that entry is somehow forbidden. Each of these occasions has found him hurrying to a rendezvous that is crucial to his worldly success; to linger in the garden would be to jeopardize his career.

As the story draws to a close, the narrator yields to this vision that seems to reflect his very soul. He disappears, and his body is found in an excavation shaft. Apparently he has fallen through a construction doorway.

Wells later wrote about "The Door in the Wall," "I am more than half convinced that he [Wallace] had, in truth, an abnormal gift, and in a sense, something—I know not what—that in the guise of wall and door offered him an outlet, a secret and peculiar passage of escape into another and altogether more beautiful world. At any rate, you will say, it betrayed him in the end. But did it betray him? By our daylight standard he walked out of security into darkness, danger, and death."

So sharply near-death experience-like (yet brilliantly masked) is this account, that we must ask ourselves if Wells himself didn't actually have such an experience, one that provided him with a profound vision of the future, and one which most likely took place at Holt. Perhaps he did not consciously remember it. If he did remember it, Wells would most likely never have spoken about it. A working class upstart who penetrated the highest levels of Britain's upper-class intelligentsia, he would have been wary of revealing anything about himself that might cast doubt on his sanity. Moreover, in general, Wells revealed little of his personal life. A notorious philanderer, he did not allow his autobiographical account of his countless love affairs, *H. G. Wells in Love: A Postscript to an Experiment in Autobiography*, to be published until every woman mentioned in the book had died. (The last to go was famed author Rebecca West in 1984.)

The list of contemporary events and (often New Age) ideas anticipated by Wells in his writings also includes astral traveling, in "The Plattner Story" (1896); remote viewing, in "The Remarkable Case of Davidson's Eyes" (1894); past-life regression and "future-life progression," in "The Dream of Armageddon" (1901); and even "cargo cults," in "Lord of the Dynamos" (1894). How can we account for such prescience? Is genius enough? Only if genius includes bursting the bonds of time and space.

This article first appeared in *Atlantis Rising* #66 (November/December 2007).

PART THREE

ANCIENT HIGH TECHNOLOGY

Great Pyramid of Giza

10

Ancient High Tech and the Ark of the Covenant

*Did Its Custodians Inherit the Powerful Legacy
of a Lost Civilization?*

BY FRANK JOSEPH

The Ark of the Covenant refers to the gold-plated, rectangular box that contained something so holy it could not be mentioned by name. According to the Old Testament, this sacred something was the pair of tablets bearing the ten commandments. But Talmudic Hebrew tradition indicates the Ark enclosed two sapphires inscribed with the "Tables of the Law." Sapphire (*sapir* in the Bible) was not meant to be taken literally as the gem, but intended only to suggest a precious stone of a "heavenly blue" color. Moreover, the original Hebrew did not specify two tablets, but rather a single, double-inscribed sapphire. Over the course of time and numerous translations, this "single, double-inscribed sapphire" became two, separate, unwieldy tablets carried by Moses as depicted most famously in Michelangelo's statue and Cecil B. DeMille's film *The Ten Commandments.*

Originally, the "sapphire" was, according to Hebrew tradition, a single precious stone featuring the Ten Commandments. This was the real and sole object inside the Ark. The "covenant" referred to a particular bond, agreement, or compact that existed between God and the Israelites. The "law" was only the mundane part of that relationship, which became uniquely special only when Yahweh materialized as a "fiery cloud" above the Ark. During such appearances, we are told, the Israelites became his "chosen people." Although custodians of the Ark for more than six hundred years, they were neither the first nor the last people to possess it. All the cultures through which it passed gave the artifact their own names. To the Israelites, it was the Aron ha-Berit, literally, the "Ark of the Covenant."

To the Egyptians before them, it appears that it was the Ben-Ben, or Bennu, the "stone of destiny," or "Phoenix stone," because of the fiery energy that occasionally glowed in the clear stone. In tracing this remarkable object from its mythic origins, through the ancient world into the Middle Ages and modern times, my book *Opening the Ark of the Covenant* (2007) argues that it was, and still is, a specimen of almost incomprehensibly sophisticated technology crafted thousands of years ago. The "stone" was in fact, I am convinced, a solid-state electronic device, a kind of ultra-sensitive capacitor able to receive, store, magnify, and discharge various forms of energy directed at it. When, for example, Joshua instructed his fellow Israelites to shout on his command and blare their trumpets, as reported in Exodus, the Ark of the Covenant resonated with their audio input, directing its amplification in an ultra-high frequency that pulverized the fortified walls of Jerico.

As such, I believe, the Ark of the Covenant could have been used as a sonic cannon, a virtual biblical "weapon of mass-destruction" that could have allowed a numerically out-numbered tribe of shepherds to overpower other peoples far more traditionally accustomed to military campaigning than themselves. Its crystal could have been sensitive to other forms of resonance. When installed inside the so-called "King's Chamber" of Egypt's Great Pyramid, as I believe evidence shows that it was, it transduced geophysical pressures, transforming seismic energies into harmless and useful electrical discharge, thereby ameliorating the worst effects of earthquake violence. At such moments, the crystal, apparently, produced a dramatic side-effect by generating negative ions that may have interfaced with the consciousness of anyone in its general vicinity.

Negative-ion therapy is today used by modern medical practitioners as an alternative to anesthesia for patients overly sensitive to conventional treatment. When the hippocampus section of the brain is subjected to an intense concentration of negative ions, people often experience otherworldly euphoria, visions of gods or angels, spiritual catharsis, mystical epiphany, plus a deep sense of inner peace and well-being. Referred to as "the God part of the brain," the hippocampus could be the seat of the human soul, or, at any rate, a psychological connection with religious feelings. It was, I suspect, this ability of the "stone of destiny" to transform human consciousness in a way that exceeded even its practical applications as a "wonder-weapon" and anti-earthquake device. Exposure to the crystal thus confirmed the reality of life's spiritual dimension on an intimately profound, personal level, making all other material considerations seem far less significant.

Accordingly, the power stone was always in the stewardship of a select group—sometimes an order or brotherhood, usually a family—of men who understood its proper use. The biblical version of these caretakers were the Levites. They alone administered to the Ark of the Covenant, and only their high priest—the Cohen Gadol—had direct access to it just once a year. Whenever he entered, say some sources, he was dressed in the *ephod*, a full-length, asbestos-like gown, his right leg shackled to a long chain held at the other end by fellow Levites hiding

The Ruined Walls of Jericho

behind the great doors of the Debir. In the event the Cohen Gadol's ephod did not adequately protect him from one of the unexpected static discharges from the ark, and he was knocked unconscious or killed, the chain was used to haul his body out of the holy-of-holies into the main hall of the temple.

These precautions were not unjustified. The Old Testament reports that thousands of Jews were killed by the capricious Aron ha-Berit. The earliest known guardians of the Ark, it is said, were the sons of Belial. This was the name Edgar Cayce learned from the akasic records he claimed to study during his "life readings." Famously known as "the Sleeping Prophet," Cayce was the outstanding psychic of the 20th century, primarily a medical intuitive, but occasionally given to visions of prehistory. Cayce often spoke of the lost empire of Atlantis, an oceanic civilization he described as more technologically and psychically advanced than anything that has come since. At the center of its magnificence was the Tuoai, or "fire stone," a great crystal once in the keeping of the sons of Belial.

Unfortunately, according to Cayce, the sons of Belial were aggressive materialists, more interested in personal than spiritual wealth, and so abused the Tuoai in their determination to excavate mineral riches; this misuse of the sacred stone unleashed geological forces that destroyed their own society. Escaping with the "fire stone" before Atlantis was utterly destroyed, a rival faction known as the children of the Law of One made their way to the distant Nile Valley. There they cooperated with the indigenous inhabitants to build a new home of the Tuoai, the Great Pyramid. This, in brief, is Edgar Cayce's story of the original Atlantean crystal and its relocation to Egypt. Remarkably, it is at least partially borne out by archaeological information he never suspected.

For example, the land on which the Great Pyramid stands, familiar today as the Giza Plateau, was known during dynastic times as the Place of the Tuoai. Cayce's name for the "fire stone" of Atlantis and its removal to the Nile Delta coincide with the same name used by the ancient Egyptians to describe the precinct of the Great Pyramid. Once installed in that immense structure, it was under the protection of an elite guard-unit, the Rosthau, or "Watchers." Like the Levites to come, they allowed no one inside, except their high priest. For nearly two thousand years after the Pyramid's construction, numerous generations of Rosthau stood watch over the mountainous monument of the Ben-Ben, or Bennu—"Phoenix Stone," as the Egyptians called the old Atlantean Tuoai.

In 1227 BC, as the story goes, the Nile Delta was attacked and occupied by fleets of "Sea Peoples," a coalition of piratical veterans displaced by the Trojan War. Taking advantage of the chaos, Ramose Khamenteru, the Pharaoh's chief vizier, or right-hand man, staged his own uprising against the Egyptian authorities by siding with the foreign invaders. Ramose's mobs swept aside the Rosthau, allowing him to break into the Great Pyramid and remove the Ben-Ben from its granite coffer in the King's Chamber. When Pharaoh's forces unexpectedly turned the tide of battle against the "Sea Peoples" and expelled them from the Delta, the ex-vizier and his followers, fearing retribution, fled into the Sinai desert with the "Stone of Destiny." According to this account, it became their own Ark of the Covenant, and Ramose became Moses.

The Aron ha-Berit, according to esoteric tradition, enabled its Hebrew handlers to survive against otherwise overwhelming opposition and to conquer their way to the promised land. There, atop Jerusalem's Mount

Moriah, around 900 BC, they erected a temple to specifically enshrine the sacred object, which had already been in the keeping of the Levites for some three centuries. Under the stimulus of earth-generated negative ions, Solomon became the wisest man of his times and Israel ascended into its golden age. Over time, abuse yet again engendered catastrophe, when the Babylonians seized Jerusalem and razed the temple to the ground in their determined efforts to possess the Ark. Prior to the city's capitulation, it is said, the Levite high priest, the Cohen Gadol, had lowered the golden box with its sacred "sapphire" through a cunningly engineered trapdoor into a shaft descending vertically 150 feet through solid limestone. Thus effectively concealed, it could not even be retrieved by the Israelites themselves when they returned to Mount Moriah after seven generations in Babylonian captivity.

Four hundred years later, King Herod I built the second temple, but he too failed to relocate the Ark. It remained lost throughout the years of the Roman empire and the fall of the Classical World, well into the Dark Ages that followed. But with the capture of Jerusalem by Crusaders in 1103, local rumors of the Ark's subterranean whereabouts began to surface. The city had been captured by Godfroi de Bouillon, who instituted the Order of the Holy Sepulcher for the purpose of locating the gold box. The order was limited to a handful of his family members, whose most prominent member, Baudoin de Boulogne, became the first Crusader king of Jerusalem. As Baudoin I, he erected a heavily fortified castle called the Royal Mountain, "*Mont real,*" in the Holy Land, to store and protect the anticipated discovery. But he died before that great find could be made.

The king was succeeded by his cousin, Baudoin de Bourcq, now Baudoin II. In 1119, he inaugurated *La milice du Christ*, "the Poor Knights of Christ," better remembered as the Knights Templar, who secretly excavated his palace grounds atop Mount Moriah. After nine years of unremitting labor, it is said, their persistence was rewarded when they retrieved the Ark of the Covenant intact from the bottom of its deep shaft where it had been hidden since the destruction of Solomon's Temple. The Templars smuggled it out of Jerusalem and into France, determined to prevent their incomparable treasure from falling into the hands of either Muslims or popes.

In early 1128, I believe they concealed the Ark at the Cistercian monastery of Citeaux, headed by Bernard de Clairvaux, today remembered

"Sacrifice of the Old Covenant" (Peter Paul Rubens, 1626)

as Saint Bernard. But close proximity to the holy object effected Bernard adversely, and the Templars removed it from his monastery, placing it into the hands of a new, related brotherhood. For the remainder of the 12th and into the 13th century, the Cathars, known widely as the *bons hommes*, or "good men," preserved their sacred charge at another "*Mont real*"— Montreal-de-Sos, in central France. The Israelites' Aron ha-Berit henceforth figured into Western European traditions of the Holy Grail, from the ancient Gallic word for "power," *gral*. Learning of its location, Pope Innocent III launched a massive crusade against the Cathars, who escaped to their mountaintop fortress in the Pyrenees.

But with the discovery of the Americas, the De Bouillon–Baudoins began to plan for the artifact's removal from endemically corrupt Europe into the purity of the New World. To that end, they formed a semi-secret society, the Compagnie du Saint-Sacrament, a covert version of Godfroi de Bouillon's Order of the Holy Sepulcher and Knights Templar. Some of its members referred to themselves as the Villa Maries, or "House of Mary," and left for Canada in 1642. In the middle of the St. Lawrence River, on a mountainous island they called Montreal after the other "Royal Mountains" used as repositories for the Ark, they broke ground for the realization of their dream—the New Jerusalem, a recreation of Solomon's Temple. After more than thirty years of difficult work compounded by the native Indians' murderous hostility, the Villa Maries had completed Bon-Secours Chapel, and sent word back to France that they were ready to receive the sacred holy-of-holies.

In 1667, Pere Jean Beaudoin, a Jesuit priest and member of the Grail family, crossed the Atlantic Ocean with the Ark to Montreal, where it was installed in the New Jerusalem. What became of the Ark forms the climax to my book *Opening the Ark of the Covenant*. For purposes of our discussion here, it is interesting to observe that, throughout its history—as long as civilization itself—this supremely holy object was always in the care of an elite priesthood, a brotherhood, or order of family-related custodians. Beginning in Atlantis, it was possessed and ultimately misused by the sons of Belial before it was saved by the children of the Law of One. I believe that they escaped with it from the destruction of their homeland to the Nile Delta, where they set it up inside the King's Chamber of the Great Pyramid, guarded day and night by the Rosthau, the "Watchers."

When they lost it during the Sea Peoples' invasion that swept over Lower Egypt, it fell into the hands of Israel's Levite priests. Godfroi de Bouillon founded the Order of the Holy Sepulcher composed of his relatives to search for the lost Ark. As the Knights Templar, they found it, returned with their charge to France, and entrusted it to yet another band of stewards, the Cathars. With their immolation, it passed back into a 17th century version of the Order of the Holy Sepulcher, the Compagnie du Saint-Sacrament. Its last caretakers were the Villa Maries, the inheritors of an unbroken tradition extending back over thousands of years and across half-a-dozen different societies to ancient Atlantis. No less compelling than this organizational legacy was the consistency of experience encountered by anyone brought into close proximity with the energized artifact.

Egyptian Pharaoh Amenhotep IV became obsessed with it, so much so, that he created a new religion, an alien monotheism around the Ben-Ben, and changed his name to Akhenaton, "Potent Spirit of the Sun." In 1355 BC, he had the "Stone of Destiny" transferred from the Great Pyramid to his private shrine at Akhetaten, a new city he built in the desert wilderness for the practice of his heretical cult. Over-exposure with Ark, I believe, drove him mad, physically deformed him, and probably resulted in his early death. When Baudoin II was irradiated by the burst of negative ions streaming from the freshly discovered Ark of the Covenant, he abdicated his throne over one of the most influential kingdoms of the Middle Ages, even though he had no son or heir, handing over the crown to his daughter, Melisande, a shockingly unprecedented move, and spent the rest of his life in monastic seclusion in Jerusalem's Tomb of the Holy Sepulcher.

A complete catalog of men and women transformed by this powerful device would be a long one. The Ark of the Covenant epitomizes the dilemma of technology, which, to paraphrase Frederick Nietzsche, is beyond Good and Evil. Technology is amoral, and, if used properly, is the tool by which mankind may ascend toward godhood. If abused, it turns against us. Here is the old story of Promethean fire, which, when misused, burns the home it formerly warmed, or destroys the food it once cooked.

The Egyptian "stone of destiny" that made civilization possible in the earthquake-prone Nile Valley drove a pharaoh to ruin; the Ark of the Covenant that made Solomon wise, electrocuted thousands of his own "chosen people"; the grail that inspired the gothic revival called down upon itself a fratricidal crusade. In the hands of well-intended persons, it illuminates the world. But controlled by ambitious men, its power becomes self-destructive. If so, then perhaps the Ark of the Covenant, given the current spiritual development of humanity, is better off undiscovered.

This article first appeared in *Atlantis Rising* #67 (January/February 2008).

11

ELECTROMAGNETISM & THE ANCIENTS

What Does the Evidence Really Show?

BY GLENN KREISBERG

I t's been suggested, at various times, that ancient humans had knowledge and use of unseen powers, forces, and energy fields. Could these unseen forces and fields consist of electromagnetic (EM) frequency waves and particle fields that make up the EM spectrum? This is not a simple question to answer.

What evidence exists, and what kind of evidence may come to light, to support such a claim?

There is no question that the EM spectrum has always existed as a naturally occurring part of our environment, comprised of a continuous sequence of electromagnetic energy arranged according to wavelength or frequency, generated by particle motion (vibrations) and pulses created from many sources.

There is also no doubt that many ancient cultures had a connection with nature and natural forces that was fundamental and could only be described as intimate and profound in ways we moderns can only attempt to comprehend.

From ancient times to today, humans have demonstrated an inherent curiosity and a desire to understand mysterious and odd phenomena, signs, and images. Spanning the vanished civilizations and cultures of Egypt, Sumer, and other early civilizations—and actually for the entire history of humankind—our connection to unseen forces seems irrefutable, and there remains many images, messages, texts, tablets, artifacts, inscriptions, engravings, schemes, and phenomena that we have yet to solve and unravel.

It has been noted by many that the designs and motifs of ancient architecture often reflect and in many ways try to mimic the patterns, signs, and signals that naturally occur in our environment. Most notable are the many variations of the basic waveforms—sine wave, saw-tooth wave, box

Saw-tooth wave representation in a native American design

Native American design with sine wave representation

The dragon or serpent is an ancient Chinese symbol for an unseen force. This one appears to take the shape of a box-tooth wave.

wave—or the endless variety of spirals and wavelike forms that adorn ancient cave walls, temples, and structures, and appear in architecture, scrolls, tablets and inscriptions throughout the ancient world.

As mentioned earlier, the EM spectrum exists naturally, occurring as a part of our natural environment. And again, acknowledging the ancients' intimacy and interdependency with nature, it would not be surprising if they possessed some knowledge of this naturally occurring "tool."

The ancient cultures of this world are known to have identified and utilized the forces of nature to their benefit, including water, fire, wind, and acoustic sound. Are we to believe that humankind is only now, in the past century, exploiting the waves and frequencies of the EM spectrum for the first time? And perhaps more importantly, if ancient cultures did possess this knowledge, where did this knowledge come from and how was it processed?

Electromagnetic radiation has been around since the birth of the universe. Light is its most familiar form. Electric and magnetic fields each form a part of the spectrum of electromagnetic radiation, which extends from static electric and magnetic fields, through radiofrequency and infrared radiation, to X-rays.

From the written historical record, it appears that many of the concepts now familiar in EM theory were explored and developed during a time when many modern high-tech investigative and detection tools and methods did not exist.

But is it possible that the ability to manipulate the particles and waves of the EM spectrum was discovered and developed even earlier than written history suggests? Could it be that many of the symbols, images, architecture, and myths of ancient cultures are representations reflecting the possession of such technological knowledge?

Observing what he believes to be power plant plans on ancient tapestry, and microprocessor design in Egyptian temple layout, Slovakian researcher Dr. Pavel Smutny (author of *Ancient Egypt and 2012*) has written, "Maybe it is unusual and surprising, but in ornaments on old carpets are woven-in schemes, and principle plans of advanced technologies, which come from vanished cultures and thousands-year-old civilizations. These residues are probably the last ones, which can help revive forgotten, very sophisticated technologies and methods for exploitation of natural electrostatic energy sources."

On the Egyptian temples Smutny continues, "If we see plans for the Valley temple at Sphinx, or of the Mortuary temple at Chephren's pyramid, or the Mortuary temple at Menkaure pyramid, or also of Osereion from Abydos, to a person familiar with the basics of computer techniques, or even better, to a person experienced with construction of microwave circuits in bands above 1 Gigahertz (GHz), he will tell you that these plans are schemes of PCBs [boards for electronic circuits]."

Some believe these figures in the Denderah temple's crypt in Egypt are actually depictions of electronic devices, perhaps cathode ray tubes, but this is not the only example suggesting ancient knowledge of the principles of electromagnetic wave propagation.

If, as Smutny suggests, these tapestry patterns and temple layouts are representations of fragmentary remnants from long lost science, what could have been the original source, other than a previously existing technologically advanced civilization? Of course, more evidence is needed before any solid conclusions can be drawn.

Turning his attention to the ancient temples of Malta, Smutny explains, "Complexes were used probably as generators of high-frequency acoustic waves. Purposes were (maybe) to arrange a communication channel among various islands." Smutny speculates about the legend of Sirens, "Their singing modulated low-frequency signals, which were generated on opposite ends of temples (in windows and in doors) simply with a bell, or with vibrating metal plates, or even with a strong wind drafted through a wall opening."

The oval multi-chambered configuration of the Maltese temples would allow signals formed from groups of air particles, before output, to be amplified in a second parallel opposite oval spaces of the temple.

As a radio frequency engineer, I find these possibilities fascinating, and while pondering them I had a bit of a revelation, namely, a birds-eye view of the temple structure and configurations in Malta. In many ways, the temple structure closely resembles an antenna propagation pattern with its main beam lobe, side lobes, and nulls (between the lobes).

Odds are, of course, this is all simply coincidence, but it poses the interesting question: Exactly what is the unique and specific temple design layout of Hagar Qim and Mnajdra temples based upon? What impetus and influence dictated those architectural configurations so long ago?

I design digital wireless networks utilizing the EM spectrum, transmitters, receivers, modulators, and antenna. I also do propagation prediction modeling using powerful computer programs. Such a program creates a model showing how a location will perform using different antenna, elevation, azimuths, and power settings. Sites are chosen based on how well the location propagates a signal.

Again, when I noticed how the land gently dropped away for a great distance from the Malta temple locations, I couldn't help but think how ideal that is for signal propagation when designing sites that can transmit great distances.

Is it possible some ancient temple locations were chosen for similar reasons? If the temple location were part of some kind of communications

Neolithic "lobe" construction of the Temple of Mnajdra on Malta (Photo courtesy *Sacredsites.com*)

or energy distribution network utilizing the EM spectrum, I'd say they were.

Is it possible a correlation exists between the Maltese temple architecture and antenna propagation patterns? Perhaps, but much more research and investigation is needed before any firm conclusions can be drawn. Certainly it can be said that the temple layout seems to strikingly conform to the characteristics of antenna propagation patterns.

If a connection were proven to exist, what would be the implications? It would require a radical rethinking of what we think we know about the level of technological sophistication that may have existed in ancient civilization, not to mention the question of how this knowledge came to the builders of the Maltese temples.

Let's assume, for a moment, the ancient builders had knowledge and understanding of wave propagation. Perhaps early post-flood cultures possessed the knowledge and understood the purpose of unseen forces but lacked the functionality to harness such forces. If it was known and handed down through generations that a force existed that could be controlled for the benefit of all humans, would not every effort be made, no matter how futile the attempt, to resurrect and re-create that functionality? This in itself could account for the existence of many megalithic structures that have puzzled modern researchers since their discovery: What could have been the purpose of these unusual structures? Why were they built?

Another example of anomalous science, which includes a possible EM spectrum connection, is the Celtic round towers of Ireland. These fascinating structures (once numbering over 100) dot the Irish landscape, the tallest measuring 34 meters in height.

The idea that the round towers were erected and used primarily as watchtowers and places of protection is strongly debated by the American scientist, Philip Callahan. In his 2001 book, *Ancient Mysteries, Modern Visions,* Callahan discusses research that indicates that the round towers

may have been designed, constructed, and utilized as huge resonant systems for collecting and storing meter-long wavelengths of magnetic and electromagnetic energy coming from the Earth and skies. Based on fascinating studies of the forms of insect antenna and their capacity to resonate to micrometer-long electromagnetic waves, Callahan suggests that the Irish round towers (and similarly shaped religious structures throughout the ancient world) were human-made antennae, which collected and transmitted subtle magnetic radiation from the Sun and passed it on to monks meditating in the tower and plants growing around the tower's base. The round towers were able to function in this way because of their form and also because of their materials of construction.

Of the 65 towers that remain as ruins, 25 were built of limestone, 13 of iron-rich, red sandstone, and the rest of basalt, clay, slate, or granite—all of these being minerals with para-magnetic properties and can thus able to act as magnetic antennae and energy conductors. Callahan further states that the mysterious fact of various towers being filled with rubble for

An Irish Round Tower with conical cap intact at ruined Kilmacduagh monastery.

UNSEEN FORCES

portions of their interiors was not random but rather may have been a method of "tuning" the tower antenna so that it more precisely resonated with various specific frequencies.

In another article "The Mysterious Round Towers of Ireland: Low Energy Radio in Nature" from *The Explorer's Journal*, Summer, 1993, Callahan gives further details of his discoveries, stating, "Another strange thing about the towers is the dirt that fills the base below the high doors. Each door has a different level of dirt filling the base, as if they were 'tuned' like a pipe organ. I had long postulated that the towers were powerful amplifiers of radio resonance from the atmosphere generated by lightning flashes around the world." Upon further investigation, Callahan concluded, "The round towers proved to be powerful amplifiers in the alpha brain wave region, two to 24 Hz, in the electrical anesthesia region, 1000 to 3000 Hz, and the electronic induction heating region, 5000 Hz to 1000 KHz. . . . It is fascinating that just above the surface of the ground to about two to four feet up there is a null of atmospheric frequencies that get stronger and stronger until at nine to 15 feet above the surface they are extremely strong."

Were Irish monks aware of these properties and were thus prompted to build their high doors? At every tower Callahan measured, there was a direct correlation between the height of the tower door and the strength of the waves. That the highly amplified waves occur in the meditative and electrical anesthesia portion of the electromagnetic spectrum is of utmost significance. In 1963, G. Walter researched brain EEG waves from 0.5 to 3 Hz (Delta region) and found anti-infectious effects.

Perhaps not unrelated to the Irish stone towers are the many anomalous ancient stone structures, chambers, and circles found through the Northeast United States in New England. In the book *Celtic Mysteries of New England* (2000), authors Phillip Imbrogno and Marianne Horrigan note and measure unexplained electromagnetic anomalies at stone chamber locations. The anomalies, described as "pulses," seem to occur in a specific frequency range beginning at 16.50 MHz with peak signal strength occurring at 1675 MHz. The authors claim this could be suggestive of a "doorway" or "portal" function of the chambers, with a burst of EM energy released whenever the door is opened or shut.

Could it be that, as opposed to a "portal" or "doorway" opening to another dimension of time and space, it might be more likely that the chamber's EM anomalies indicate a communication channel opening for use in some way?

Someone once said that science is like a game of darts. The surface of the dartboard, albeit perhaps infinite, represents all the science there is to know. Each theory confirmed, through experiment and scientific method, represents a dart hitting its mark on the dartboard of science. While the surface of the board may have many darts in it, most of it, as of yet, remains untouched by a dart. And of course, sometimes one dart thrown may knock out a previously thrown dart from its apparently secure location. In other words, there is still a great deal of true science yet to be discovered and confirmed, and perhaps some ideas that may need to be unlearned. Above all, the perspective with which we search is perhaps the key to what we discover.

An important lesson may be learned from the device known as the Antikythera Mechanism. The device, discovered over 100 years ago on the floor of the Mediterranean Sea, has been dated by archaeologists to be at least 2,000 years old. Because the device suggests that the ancient Greeks had the mechanical sophistication of 18th century Swiss watchmakers, historians and scholars have generally ignored and dismissd it. Could this device be evidence that a period of technological *devolution*, as a general trend, took place over many thousands of years in fields such as mathematics, mapmaking, mechanics and more? Can the same claim be made for wave and particle theory? Was much more known, much earlier on, than what current evidence supports and the academic world is willing to accept? And if this downward trend in knowledge occurred—why?

Nothing less than a major shift in the approach to these mysteries needs to occur in order for a full debate and examination of the facts and theories to take place within the established academic community. The fact is, the Antikythera device exists, as do many other anomalies of science and history. No, they do not fit into the context of established history, but to not consider them as part of a larger picture, that is far from complete, does a great disservice to the pursuit of knowledge.

This article first appeared in *Atlantis Rising* #56 (March/April 2006).

12

MERCURY: METAL OF MYSTERY

Are Today's Scientists Taking a Page
from Ancient Alchemists?

BY PETER KING

W ho has not been entranced by their first encounter with mercury? Those silvery globules racing around in a madcap chase
more than justify this elemental metal's other name of "quick-
silver," while its elusiveness and eternal motion are qualities that affirm its
refusal to be captured. It's as if this unique metal is determined to preserve
the secrets of its mysterious substance.

The very fact that mercury is a liquid metal is in itself a paradox. How
can a metal be liquid? It is one of the many characteristics that make mercury singularly mysterious.

The ancient alchemists regarded mercury with awe, recognizing
immediately its mystical aura. They bestowed the name of mercury on
it because of its resemblance to the god Mercury—"winged and fugitive,"
they described it.

The metal was used extensively by alchemists in both the Eastern and
Western worlds and was crucial to many chemical experiments. It was particularly valued because of its ability to combine with most other metals.

The renowned Chinese alchemist, Ko Hung, wrote a book in the 4th
century that referred frequently to his use of mercury. In the Arab world,
Ar-Razi, in the 10th century, experimented with the liquid metal extensively.

In 13th century Spain, the Franciscan friar and mystic Ramon Lulli
wrote extensively on scientific subjects and eagerly sought the Philosophers' Stone—the substance that would transmute base metals into gold.
He became a technical adviser to Pope John XXI, then later spent months
in a laboratory in the Tower of London where it was said that he transmuted mercury into gold for King Edward in the amount of six million
crowns. "Were there enough mercury," Lulli wrote, "I could transform
whole oceans into gold."

A bottle holding liquid mercury

During the same century in England, another alchemist was at work with mercury: Roger Bacon, a Franciscan friar and also an Oxford don of extraordinary learning and achievement. A dedicated alchemist, Bacon was a fervent believer that the mercury–sulfur combination was the key to transmutation—though he never succeeded in producing gold.

One of the most renowned of the Western alchemists of the 15 century was Paracelsus. Of Swiss origin, he believed that things were not merely inert lumps of matter but that they all possessed unknown powers and were merged in the magic of an unseen world. He reached the conclusion that there were three basic alchemical elements—mercury, sulfur, and salt.

Successors to Paracelsus expanded his beliefs to assert that there were seven elements, basing this number on the fact that the sky contained seven heavenly bodies. Again, mercury was one of the seven selected.

When Pope John XXI died, he was succeeded by John XXII, a noted alchemist. He built a laboratory in Avignon, the new Vatican, and wrote books on the transmutation of metals, which identified mercury as the dominant chemical agent. When he died, he left eighteen million florins in gold—an unprecedented amount for the impoverished papacy at that time—and it was universally believed that he could have accumulated such wealth only by transmutation.

In 1782, the Royal Society of London was startled when one of its members, a chemist named Charles Price, claimed to have solidified pure mercury and then turned it into gold. He was called upon to repeat this feat before selected committees of the Royal Society and did so several times to the astonishment of all present—members of the House of Lords, senior dignitaries of the Church of England, and master gold refiners. Price used a white powder as the catalyst in this process but naturally refused to divulge what this was. He took his own life by drinking cyanide before his veracity could be established.

The core of the solution to the centuries-old search for the Philosophers' Stone was believed by many to consist of two steps. The first step was to combine mercury and sulfur, and then . . . but that second step eluded even the most gifted of the alchemists. Modern researchers have valid reason to believe that their efforts could be successful. While it was long considered that there were 92 elements and that the entire universe did not contain any more, nuclear bombardment was able to produce what are known as "the trans-uranium" elements, uranium being number 92.

Elements from number 93 onward—a total now of 26 additional elements—are man-made, which distinguishes them from the "natural" elements in the atomic table. Nevertheless, some researchers argue that this proves that elements can be transmuted and that in theory, base metals can be converted into gold. Perhaps someday, this scientific dream will be realized—and that realization has some basis in scientific fact. Consider the following:

The atomic number of mercury is 80. Gold, which is next to mercury on the table of periodic elements, has an atomic number of 79. This means that mercury has one more proton than the atomic structure of gold. If one proton and its corresponding electron could be knocked out of the mercury atom, it would be identical to the gold atom. Such an atomic restructuring is theoretically possible. Today's scientists (21st century alchemists?) believe that this can be achieved with the aid of the new and immensely powerful particle accelerators.

Mercury occurs only rarely in its elemental form in nature. Alchemists of the Middle Ages believed it occurred wherever the planet Mercury had the most influence. Still, they described its appearance accurately and correctly identified the types of rock in which solid mercury was found. Its principal ore is cinnabar, which consists of mercury and sulfur. The ore can be heated in air so as to oxidize the sulfur and leave the globules of mercury metal. This has been a common practice since as early as 1500 BC; consequently it was readily available to Paracelsus and the other practicing alchemists.

Metallic mercury guards its secrets; it is not a human-friendly element. It is, in fact, a dangerous poison and is easily absorbed through the membranes of the nose and mouth, the stomach, and even through unbroken skin. Mercury at room temperatures is moderately safe, but any increase in temperature produces mercury vapor, which is highly toxic.

Mercury was found to be dangerous in another way too.

The expression "mad as a hatter" has been an expression in common use for some time and it took many years for the realization that an inordinately large number of hat-makers did in fact become insane. The reason was eventually found to be due to the mercury compounds used in hat-making.

The alchemists and doctors of the time were aware to some extent of the dangers of mercury, but they were also aware that what can kill man can also kill man's diseases. Used cautiously, mercury-based chemicals were powerful weapons in the hands of the early health practitioners.

Mercury's mysterious properties have led people to place credence in its ability to sustain—and even prolong—life. One modern group that has followed this persuasion call themselves "Hermeticists." Among them was a man named Swami Purna, an Oxford scholar who later lived in London.

Swami Purna alleged to have graduated in 1845 (which would have made him over 100 years old), and he maintained that his longevity was due to a small image of the Hindu god Shiva that he had himself carved from a block of solidified mercury, and which was then implanted in his flesh.

Sir Isaac Newton was perhaps the greatest scientist in history. His discoveries in gravity and light are the cornerstones of much of our current scientific knowledge. Less known, however, is his passionate interest in alchemy. He amassed one of the finest private alchemical libraries ever collected and at the same time wrote more than one million words on the subject. The best biography of Newton (written by Michael White, 1999) is aptly titled, *Isaac Newton: The Last Sorcerer.*

Newton was a devoted experimenter and his friend and contemporary, Lord Atterton, reported excitedly on one occasion that "Newton has unlocked the secret of mercury." What he meant by that has been long debated although it was known that mercury was widely used in Newton's work. The British nuclear physicist, Edward Neville da Costa Andrade, gave a speech at Cambridge University in July 1946 making reference to Newton's knowledge of mercury's secrets. He said, "Modesty teaches us to speak of the ancients with respect, especially when we are not familiar with their works. Newton, who knew them practically by heart, had the greatest respect for them and considered them to be men of genius and superior intelligence who had carried their discoveries in every field much further than we suspect today."

Andrade continued, quoting Newton and saying, "Because of the way mercury may be impregnated, it has been thought fit to be concealed by others that have known it and therefore may possibly be an inlet to something more noble, not to be communicated without immense danger to the outside world." Did Newton refer to gold in his mention of "something more noble"? and what is the "immense danger" to which he alluded?

Possibly the most extensive references to mercury in earlier times are those in the Vedic literature of ancient India. The Mahabharata, the Ramayana, and the Puranas all give detailed descriptions of flying machines. There are literally hundreds of these texts; some have not yet been translated from the old Sanskrit. These works tell of a world 10,000 to 15,000 years ago, they have not been given a great deal of credence—until recently. The reason for this is the remarkable similarity of the powers possessed by these Vimanas or "sky chariots" to those ascribed to UFOs.

Vimanas are described as circular flying machines with a double-deck, portholes for look-out, and a dome. The Vimanas are about 20 feet in diameter and according to the ancient texts have a "strong and durable body like a great flying bird made of light material." But it was their descriptions of the engines that are extraordinarily fascinating:

"Inside the Vimana must be placed the mercury engine with its iron heating apparatus beneath it. By means of the power latent in the mercury which sets the driving whirlwind in motion, a man sitting inside may travel a great distance in the sky in a most marvelous manner."

The account in the Samarangana Sutra-dhara goes on to state that Vimanas could be built as large as a temple: "four strong mercury containers must be built into the inner structure. When these have been heated by controlled fire from the iron containers, the Vimana develops thunder-power through the mercury . . . it develops power with the roar of a lion."

Did the Hindus of 10,000 to 15,000 years ago have such technology? We do not know today exactly what was meant by "a mercury engine" but current development work on ion propulsion techniques suggest that a mercury engine may be not only a power source of the past but a valuable power source of the future.

Millions of dollars are now being spent on bringing ion propulsion technology to practical fruition. Hydrogen gas was used as the fuel in the earliest ion experiments but xenon gas has now become the preferred choice. In a space propulsion engine, the gas is ionized in a magnetic chamber and expelled from an exhaust, driving the craft forward. Though the mass expelled is very low and provides only a barely measurable amount of thrust, the concept has been proven valid. What remains is to increase that thrust.

Ten years ago, NASA's Deep Space probe designated DS1 operated for more than a year using the ion propulsion method in the near-vacuum of

NASA'S Deep Space 1 with the NSTAR Ion Engine (NASA)

space and millions of miles from earth. Based on experienced gained from this project, the construction of engines with higher thrust capabilities was then ardently underway, and DS2 was subsequently launched. (Unfortunately the program came to a halt in 2009 when Congress cut funding.)

Gases have very low atomic weights and a shift from xenon gas to a heavy metal such as mercury would increase the amount of thrust by several orders of magnitude. Mercury is easily vaporized and, in liquid form, readily stored and easy to meter into a combustion chamber. As a result, it would be an ideal propellant. Is it possible that the ancients had already made such discoveries?

In 1970, a Soviet periodical, *The Modern Technologist*, published descriptions and illustrations of mysterious pots found by a Soviet archaeological team in a cave near Tashkent in what is now Uzbekistan. These were conical ceramic jars, each carefully sealed and each containing a single drop of mercury. There was no clue as to the purpose of the pots or their age. Were they some kind of power generator? Small batteries today use a tiny amount of mercury—had the ancients discovered how to use the metal for that same purpose?

In the 15th century, that indefatigable and brilliant inventor, Leonardo da Vinci, made use of mercury in his design for a perpetual motion machine. It consisted of a wheel with four radial arms. At the end of each arm was a hollow sphere containing a small amount of mercury. As the wheel turned, the theory was that it would always be heavier on the side of the axle and thus keep turning.

Da Vinci was an intensive researcher and was always ready to apply the development work of earlier researchers. However, it is unlikely that he was aware of the writings in the Sysyadhivrddhida Tantra in AD 748, an ancient Sanskrit document, as translations from Sanskrit to Latin or Italian had not been made. We now have such translations and this work tells us that the Hindu astronomer Lalla built a self-rotating wheel driven by mercury running inside its curved spokes.

Such a method of transference of energy is the same basic concept as that of da Vinci and it proved to be a popular one. In AD 1150, the Hindu Bhaskara proposed a wheel that had containers filled with mercury around its rim. As the wheel turned, the mercury moved, keeping the wheel turning forever—in theory.

None of these thoughtful ideas translated into practical reality as far as perpetual motion was concerned.

All of these—and many other—wheel notions saved energy and made the apparatus more efficient but they did not produce energy from nothing, which a perpetual motion machine is expected to do.

So mercury continues to baffle us, even as we are able occasionally to add to our store of knowledge and make advancements in areas of science that in the past would have been considered as witchcraft. There can be no doubt that mercury will be a major contributor to numerous fields of research, not only in aerospace and engineering but in more mundane applications to everyday life.

Such advances will undoubtedly be difficult to achieve—for mercury can be expected to continue to exhibit a determination to hold on to its secrets in the future as it has in the past. Man has spent centuries probing its mysteries but has still not pulled aside the curtain that resolutely hides what may be more arcane properties than even the most unconventional experimenters have ever suspected.

This article first appeared in *Atlantis Rising* #59 (September/October 2006), and has been updated here to include recent developments.

13

TELESCOPES AND THE ANCIENTS

A Forgotten Case for Ancient Achievement Revisited

BY LARRY BRIAN RADKA

The word *telescope* is derived from the ancient Greek word *tle*, meaning "far off," plus *skopein*, meaning "to look." The primary definition of a telescope, according to the 1927 *Encyclopedic Edition of the Winston Simplified Dictionary*, is: "An optical instrument for viewing distant objects, especially heavenly bodies: called refracting if bringing the rays to a focus by a lens, reflecting if by a concave mirror." However, this authority's editors (Yale's Dr. H. S. Canby, the editor of *The Saturday Review of Literature,* Dr. T. K. Brown Jr., formerly of Haverford College, and Dr. W. D. Lewis, formerly the Superintendent of Public Instruction for the Commonwealth of Pennsylvania) made no mention of who invented the telescope, perhaps because of the previous controversy surrounding the subject.

"The credit of the discovery of the telescope has been a fruitful subject of discussion," declared the 1911 edition of *Encyclopaedia Britannica.* "Thus, because Democritus announced that the Milky Way is composed of vast multitudes of stars, it has been maintained that he could only have been led to form such an opinion from actual examination of the heavens with a telescope. Other passages from the Greek and Latin authors have similarly been cited to prove that the telescope was known to the ancients."

One of these passages is found in *The Face of the Moon*, written by the 1st century Greek biographer Plutarch. He claimed, "The Moon is very uneven and rugged." How could he have determined this if the ancients were not using telescopes to observe its terrain at the time?

In another passage, on the wisdom of Pythagoras in the 6th century BC, the ancient philosopher Iamblichus suggested that the Greeks used telescopes by spelling out the word when he announced, "Sight is made precise by the compass, rule, and telescope."

The ancients apparently used the telescope long before Pythagoras. Babylonian astronomers catalogued the non-planetary fixed stars, observed and recorded their observations on occultations of the planets by the Sun and Moon, and determined correctly within a small fraction the length of the synodic revolution of the moon. They also knew the true length of the solar year was 365 days and one quarter. In fact, the exact length of the ancient Babylonian year has been determined to have been 365 days, 6 hours, and 11 minutes, which varies less than two minutes from the sidereal year. They also ascribed eclipses of the Sun to the interposition of the Moon between the Sun and the Earth, and they apparently knew the arrangement of at least seven planets and spotted some of their moons— which certainly requires the use of a telescope.

Their long line of astronomical records on clay tablets stored in the British Museum, dating back to 747 BC, indicate they observed some of the moons of Jupiter and Saturn. "There is said to be distinct evidence that they observed the four satellites of Jupiter, and strong reason to believe that they were acquainted likewise with the seven satellites of Saturn," wrote the English Orientalist George Rawlinson in the 1860s. "It has generally been assumed that they were wholly ignorant of the telescope," added this Camden professor of ancient history. "But if the satellites of Saturn are really mentioned, as it is thought that they are, upon some of the tablets, it will follow—strange as it may seem to us—that the Babylonians probably possessed optical instruments of the nature of telescopes, since it is impossible, even in the clear vaporless sky of Chaldea [ancient Babylonia], to discern the faint moons of that distant planet without lenses."

Some of their ancient astronomical instruments likely consisted of single-lens refracting telescopes, larger and more sophisticated than the ancient Babylonian lens that was found by A. H. Layard at Nimrud, and brought to England in 1853. Since then, in *The Crystal Sun* (2000), Robert Temple has identified and provided photographs of several previously unrecognized ancient lenses, scattered around in various museums. In this scholarly work, he also included a photograph of a more than 2,000 year old fragment of Greek pottery in the Acropolis Museum at Athens and on it, there is a man peering up through what appears to be a set of telescoping tubes, which looks amazingly like one of our more modern refracting telescopes.

Modern telescopes, however, need no tubes to fulfill their purpose. "Refracting telescopes may consist of a double-convex lens placed upon a stand, without tube or eyepiece," states the 1873 revised edition of Elijah H. Burritt's *Geography of the Heavens and Class-Book of Astronomy.* "Indeed, a pair of ordinary spectacles is nothing less than a pair of small telescopes, for aiding impaired vision."

Sometimes called binoculars, spectacles were also known in antiquity. Polybius, a 2nd century BC Greek historian, in his work "Fragents" speaks of "a telescope with two tubes." Furthermore, in arguing the Earth's position in the universe, in the 1st century the Roman encyclopedist Pliny the Elder confirmed their use in his day by maintaining, "Binoculars confirm this very powerfully."

Before introducing the Julian calendar in 46 BC, Julius Caesar may also have used binoculars to confirm the Earth's position. After all, according to Roger Bacon, a Medieval Franciscan monk of Ilchester, before crossing the English Channel nine years previously, he used some sort of telescope to survey the shores of Great Britain from Gaul (France).

He may have used just a simple double-convex lens, similar to the telescope described below, which Burritt's revised textbook on astronomy explains as follows: "Here the parallel rays are seen to pass through the lens at A, and to be so converged to a point as to enter the eye of the beholder at B. His eye is thus virtually enlarged to the size of the lens at A."

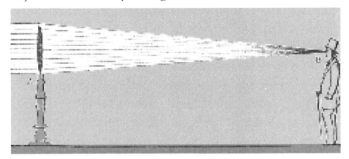

"Having some time ago procured a very large lens, 26 feet in focal distance and 11 inches in diameter, I have tried it with various experiments of this kind upon different objects," claimed Dr. Thomas Dick, in an 1857 article titled, "Telescope formed by a Single Lens."

Dick continues, "Standing at the distance of 25 feet from it, I can see distant objects through it magnified about 26 times in diameter, and consequently 676 times in surface, and remarkably clear and distinct, so that I can distinguish the hour and minute hands of a public clock in a village two miles distant," he added. "This single lens, therefore, answers the purpose of an ordinary telescope with a power of 26 times."

Nevertheless, the ancients did not need to rely on this type of telescope. They also made reflectors, which work even better. "In employing a mirror if the thickness of the metal has been polished and beaten out into a slightly concave shape," wrote Pliny, "The size of the objects reflected is enormously magnified." This observation certainly proves that the ancients invented the telescope!

In fact, astronomers still use Pliny's concave type of mirrors to prevent precious light from being absorbed by additional lenses and/or mirrors often employed in modern telescopes. They ignore these extra optical devices, and revert to a simple concave mirror to make photographic plates of the stars and the highly magnified results prove its efficiency and effectiveness.

Despite this blatant fact, recent dictionaries and astronomy books still fail to define simple concave mirrors (or double-convex lenses) as telescopes. Yet, years ago, as Winston's Dictionary has fully affirmed, with its definitions of a telescope, this was not always the case. And other, older authorities, like astronomers Dick and Burritt, also pointed out the fact. The revised edition of Burritt's work plainly exemplifies this by stating: "The Reflecting Telescope is one in which the light is converged to a focus by means of a concave metallic reflector or speculum. Like Refractors, they may be constructed with very little mounting, though for convenience in use it is necessary to place the reflector in a tube." And it goes on to explain the image below, by relating that "In this cut, the light A is seen passing from the object on the right, and falling upon the concave surface of the reflector B, from which it is reflected back to a focus, and enters the eye of the observer at C. This telescope has no eye-piece."

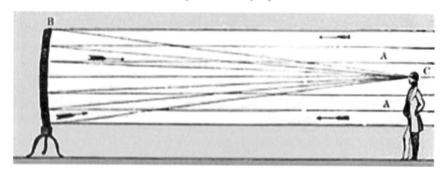

"This mode of viewing objects is extremely easy and pleasant, especially when the mirror is of a large diameter, and the observer is at first struck and gratified with the novel aspect in which the objects appear," wrote Dr. Dick. "Were a concave mirror of this description—whether of glass or of speculum metal—to be formed to a very long focus, the magnifying power would be considerable. One of 50 feet of focal length, and of a corresponding diameter, might produce a magnifying power, to certain eyes, of about 75 times and, from the quantity of light with which the object would be seen, its effect would be much greater than the same power applied to a common telescope."

"Sir W. Herschel states that, on one occasion, by looking with his naked eye on the speculum of his 40-foot reflector, without the interposition of any lens or mirror [eyepiece], he perceived distinctly one of the satellites of Saturn, which requires the application of a considerable power to be seen by an ordinary telescope," added Dr. Dick, in his article entitled "A Reflecting Telescope, with a Single Mirror and No Eyepiece." "Such an instrument is one of the most simple forms of a telescope, and would exhibit a brilliant and interesting view of the moon, or of terrestrial objects."

Speaking again of Herschel, who discovered Uranus and several of its moons in the 18th century, he pointed out another occasion when he bypassed the eyepiece of one of his telescopes and just used its large mirror as a telescope. "Being sensible of the vast quantity of light which is lost by a second reflection from the small speculum, he determined to throw it aside altogether, and mounted this 20-foot reflector on a stand that admitted of being used without a small speculum in making front observations, that is, in sitting with his back to the object and looking directly towards the surface of the speculum. Many of his discoveries and measurements of double stars were made with this instrument."

Thousands of years before Herschel's time, a similar telescope stood atop a tower near the island where the Pharos Lighthouse was later built. According to Makrizi, it served as the prototype for the mirror that was later placed atop the Pharos Tower in the third century BC. "In the ancient city of Rakoti [Rhakotis] there is said to have been a dome on pillars of brass, all gilded, and above this dome rose a lighthouse, on which was a mirror of composite metal [speculum], five spans [about 45 inches] in diameter."

Another large telescope, a mobile military type, from Pythagoras' time, is illustrated at the top of page 97. Here, the concave mirror is tied down horizontally upon the hands of a statue by ropes so that a strong wind would not catch it enough to overturn the wagon. When the reflective telescope was ready for use, the guards protecting the prize had to release the ropes, and the mirror swung down in a vertical position to enable the spotters riding in the wagon to see its images easily. This little replica of an ancient telescope is stored in a museum in Strettweg, Austria. It represents one that was perhaps six actual feet in diameter, and it displays signs of Italian workmanship. However, nobody knows where, or by whom, it was made.

A bronze replica of a gigantic mobile telescope of the 7th century BC.

The bronze replica shown here was found in a Danish peat bog at Trundholm in 1902, and still partially decorated with gold leaf.

Both bronze and gold are highly reflective metals, and in antiquity, both were readily available for use in large telescopes, like the one on the Pharos Tower. However, because of atmospheric effects, the metal in bronze mirrors quickly becomes dull and often requires cleaning. This is not the case with gold because it does not tarnish or corrode. Except for periodically wiping off the accumulation of dirt, it requires no additional cleaning—and it lasts forever. Gold coins found in old sunken galleons are as bright and shiny as the day they were cast. The gold recovered from Tutankhamun's tomb is as lustrous as the day it was buried with the young Egyptian king, thousands of years ago. .

However, gold does not reflect as much light as the corrosive but cheaper metal alloy called speculum (copper, tin, and arsenic). It also does not reflect nearly as much as corrosion-resistant tinned glass. And the ancient Alexandrians, noted for their production of modern types of glass, probably manufactured both. "We meet, in ancient classical writers, with very ample and repeated testimony, that the Egyptians, in the glass-houses of Diospolis, knew how to fabricate mirrors of stupendous magnitude," wrote Thomas Maurice. "And, though hence it does not absolutely follow that these mirrors should be tinned glass, yet the use to which they applied, at least, two of these mirrors, afford very strong reason for that supposition since, if composed of any metal-line substance, the situation in which they were placed must unavoidably have exposed them to obscuration or corrosion."

"One of these mirrors, according to Strabo (lib. xvii. p. 492), was elevated on the summit of the great temple of Heliopolis, or the city of the sun, to reflect into that temple the full splendor of its meridian beam," added the nineteenth-century Assistant Keeper of Manuscripts in the British Museum. "Another of still more prodigious dimensions was, in later periods, erected on the Pharos of Alexandria, and so placed as to reflect ships approaching Egypt at a vast distance, and imperceptible by the eye from the loftiest pinnacle."

In her 1877 edition of *Isis Unveiled*, H. P. Blavatsky pointed out, "If the mirror really existed, as I firmly believe it did, to the ancients belong the honor of the invention of the telescope."

This article first appeared in *Atlantis Rising* #59 (September/October 2006).

UNSEEN FORCES

14

ENIGMA OF THE CRYSTAL SKULLS

The True Story that Preceded the Hollywood Fantasy
Offers No Shortage of Mystery and Drama
on Its Own Account

BY DAVID H. CHILDRESS

With the opening in 2008 of the movie *Indiana Jones and the Kingdom of the Crystal Skull*, millions learned for the first time about one of the most remarkable stories in the annals of archaeology, the mystery of the crystal skulls. The movie may be fiction, but the tale of the crystal skulls is not only filled with plenty of Hollywood-style adventure, a lot of it is also true.

One of the most fascinating substances in nature, crystal lends itself uniquely to various adaptations, including information storage. Today crystal technologies are at the cutting edge of advancements in nanotechnology and computing. As for the skulls, themselves, does the fact that they are carved from crystal enable them to store information and interact with human thought waves? Strangely, there is evidence to suggest this could be so.

Moreover, the history of Mesoamerica, where the skulls are said to originate, is rich with the mystical, magical sorcery of the Olmecs, Zapotecs, Maya, and Aztecs. Indeed, the turbulent times of the Mexican Revolution form the backdrop for much of the most recent part of the tale, including the saga of F. A. Mitchell-Hedges, the notorious adventurer who emerged from the jungles, it was said, with the most famous of the crystal skulls—the so-called "Skull of Doom."

There are genuine enigmas associated with crystal skulls. Some seem outlandish, while others would appear to make sense but aren't necessarily true. Studies of crystal skulls run from exacting scientific examinations to bizarre psychic readings that could never be proven. Much of the material on crystal skulls may be fabricated or deceptive, and the age and origins of the objects obscured—but one thing is certain: crystal skulls are real!

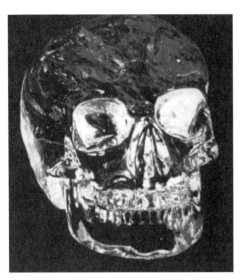

The Mitchell-Hedges "Skull of Doom" {British Museum}

Quartz is the second most abundant mineral on the Earth after feldspar, and has even been found in meteors. It is a large component of sand and sandstone, and is part of almost every rock, be it igneous, metamorphic, or sedimentary. It is the main mineral in most gemstones.

Quartz is extremely hard, with a Mohs scale of 7. Since diamonds are one of the few minerals that exceed quartz in hardness, diamond-tipped tools or dust are thought to have been used to make most crystal skulls.

The structural framework of quartz is a lattice of "silica tetrahedra"; this structural lattice forms into a six-sided prism terminating with six-sided pyramids at each end. Its crystals can grow together and become intertwined and therefore show only part of this shape, looking like a giant crystal mass. But the underlying crystalline structure, one in which internal patterns of molecules are regular, repeated, and geometrically arranged, gives quartz many of its striking properties, and makes it possible for one to believe that crystal skulls may actually be the depositories of ancient wisdom.

Eric Smalley, in an article about quantum computers in *Technology Research News* (online at *trnmag.com*) reports that a research team from the U.S. and Korea succeeded in storing a light pulse in a crystal, and then reconstituting it. This was significant because quantum information is notoriously fragile, and the ability to store it in a crystal would advance the feasibility of building a quantum computer (which would theoretically work at far faster speeds than are now possible).

Although there is much work to be done to develop a quantum memory chip, experiments with crystal seem promising. More recent research takes the use of crystals in information processing a step further, experimenting with perhaps the ultimate material in information storage, DNA.

UNSEEN FORCES

According to *Science Daily,* "Crystals promise a new way to process information." An article in February, 2003, reported, "A team led by Richard Kiehi, a professor of electrical engineering at the University of Minnesota, has used the selective 'stickiness' of DNA to construct a scaffolding for closely spaced nanoparticles that could exchange information on a scale of only 10 angstroms [an angstrom is one 10-billionth of a meter]."

More incredible research involving DNA and its crystal structure has been carried out in an attempt to solve the mysteries of evolution and the origins of life. In the meantime, IBM, in conjunction with DARPA, the Defense Advanced Projects Research Agency, has been involved in developing holographic data storage systems. Through a process of shooting laser beams into the crystal, they have successfully stored thousands of holograph images on a single lithium niobate crystal.

Clearly, on the cutting edge of science, crystals of various types are being used to store and process information, and success is due to the very nature of crystals themselves. Information can be stored in an orderly fashion, replicated, and retrieved. Is it then so far-fetched to think that a technologically advanced earlier civilization could have developed these capabilities, and perhaps used crystal skulls to record information? Or even that the same ends may have been met intuitively?

In order to make a large-size crystal skull—say, one nearly the size of a human skull—the crystal carver would need a pretty large piece of quartz crystal. Some quartz crystals can reach several meters in length, and weigh tons. Obtaining large, translucent quartz crystals would be very difficult, especially in ancient times. We know that deposits of large crystals of different grades occur in Brazil, Peru, Mexico, California, Arkansas, and other areas of the Americas. Deposits of large quartz crystals are also found in Africa, Europe, and Asia, but much of the high quality, translucent quartz crystals today come from Brazil.

Gold and silver are often found around quartz, and quartz crystals can have beautiful gold threads inside them, having grown with the crystal. Quartz crystals have an axis of rotation and they have the ability to rotate the plane of polarization of light passing through them. They are also highly piezoelectric, becoming polarized with a negative charge on one end and a positive charge on the other when subjected to pressure.

Quartz crystals vibrate when an alternating electric current is applied to them, and for this reason they have proven to be highly important in commercial applications. Quartz oscillators were developed in 1921 and one early use was in phonograph needles. Their piezoelectricity also makes them ideal for use in making microphones, speakers, pressure gauges, actuators, resonators, and clocks.

The many astonishing qualities of quartz seem to make it an ideal material for "psychic" and "light" experiments. In theory, a piece of crystal quartz, or a crystal skull, could and would react to what was around it, including light, electricity, pressure, sound, vibrations of all sorts, and possibly human thought waves and the human electrical field.

Marcel Vogel, an IBM researcher, spent 17 years testing crystals and their interaction with human energy. He perfected the "Vogel-cut" of crystals to maximize their ability to convey psychic and healing influences. His work is perhaps best summarized in this quote from him: "The crystal is a neutral object whose inner structure exhibits a state of perfection and balance. When it is cut to the proper form and when the human mind enters into relationship with its structural perfection, the crystal emits a vibration which extends and amplifies the power of the user's mind. Like a laser, it radiates energy in a coherent, highly concentrated form, and this energy may be transmitted into objects or people at will."

Many unusual phenomena have been associated with crystal skulls. According to Frank Dorland, a San Francisco art expert and restorer who studied the Mitchell-Hedges crystal skull for six years, the skull would often be seen with its eyes unusually lit up. The eyes would flicker as if they were watching the observer, and visitors reported odd odors and sounds, as well as various lighting effects coming from the skull. Bizarre photographs were taken of "pictures" which sometimes formed within the skull, including images of flying discs and of what appears to be the Caracol observatory at the Toltec Mayan site of Chichen Itza. The astonishing ability of crystal skulls to create unusual phenomena is now well known.

It is nearly impossible to discuss crystal skulls without looking into the life of F. A. "Mike" Mitchell-Hedges. A fascinating individual, Mitchell-Hedges was very much the prototype for the Indiana-Jones character. After adventurous younger years with Pancho Villa in Mexico, he returned to his native England and then later appeared in Canada where he adopted a young daughter named Anna. Later he traveled throughout Mexico and Central America investigating Atlantis and other ancient mysteries. In the 1920s and '30s he wrote many books and articles about his adventures and lost ancient cultures.

When he was not traveling, Mitchell-Hedges did a lot of lecturing and radio shows. He was known to be a tall-tale teller, as well as something of a braggart. On a number of occasions he was accused of lying. While he did, apparently, fabricate some tales, it should be pointed out that stories like his involving adventures in wild, remote places are inherently hard to document. The fact that he maintained sponsorship by the likes of the Heye Museum, the British Museum, and the *Daily Mail*, indicates a respected number of others had a considerable amount of trust in him and that he actually

Anna Mitchell-Hedges holds the skull which she is credited with finding when she was a teenager in the 1920s.

performed to their satisfaction. He is known to have contributed artifacts to the British Museum.

Some surmise that Mitchell-Hedges may have been a British agent, funded by the government, and, therefore, subject to the Official Secrets Act, which mandated two years hard labor for violators. He may actually have been forced to make up stories and change facts in his books in order to not violate this mandate.

His books were popular during their time and *The White Tiger* (1931) was republished in a number of mass-run mini-hardbacks for the troops and other far-flung readers during WWII. Mitchell-Hedges continued to write after the war.

Many researchers have wondered why, in all of these books, the crystal skull—the Skull of Doom—is never mentioned, until *Danger, My Ally* (1954). Is it because the authors were sworn to secrecy over the skull's origin? Did Mike Mitchell-Hedges only acquire the skull late in his life, after all of his other adventures, remarkable as they were? Had it some secret occult origin he could not reveal?

Strangely, he devotes only three paragraphs to the skull in his book and even these were removed from the American edition, published later. He says, referring to a trip to South Africa in 1947, "We took with us also the sinister Skull of Doom of which much has been written. How it came into my possession I have reason for not revealing.

"The Skull of Doom is made of pure rock crystal and, according to scientists, it must have taken over 150 years—generation after generation working all the days of their lives, patiently rubbing down with sand an immense block of rock crystal until finally the perfect skull emerged.

"It is at least 3,600 years old and according to legend was used by the high priest of the Maya when performing esoteric rites. It is said that when he willed death with the help of the skull, death invariably followed. It has been described as the embodiment of all evil. I do not wish to try and explain [these] phenomena."

The popular story of the skull's discovery is that it took place in the latter period of excavations at Lubaantun in 1927. Anna was supposedly digging in a collapsed altar and adjoining wall on her 17th birthday when she found the skull. Three months later a matching jawbone was discovered 25 feet away. And thus, one of the world's strangest ancient objects came to light. But, in fact, not a word was said about it for years afterward. Could its origin be more mysterious than the public was led to believe?

Another possibility is that it came from another Central American ancient city, or possibly one in Mexico, and was looted from some pyramid. In this story Mitchell-Hedges would have bought it as a stolen artifact; thus, his statement that he had reasons for not revealing how he acquired it.

One theory was that the skull was a 12,000-year-old relic from Atlantis that had been handed down through the Knights Templar and ultimately came into the possession of the inner circle of the top Masonic Lodge. Mitchell-Hedges was an inner Mason and may have somehow acquired the skull either through the secret society or as part of a gambling debt. He then, it is suggested, introduced it to the world through the ingenious device of a lost city.

Wherever he got it, Mitchell-Hedges' "skull of doom" has certainly been the target of considerable interest and not a little scientific research since. In 1970, Frank Dorland was given permission by the Mitchell-Hedges estate to submit the skull to tests conducted at the Hewlett-Packard Laboratories at Santa Clara, California.

In the last days that Dorland had the skull, it was submersed in a benzyl alcohol bath at the Hewlett-Packard Laboratories, with a beam of light passing through the submerged skull. It was during this test that is was noted that both the skull and jaw piece had come from the same quartz block. This made the carving even more remarkable.

Crystallographers at Hewlett-Packard also discovered that the skull and jaw had been carved with total disregard to the natural axis in the quartz. This might be expected of ancient skulls, but not so much of modern ones. The reason is that the tools used in modern crystal cutting vibrate, and can fracture and break a crystal if it is cut wrong. Therefore, the first procedure is always to determine the axis, and during the subsequent shaping process to work along with it.

According to Dorland, no evidence of the use of metal tools could be found. Using a high-powered microscope for analysis, he looked for any tell-tale scratch marks. From tiny patterns in the quartz near the carved surfaces, Dorland determined the skull was first meticulously chiseled into a rough form, probably using diamonds. The final polishing and shaping, he believed, was done by applying innumerable applications of solutions of water and silicon-crystal sand. In theory this was done by hand—say, by polishing the skull with a leather rag that had been doused in the solution, over and over again.

The problem with that, Dorland suggested, was if these were the processes used, then, he calculated, it would require a total of 300 man-years of continuous labor. Mitchell-Hedges in *Danger, My Ally* suggested that it took 150 years to make. If it took centuries to make such a skull, the implication is that these objects were very important to the cultures that produced them. But that is assuming that the Mitchell-Hedges skull, and other similar skulls, are indeed ancient.

For now, most of the major questions regarding the true origins and purpose of the crystal skulls remain unanswered.

This article first appeared in *Atlantis Rising* #71 (September/October 2008).

15

MEXICO'S AMAZING PYRAMID

Is There an Egyptian Connection?

BY FRANK JOSEPH

"There are in Mexico the ruins of a prehistoric sacred city [Teotihuacan] which apparently in that country had the significance that Mecca possesses for Moslems, or Lourdes for Catholics." This was the observation of mid-20th century Atlantologist, Alexander Braghine.

Thirty-three miles north of Mexico City lies the grandest archaeological zone on the continent, Teotihuacan. At the zenith of its power, believed to be about fourteen centuries ago, the ancient megalopolis may have embraced as many as 300,000 inhabitants, who dominated Middle America to a greater extent than any people before or since. Covering an area approximately of eight square miles, a nearly two-mile long, 130-foot wide ceremonial highway known as the Avenue of the Dead leads to a stupendous set of stone monuments, the largest of these being the Pyramid of the Sun. Originally rising in four massive stages above the arid environment, the pyramid contains approximately one million cubic yards of stone mostly faced with hewn tezontle, a coarse, reddish volcanic rock.

Other than a generally comparable massiveness, the Mexican structure appears at first glance wholly unlike ancient Egypt's foremost structure, the Great Pyramid of Khufu on the Giza Plateau. But a closer examination reveals some startling similarities. There is only a six-foot difference in their base diameters on both sides, and the Pyramid of the Sun was (before modern restoration) just 14.39 feet over the mid-height of the Great Pyramid of Giza. While not identical, these dimensions are intriguingly close.

The fundamental arithmetical function of Khufu's Egyptian Great Pyramid incorporates the value of pi, the ratio of a circle's diameter to its circumference, a concept used to solve problems about the size, shape, and weight of the Earth. The concept works when we multiply the structure's radius by 2 pi. Mexico's Pyramid of the Sun achieves the same result through precisely twice the Egyptian formula. Multiplying its true height by 4 pi makes an incredibly accurate (less than one-half inch from exact) reading of its perimeter. The very precision of this computation renders chance arrangement unlikely.

The late 19th-century pioneer in Mesoamerican archaeology, Augustus Le Plongeon, found that the Mayan chief unit of measurement was one forty-millionth of the circumference of the Earth. It is not known if Teotihuacan's Pyramid of the Sun incorporates this geodetic unit, although the structure was in use during the flourishing of the Mayan empire. Le Plongeon was pilloried during his lifetime by conventional colleagues, who took scant interest in his priceless collection of Maya artifacts, in large measure because he refused to observe their disregard and dislike of public discussion about Atlantis.

Both Egypt's Great Pyramid and Mexico's Pyramid of the Sun are oriented to the four cardinal directions, an alignment that produces a shared phenomenon. At high noon of the vernal and autumnal equinoxes, the Great Pyramid of the Nile Valley and America's greatest pyramid in the Valley of Mexico cast no shadow—an effect that recalls the similarity of their

The Pyramid of the Sun at Teotihuacan

Great Pyramid of Giza Superimposed over Pyramid of the Sun

names; the former was commonly known as the "Mountain of Ra," the sun-god, just as the latter is still remembered as the Pyramid of the Sun. According to Dr. Gunnar Thompson, "Mexican historian Mariano Cuevas believes the Egyptian structure served as a model, because both have the same geographical alignment. Furthermore, archaeologists have identified the 'Re' serpent/sun glyph at Teotihuacan." Reproductions presented by Thompson show a fundamental similarity between the "Re glyph" and the "Mexican Serpent Sun Eye."

Beneath the Pyramid of the Sun is a 300-foot-long, seven-foot-high lava tube leading to a natural cave, terra-formed by its ancient builders into a quartet of chambers. Its arrangement roughly parallels the descending passageway and chambers of the Great Pyramid. More exactly like the Egyptian King's Chamber, the Mexican passageway terminates into its cluster of chambers just off center from the Pyramid of the Sun's geometrical mid-point. Its two upper levels contained a huge sheet of mica. The function of this bizarre find could not have been decorative, because its position was situated between layers within the uppermost reaches of the apex. Unfortunately, the mica disappeared after its discovery in 1906.

But another, much smaller structure not far from the Pyramid of the Sun was found to contain two enormous mica wafers, each 90 feet square. This building may have been used to store the mica for use in the nearby Pyramid of the Sun.

The mineral was certainly valued most highly, because it had to be imported with great care all the way from Brazil, 2,000 miles by land and sea. Even so, it does not appear in a religious or ceremonial context anywhere else in Teotihuacan, or the rest of Mesoamerica, for that matter. How could it, concealed away from view within the apex of the Pyramid of the Sun? Yet, its presence provides an answer when we realize that mica has been valued since the beginning of our modern age of electricity for its use as a chief component in the production of capacitors. As Corliss points out, "Since large slabs of mica have considerable value for their electrical properties, it is hardly surprising that this artifact quickly disappeared."

In his landmark work, *The Giza Power Plant* (1998), Christopher Dunn demonstrated that Egypt's Great Pyramid was never a tomb, but a solid-state electrical device powered by the natural forces of the Earth itself. Following up on his convincing evidence, I concluded in *Opening the Ark of the Covenant* (2007) that the Great Pyramid was a geo-transducer purpose-built to transmute seismic violence into electrical discharge. Like Egypt's Great Pyramid, its Mexican counterpart is similarly positioned over a major earthquake fault, the most active in Middle America, and the culprit responsible for so many seismic upheavals that have done terrific damage to Mexico City for centuries. As in any transducer, in order for it to have functioned, a large and suitable crystal had to be installed in the granite "sarcophagus" of the structure's King's Chamber. In fact, Arab tradition recounted the former existence of just such a crystal in the Egyptian pyramid.

Did the huge mica sheets in Mexico's Pyramid of the Sun similarly ameliorate the harmful energies unleashed by earthquake activity? Corliss admits that "a tenuous and subtle connection can be made between the Teotihuacan mica sheets and the strange cavities filled with sifted, mineral-enriched sand in the Great Pyramid." There are, in fact, many and significant geodetic comparisons between both structures: The fundamental similarity of their internal configurations, their positioning over major earthquake faults, and a shared use of capacitor minerals at their apexes lead one to conclude that the two pyramids were engineered as geo-transducers by the

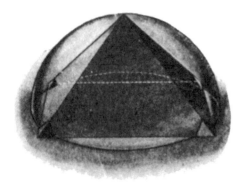

This is the relationship of the Great Pyramid of Egypt to a hemisphere. The Pyramid of the Sun has the same ratio, times two.

same designers. Their differences are equally important, because each structure, while incorporating important common features, reflects the particular topography and geology of their separate locations. An exact reproduction of Egypt's Great Pyramid would not fit in the Valley of Mexico because, among its other geodetic features, it defines the geographical dimensions of the Nile Delta. On the other hand, the Pyramid of the Sun was, as it were, tailored to the related though peculiar situation of Middle America.

But what can account for their fundamental similarities, separated as they are by thousands of miles and a vast ocean? A hint may lie in Teotihuacan's location. Perhaps the most overtly antediluvian site on the continent, it lies an incongruous 130 miles from the nearest coast, it abounds with maritime themes. Murals and stone friezes are obsessed with portraying conch, scallop, and olive seashells. At the base of the Pyramid of the Moon, on its own massive altar in a unique place of honor immediately fronting the ultimate monument of Teotihuacan, is a great conch shell superbly sculpted many times its natural size. Why should the lone symbol of the sea have been provided with so extraordinary a place in this desert kingdom, if not to epitomize some deeply significant connection between its creators and the ocean?

The Atlantean character of the site begins to reveal itself in the city's alignment with the setting of the constellation Pleiades, also known as the Seven Daughters of Atlas (*Atlantis* means "daughter of Atlas"). Reaffirming the importance of this orientation, the builders of Teotihuacan even altered the course of the nearby San Juan River to align with the Pleiades. Close to the Pyramid of the Sun stood a colossal basalt statue of Chalchiuhtlicue, the water-goddess who was said to have caused the great flood that destroyed a former age. She was massively portrayed at Teotihuacan as an "Atlantean" figure supporting a lintel signifying the sky.

Another "Atlantean" figure, the bearded rain-god, Tlaloc, who bore the sky on his shoulders, is depicted in an important mural at Teotihuacan's Tetitla Palace. Several buildings down from the Pyramid of the Moon stands the Temple of Quetzalcoatl, the yellow-bearded, fair-skinned culture-bearer who arrived with his fellow artists and scientists of the Old Red Land from over the Sunrise Sea to found civilization in the Valley of Mexico. And when we observe that the monuments of Teotihuacan are built with the same kind of red, white, and black volcanic stone Plato said the Atlanteans preferred as the construction materials for their sacred buildings, implications of Atlantis are difficult to ignore.

Comparisons with the Great Pyramid, however compelling, are challenged by the relative dating of both structures. The Egyptian edifice is at least 4,500 years old, perhaps much older. According to archaeologists, Mexico's Pyramid of the Sun was built approximately 2,000 years ago. The twenty five centuries (at least) that supposedly separate the two sites would seem to render any connection between them most unlikely. Yet, there may be a reason for this apparent discrepancy in time.

Researchers are divided over the true age of Teotihuacan. Standard texts describe the earliest human habitation there around 200 BC, but as long ago as the 1950s, one of Mexico's leading archaeologists, Manuel Covarrubias, arrived at firm radiocarbon dates for 500 years earlier. According to David Childress, "further radiocarbon tests gave a date of 1474 BC (with a possible small error either way). A date of circa 1400 BC is now widely accepted." But even a 15th century BC time parameter for the city would still make its Pyramid of the Sun more than a thousand years younger than the Great Pyramid of Egypt.

The most plausible date for Teotihuacan was arrived at through a study of the area surrounding the ceremonial center. The land is far too poor to have ever supported a population upward of 300,000 inhabitants. Investigators continue to wonder why the megalopolis was founded in so unproductive and remote a location. But its natural surroundings were not always arid. Once the soil was rich, rivers ran across the plain, lakes were home to abundant wildlife, and there were forests and meadows. The establishment of Teotihuacan would have made sense in such a supportive setting. This Edenic environment was drastically transformed to its present desert-like condition by the massive eruption of a nearby volcano. A minority of geologists argue that Teotihuacan must have flourished before Mount Xitli's massive out-gassing. The date for its eruption around 4000 BC dates the Pyramid of the Sun far beyond the parameters calculated by available radiocarbon testing, and places it within the general time-frame of Egypt's Great Pyramid.

Certainly, Teotihuacan went through major construction phases between AD 200 and 450, and rose to the zenith of its influence over the next three centuries. But perhaps the technological foundation of its foremost structures was already in place for several millennia before. It may have been subsequently built upon and expanded by later cultures. If so, then the Mexican and Egyptian pyramids could have a common origin after all. As Peter Tompkins suggests in his monumental work on the subject, *Mysteries of the Mexican Pyramids* (1976), "it seemed reasonable to assume that any Earth-commensurate unit used in Mesoamerica be related to the unit used in the building of the Great Pyramid of Cheops, or at least to have been derived from some common source."

Like the Egyptian structure, Mexico's Pyramid of the Sun may have served metaphysical purposes. While its mysterious builders vanished around AD 650, a suggestive echo of their structure's similarly spiritual qualities survives in the name of the city it still dominates: Teotihuacan. In Nahuatl, the Aztec language, it means "The Place where Men become Gods." Perhaps men did indeed feel like gods when they experienced the extrasensory effects generated by the Pyramid of the Sun.

This article first appeared in *Atlantis Rising* #65 (September/October 2007).

16

HIDDEN IN PLAIN SIGHT

If We Found Evidence of a Highly Advanced
Ancient Civilization, Would We Know It?

BY WILLIAM B. STOECKER

Would we recognize the ruins of a forgotten indigenous human civilization or the evidence of an advanced technology here on Earth if we found it? Can we even define "civilization"? Suppose a technology was not like ours, on the same line of development and perhaps less advanced than ours or more advanced, but on a completely different path? Suppose machines were made of stone rather than metal and designed to harness the chi, or kundalini force (it has many names) the very existence of which is denied by most mainstream physicists?

Conventional archaeologists and historians long assumed that the first civilizations began between 5,000 and 6,000 years BP (before the present) in the Fertile Crescent. They assumed that several elements appeared together and that the presence of all, or at least most, of these are what defines civilization. These elements are agriculture, woven fabrics, metal tools, weapons, fired ceramics, and large buildings of brick and/or cut stone. It is believed that the development of writing and, hence, the dawn of recorded history, followed shortly after.

The walled city of Jericho dates back to 10,000 BP; agriculture is now generally believed to be at least 12,000 years old; and woven fabrics and fired ceramics have been around for about 28,000 years . . . or longer. The age of our species has been pushed back until many conventional archaeologists and anthropologists now admit to a date of 275,000 BP. Seafaring, it was once believed, is a fairly recent innovation. But Polynesians with no metal tools sailed for thousands of miles across the Pacific; Australia and New Guinea were settled at least 50,000 BP; and now even some professional archaeologists are speculating that North America's Clovis Points, dating back to the last ice age, may have been brought across the Atlantic by seafaring people from what is now France. And, incredibly, hand axes of the type made by *Homo erectus*, a supposedly primitive ancestor or relative of *Homo sapiens*, have been found on Crete and dated back to at least 130,000 BP. There was no way to get to Crete except by sea.

Cultures with some, but not all, of the elements of civilization date back to very early times. Towns have been found on the continental shelf of India and dated, based to the depth of their submergence, to at least 9,000 BP. These towns had stone buildings and left a great many stone tools, rather than metal (although metals might not survive thousands of years in corrosive sea water). Gobekli Tepe, in what is now Turkey, is the site of large structures of carved and cut stone built over 11,000 BP by a people who left no evidence of metal or ceramics or agriculture and who appear to have been hunter-gatherers rather than farmers. This is contrary to everything we thought we knew. Archaeologists are finding the ruins of a widespread culture in the Amazon Basin, which seems to have made little or no use of metal and had no stone buildings (there is very little stone available in the region) yet they built immense earthworks and canals and practiced an advanced form of agriculture, somehow creating and preserving fertile soil in a region that, today, is only marginally suited for agriculture. These are examples of cultures we would deem to be advanced in some ways but which lacked many other attributes of civilization.

Carvings at Gobekli Tepe

Some ancient technology is easily recognizable as such. An ancient shipwreck off the Greek island of Antikythera contained a complex but badly corroded mechanism that has been dated to 2,100 BP; it may be much older. It consists of at least 30 gears and could have been used to calculate lunar, solar, and some planetary positions in the sky as seen from Earth. Possibly ancestral to later clocks, it may have been capable of determining the position of the Moon on a particular day, thus enabling ancient mariners to determine longitude. Supposedly such a precise determination of longitude was not possible until John Harrison perfected his chronometer in 1761. This is well known, as are the ceramic jars with metal components, originally found in Bagh-dad in 1936 and afterward, by Wilhelm Konig, the German director of Iraq's National Museum. These ceramic jars, it has been proven, could have functioned as electric cells and may have been used for electrolysis or for some kind of medical treatment. Both electric cells and geared mechanics as precise and complex as that from Antikythera had previously been thought to have been much more recent developments.

Could the ancients have had an understanding of aerodynamics? Could they have built aircraft? A gold artifact, dated to about 500–800 BP and found in Colombia, resembles a model of an airplane with a delta wing and a separate tail assembly, including a vertical stabilizer. It even has the suggestion of a cockpit and bears no resemblance whatever to a bird or to a stingray. In 1898, archae-ologists found a wooden model air-plane or glider in a tomb at Saqqara

The Antikythera device

in Egypt, dated to about 2,200 BP. It has very advanced high lift reverse dihedral wings; and, although it is painted to resemble a bird, it has a verti-cal tail stabilizer—no bird has such a tail. If a horizontal tail plane is added, the glider flies perfectly; models have been built and tested. None of these models or carvings show a jet or a propeller, so were they intended merely to depict gliders or could there have been some exotic propulsion system contained internally? And did early man understand aerodynamics?

Often overlooked is the fact that true boomerangs, both returnable and nonreturnable, are airfoils with a flat underside and a curved topside to generate lift. The more sophisticated asymmetric and returnable ones were used in Australia and in Egypt as far back as 3,000 BP. There are accounts of boomerangs dating back to 10,000 and even 30,000 BP, but it is not clear whether or not these were true airfoils. Taking all of the above into account, the pattern of evidence shows that ancient man probably built, or at least knew of, aircraft or gliders. But, aside from the possible exotic propulsion systems, all of this, while startling, is clearly recogniz-able as technology in many ways resembling our own.

The ability of the ancients to quarry, transport, shape, and lift enormous stones, or megaliths, has been discussed *ad nauseam*, with true believers insisting that no amount of human or animal labor and no combination of levers, pulleys, or ramps could possibly have moved stones weighing up to one, or even two, million pounds or more, as in the platform at Baalbek, Lebanon (which, by the way, is of unknown age and built by a completely unknown civilization). By contrast, conventional archaeologists and historians insist that human labor, ingenuity, and patience could have done the job. The truth lies between the extremes.

Often overlooked is the fact that the ancient Romans and Greeks, and the later Europeans, prior to the Industrial Age often quarried, transported, and lifted stones weighing many tons, like the cylindrical marble blocks forming the high columns of the Parthenon. The Greeks and Romans left behind detailed descriptions and drawings showing the man-powered pulley systems that were used. The Romans also brought a number of Egyptian obelisks weighing hundreds of thousands of pounds to Rome and Constantinople (now Istanbul) and re-erected them. One of these weighed some 460,000 pounds. One Roman obelisk was moved and erected again in Vatican City precisely to the east of St. Peter's Cathedral by the architect Domenico Fontana in 1586 using a huge and complex assembly of scaffolding and ropes pulled by hundreds of horses and men. The Alexander Column in Palace Square in St. Petersburg, Russia, includes a cylindrical pillar weighing about 1,322,760 pounds, erected in 1834 under the direction of French architect Auguste de Montferrand, using the labor of thousands of men and no steam engines.

So immense weights can be handled with "primitive" technology, but, it must be remembered, there are limits. One thing most people never think of is simple geometry. The surface area of a stone, for putting ropes around it and rollers or levers under it, varies with the square of its dimensions, but the volume and weight vary with the cube. Eventually the weight increases so much, and the area so relatively little, that it is impossible to move. Note that the obelisks are long and slender, allowing relatively more men and ropes and rollers than is the case with a more nearly cubical stone.

In addition, it is hard to shape large stones with precision, and hard to emplace them exactly, and all of these difficulties combine. At Ollantaytambo in the Urubamba River valley in Peru, I have seen stones weighing up to 70 tons that were taken from a quarry on one side of the river and

Monoliths at Ollantaytambo

emplaced hundreds of feet up above the steep opposite side. At Sacsahuaman, there are many stones weighing over 10 or 20 tons, and one weighing about 100 tons, that were quarried 25 miles away and transported over rough country, and raised 700 to 800 feet up to the top of the ridge where they now stand. Many of them have complex "jigsaw puzzle" shapes and fit perfectly on one another; it is not hard to visualize the incredible difficulty of this achievement. We have to take seriously the possibility that such structures are evidence of a technology utterly alien to us, perhaps, as many have claimed, involving some form of levitation.

And there are many ancient structures whose shapes are so strange and complex that even today, even to us, they resemble nothing so much as machines of stone, built for unknown purposes. Certainly this is true of the Great Pyramid at Giza, which has no paintings or decorations (its exterior limestone casing blocks may have been painted) but whose internal structure is hard to explain. Over the so-called King's Chamber, with its precisely cut "sarcophagus," is a complex assembly of huge, angled blocks with spaces between them, usually explained by conventional archaeologists (people generally ignorant of engineering) as a way of relieving the

The pyramids at Giza

weight on the chamber and preventing its collapse. Christopher Dunn, an engineer and expert in machining, among others, has pointed out the absurdity of this from an engineering standpoint; he also noted that the deeper Queen's Chamber, with a greater weight of rock above it, has no such relieving structure.

Other people, agreeing that the structure seems to be a machine, have other ideas as to its purpose. I suggested years ago that it may be analogous to a lens, focusing and altering not visible light but the chi force. This energy may have been used for a number of purposes, including, perhaps, altering the consciousness of initiates to the priesthood, who may have lain in the "sarcophagus." Depending on the size of various cubits, which tended to vary, the Ark of the Covenant, structured like a large capacitor, might have fitted into the sarcophagus, and a man with his knees drawn up might have fitted into the Ark. Of course, all of this is mere speculation and none of us knows for certain what the Great Pyramid did.

The Pyramid of the Sun at Teotihuacan in Mexico has a base almost equal to that of the Great Pyramid but is roughly only about half as high. Could it have had a similar function, and, if so, how could it do so? When this structure was first excavated, a layer of mica was found; most of this was stolen by looters. Mica is a sheet silicate mineral with several varieties, and it has near perfect basal cleavage and is a highly effective dielectric, often used in capacitors. Supposedly the mica at Teotihuacan came all the way from Brazil. If true, this is evidence of seafaring and long distance trade, but what was the purpose of the mica? Could it have aided in focusing or altering the chi energy, helping to compensate for the pyramid's reduced height?

There are numerous other bizarrely shaped ancient structures. At Puma Punku in Bolivia near Lake Titicaca, there are rows of precisely cut sandstone blocks, along with some of andesite. The blocks, cut from a quarry some ten miles away, are so precise and so identical that they seem to have been mass produced, perhaps using machine tools—perhaps Christopher Dunn will investigate this one day. The largest stone weighs some 131 metric tons, or 288,724 pounds. Many of the stones were held together by clamps of a peculiar alloy of copper and nickel with a (perhaps accidental) trace of arsenic.

Strangely shaped structures are almost commonplace, like Sacsahuaman, which makes no sense as a fortress and much of which may be underground, with tunnels blocked to the public; either the authorities are refusing to explore them or they are keeping their explorations secret—rather like the Giza underground. Ollantaytambo is almost as mind-boggling to see as Sacsahuaman; the mind tries, and fails, to fit these creations into some familiar pattern. I have also seen a partly excavated adobe pyramid in Lima, Peru, and its complex shape is as strange as that of the Akapana pyramid.

While the shape of some of these structures may be artistic or ceremonial in nature, the overall patterns do indeed suggest that the ancients, or at least some of them, built machines of stone and may have used some form of levitation. But could there be even stranger civilizations and technologies? Given that, as shown above, some early cultures had some, but not all, of the attributes that supposedly constitute civilization, can we even define the term? If an early culture of farmers or even hunter gatherers were a highly moral people, engaging only in defensive war when unavoidable, maintaining law and order within the tribe, and never practicing human sacrifice, cruelty to animals, or abuse of children and women, would they not be civilized in a very real sense? Yet they would have left no real evidence for their way of life and would be unknown to us today.

Taking the idea further (and this, I admit, is pure speculation), suppose this hypothetical people's shamans were in contact with benevolent tutelary spirits and had herbal remedies and other medical treatments in many ways superior to our own. Suppose that they could travel out of the body and had detailed knowledge of other parts of the Earth and even of other planets. Or suppose some early culture made machines, interpreted by us as primitive ritual objects, that could help them to harness their own latent psychic powers for healing, transportation, or levitation. Again we would recognize none of this. We may be all but surrounded by the remnants of advanced early cultures and never know it.

This article first appeared in *Atlantis Rising* #83 (September/October 2010).

PART FOUR

EGYPT THE UNKOWN

19th century conjectural image of the Lighthouse at Alexandria

17

IN THE SHADOW OF ATLANTIS

The Great Sphinx and Indelible Clues
to a Forgotten Civilization

BY FRANK JOSEPH

The pyramids of Khufu and Khafre together form the hieroglyph for "horizon," appropriately enough, but only when viewed from the Great Sphinx one day each year, at sunrise of the summer solstice. During the winter solstice, an observer standing in the doorway of a nearby temple will see the Sun perfectly skirt the whole length of the headdress of the Sphinx on its right side beginning at the crown. The Sphinx lies 481 feet from the base of the Great Pyramid; 481 feet is the original height of the Great Pyramid. The Sphinx is 240.5 feet in length, exactly half its distance to the Great Pyramid and half its height. These unquestionably deliberate alignments connecting the major structures prove they were built together as different parts of a larger whole. They suggest, too, that the Great Sphinx predates the other structures, which were aligned from its position. It was originally a 66-foot-high out-cropping of natural rock that ancient artists fashioned into the form of a mythical beast.

"Sphinx" is Greek for something entwined or bound together, combining various elements, drawn from the man's head on a lion's body. But the monumental Seshep-ankh, or "Living Image," as the Egyptians knew it, commemorated the Great Deluge that was repeated annually in the beneficent swelling of the river. As standard literature on the Sphinx explains, "This association probably derived from the zodiacal sign of Leo, since it was during his summer month that the Nile began to flood." But early Islamic writers obviously had a different flood in mind when they wrote of the Great Sphinx.

The 15th century Moslem scholar, Makritzi, relying on older, unnamed sources, described the Deluge and how a "fire was to proceed from the sign of Leo and consume the world." According to Medieval Egyptian Coptic historian, Masudi, the natural catastrophe that Surid, builder of the

Great Pyramid, was warned against emanated in Leo. Masudi apparently received his information from an earlier source, the *Abou Hormeis*, the 9th century Arabic translation of a dynastic document, which recorded that "the Deluge was to take place when the heart of the Lion entered the first minute of the head of Cancer." These Leonine indications appear to describe the direction of the sky from which the cataclysm came, not the time it arrived. As such, the Great Sphinx that sprawls before the Pyramid is in fact symbolic of that same constellation and associated with a world-class inundation.

In *Gods of Eden* (1998), author Andrew Collins shows that the Great Sphinx would have been perfectly aligned with the rising of the constellation Leo in the pre-dawn of the vernal equinox, 21 March 9220 BC. This is the same time period given by the Egyptian high-priest for the destruction of Atlantis in Plato's account. If so, then the monument was obviously meant to symbolize Leo, and its orientation to that stellar configuration on the first day of spring in the year of the Atlantean catastrophe signifies human survival and rebirth at the Nile Delta.

Scholars know, however, that the Great Sphinx has been often modified, sometimes radically, over the last 4,000 or more years, so much so, that modern observers might be shocked to see its original condition. For example, its first identity may not have been feline at all, but entirely canine. The Koran refers to the Great Sphinx as dog-headed Anubis fronting the Great Pyramid, and "laying at the entrance with his feet outstretched." The "Text of Unas" in the Egyptian Book of the Dead appears to identify the Great Sphinx with Anubis: "O, you who have lain down . . . you Apuat." Known in Egyptian myth as Apuat, the "Opener of the Way from the West, or simply, the "Westerner," Anubis was said to have "written annals from before the flood" that destroyed his island-home in the Distant West, from whence he arrived to reestablish his worship in Egypt. He was also known as the "Great Five," the sacred numeral of Atlantis, according to Plato. As such, the Great Sphinx's original guise as Anubis would have especially exemplified the Giza Plateau's Atlantean and geodetic qualities.

Perhaps during the early Old Kingdom, when some 3rd dynasty pharaoh replaced the monument's facial features with those of his own, it was transfigured from a single god into the divine trio of Horakhty, Khepra, and Atum. The Great Sphinx looks east over the Nile, so its association with Horakhty, "Horus-of-the-Horizon" (that is, the dawn), is apparent.

The Great Sphinx of Egypt

Khepra, however, epitomized the "First Time," the Tep Zepik, a golden age when gods and men lived together on this kingdom in the sea, until humans became degenerate. Atum, who created the island, was called upon to destroy this first home of mankind, the "primeval hill," as it is described in The Book of the Dead, with a Great Flood, from which the immortals and a few chosen men escaped to eventually land at the Nile Delta, where they sparked "Pharaonic Civilization." Mythological and philological correspondences between Atum and Atlas define the Atlantean identity of the Egyptian god.

That the Great Pyramid is not a thing in itself but the centerpiece for a set of related structures was substantiated by physicist John Legon and geologist Robin J. Cook. Legon demonstrated that the three pyramids fit precisely within a rectangular perimeter formed by a basic modular unit of one thousand cubits (approximately 1,833 feet), a harmonious arrangement beyond mere coincidence. This site-plan uniformity extended beyond the Giza Plateau to include other, even much-later structures. Although it arose with the birth of Dynastic Egypt, the geodetic and, hence, sacred measurement principles incorporated throughout the

Great Pyramid persisted in another of the Seven Wonders of the Ancient World, as retold in a brilliant book on the subject, *The Electric Mirror on the Pharos Lighthouse* (2006). According to author Larry B. Radka, at the command of Ptolemy I, Egypt's first Hellenistic ruler and former general in the army of Alexander the Great, construction began around 300 BC under the direction of Sostratus of Cnidus, the architect-in-charge. The site he chose, Pharo, was an islet just off the coast connected to the mainland, and which formed one side of the great harbor at Alexandria.

Relying on the arcane wisdom that brought the Great Pyramid into existence 3,000 years before, Sostratus raised a tower in similarly colossal blocks of white stone, beginning with a massive, square platform surmounted by a taller octagonal section. The topmost addition was a contrasting, circular design. At its apex, a gigantic mirror reflected sunlight during daylight hours. But after sunset, a large beacon was lit, and its projected beam was visible for 32.5 nautical miles. From this distance, Radka deduces it stood about 600 feet above sea level. While he believes this was probably the structure's actual overall height, more likely, a smaller tower stood on a precipice or raised plateau, as did the Great Pyramid at the Giza plain, bringing its beam to approximately 600 feet above sea level.

Contemporary Alexandrian coins portraying the Pharos Lighthouse show it was adorned with four colossi of tritons blowing horns, one on every corner of the building, and surrounded by minarets, which Islamic architects copied much later in standard mosque design. Its mirrors were so large they could be swiveled into position during a daytime attack to set enemy ships on fire by concentrating the sun's rays on sails and rigging. Conventional scholars dismiss any such military application for the Pharos Lighthouse, insisting it must have been entirely legendary, citing the allegedly low quality of reflective technology at the time. But their poor assessment of ancient optics is contradicted by Pharaonic Egyptian lenses superior to modern examples. During the late 1990s, the quartz crystal eyes of early dynastic statues were examined by Jay Enoch (School of Optometry, University of California, Berkeley) and Vasudevan Lakshminarayanan (School of Optometry, University of Missouri, St. Louis).

They were surprised by the intricacy of anatomical detail found in the artificial eyes of the 4th dynasty representation of Prince Rahotep and a sculpted scribe from a 5th dynasty tomb at Sakkara, which the scientists tried to reproduce with the latest optical technology. "Amazingly," writes

Edward Malkowski in his report on their attempt, "the ancient Egyptian lenses were of better quality than the duplications." Enoch and Lakshmi-narayanan concluded "that because of the performance quality and design complexity, it is highly doubtful that the lenses used to re-create eye structures in ancient Egyptian statues were the first lenses created, despite the fact that they are 4,600 years old."

Their research was complimented by a nearly thirty-year investigation, published by Robert Temple in 2001. "The earliest actual lenses which I have located," he stated in Australia's *New Dawn* magazine, "are crystal ones dating from the 4th dynasty of Old Kingdom Egypt, circa 2500 BC. These are to be found in the Cairo Museum and two are in the Louvre in Paris. But archaeological evidence showing that they must have been around at least seven hundred years earlier has recently been excavated at Abydos, in Upper Egypt. A tomb of a pre-dynastic king there has yielded an ivory knife handle bearing a microscopic carving which could only have been done under considerable magnification (and of course can only be seen with a strong magnifying glass today)."

Temple makes a connection between the mirrors in the Pharaos Lighthouse and construction of the Great Pyramid: "The technology for surveying the Great Pyramid existed at least as far back as 3300 BC, and doubtless earlier than that, since we can hardly presume that the ivory knife handle was the first such object to exist, as it is already highly sophisticated and suggests a long-standing tradition. Thus, we know that magnification technology was in use in Egypt in 3300 BC [The Great Pyramid] is so perfectly oriented to the geographical points of the compass that no one has ever been able to understand how this was done, for the accuracy exceeds any hitherto known technology of ancient Egypt. Then there is the equally famous question of how the extreme accuracy of the construction of the Great Pyramid was possible.

"In 1925, J. H. Cole discovered in his survey that the great pavement, upon which the Great Pyramid partially rests and which surrounds it, is flat to within 15 mm. Earlier scholars had commented that the accuracy of the surface of the Great Pyramid was equivalent to the accuracy of the grinding of an optical reflective mirror in a giant modern telescope. The original (now largely destroyed) casing stone sides of the structure have been compared in their precision to the mirror of the Mount Palomar Telescope. How were such feats accomplished? Back in the 1960s and 1970s, the Argentine physicist Jose Alvarez Lopez claimed that it was physically impossible for the Great Pyramid to have been constructed without extremely accurate optical surveying techniques such as are used in theodolites. The Great Pyramid was clearly surveyed with early forms of optical surveying instruments that we could call prototheodolites."

Flinders Petrie marveled at "an amount of accuracy equal to most modern opticians' straight edges of such a length" in the Great Pyramid, and his views were supported a century later when Peter Lemesurier observed that its 21 acres of polished limestone outer casing "was leveled and honed to the standard of accuracy normal in modern optical work." Egyptian records themselves describe a level of reflective technology mainstream scholars are still reluctant to consider. At sixty feet in height, the 121-ton obelisk at Heliopolis, raised for Pharaoh Sesostris I's jubilee in 1942 BC, is the oldest of its kind, and is inscribed with a hieroglyphic text describing "thirteen thousand priests chanting before a huge mirror of burnished gold."

The Lighthouse survived the fall of Classical Civilization, but could not withstand two earthquakes; the first in AD 1303; the next, twenty years later. Qaitbay, the Egyptian Sultan, demolished what little remained of its squarish first section to build a fortress, using fallen stone and marble, in AD 1480. But while it stood, the Pharos Lighthouse rose to 280 Old Kingdom royal cubits, or 481 feet, the precise height of the Great Pyramid. Such a salient comparison was not coincidental, demonstrating that both structures, despite the millennia separating their construction, were built according to the same principles of sacred geometry.

This organizational unity began with all three pyramids of the Giza Plateau. They are linked by the Golden Ratio. Rediscovered by Leonardo da Vinci, who provided the name, the Golden Ratio is a spiral in the canon of ancient geometry used for the design of sacred architecture. It was valued as the most desirable proportion, because it is expressed in the patterns of

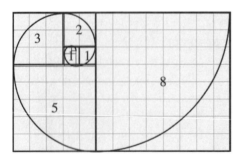

natural forms. These include cosmic nebulae, in the ratios between planetary orbits, animal horns, sea mollusks, the formation of the human fetus, in the laws of Mendelian heredity, heliotropism (the

The Golden Ratio (also known as the Fibonacci Sequence)

UNSEEN FORCES

movement of flowers following the path of the sun), and whirlpools, together with thousands of other examples observed in nature. It appears in a nautilus shell, its exterior wall removed to expose the Golden Section spiral inside. This was the Wind Jewel, the personal emblem carried by the Mayas' Kukulcan and the later Aztecs' Quetzalcoatl—the "Feathered Serpent," who long ago brought the principles of civilization to Mexico from his sunken kingdom across the Atlantic Ocean.

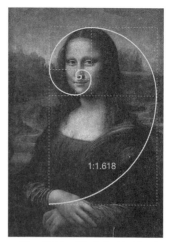

The Golden Ratio in Da Vinci's "Mona Lisa"

Temple was the first to notice that "a shadow is cast by the second pyramid, known as the Pyramid of Khafre, upon the Great Pyramid at sunset on 21 December. The shadow if truncated by a vertical line running up the middle of the south face of the Great Pyramid, does actually form a golden triangle. There is actually a purposeful slight indentation of a few inches in the construction of the side of the pyramid, discovered in measurements made by Petrie. This 'apothegm,' as geometers call such vertical lines, forms the right angle to transform the solstice shadow into a perfect Golden Triangle."

That this shadow was thrown on the Great Pyramid by the Pyramid of Khafre each winter solstice to form "a perfect Golden Triangle" can hardly have been fortuitous, and further illustrates that all three pyramids were built simultaneously as part of a unified plan, over which the Great Sphinx still holds court.

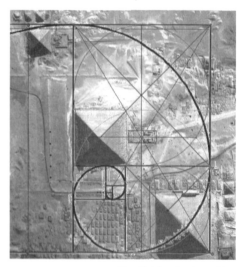

The Golden Ratio at Giza

This article first appeared in Atlantis Rising #60 (November/December 2006).

18

IN THE FIELDS OF THE BLESSED

*Do the Reeds of Papyrus on the Banks of the Nile
Hold the Secrets of Hidden Dimensions?*

BY WILLIAM HENRY

In numerous ancient traditions there is a description of a hidden and blessed place linked by a chain of symbols, a repetition of place names (the Reed Place), and references to this place as a door to a parallel dimension. As I document in my book, *Starwalkers and the Dimension of the Blessed* (2008), whether we look to the Maya, the Egyptians, the early Christians, or the Holy Grail legends, we find a recollection of an essential teaching about this "blessed" place.

For instance, in the ancient Egyptian records of Amenta, the "Hidden Place," we learn of two mounts. Atop the higher mount we find the gate to the Field of Reeds, also known as the Aarru Fields of Heaven. *Aarru* means "blessed." The ancient Egyptian's direct experiences of this blessed realm are recorded in texts and in scenes on temple walls.

> "The doors of the sky are opened, the doors of the firmament are thrown open at dawn for Horus of the Gods. He goes up to the Field of Reeds, he bathes in the Field of Reeds."—Utterance 325, Pyramid Texts

Ancient traditions the world over are also loaded with stories about beatified beings that travel between our world and the blessed realm. Sages, shamans and bodhisattvas who used spiritual technology—dreams, visions, hallucinogens, remote viewing—to expand consciousness to explore this realm left us these descriptions. They who learned about it also spent much of their lives preparing spiritually to enter it.

In *Lost Secrets of the Sacred Ark* (2003), Laurence Gardner makes a valuable contribution to the understanding of this "Field" (plane, zone) by declaring that Aaru is also called the Dimension of the Blessed. Science fiction television shows and movies often mention the concept of dimension. In the common mind, this word connotes parallel universes, alternate universes, and planes of existence. Was the ancient mind also tuned to the concept that one could travel to parallel/alternate universes/planes/fields? As many stories say (and physics theorizes), these universes are closer to us than we realize.

Hesiod called this dimension the Isle of the Blessed and the Elysium. Those mortals who were fortunate enough went to dwell on the Blessed Isle for eternity. Elysium was an "Apple-land," like Avalon or Eden.

In the *Aeneid*, Virgil referred to it by additional names, including "Land of Joy," "the Fortunate Wood," and the "Home of the Blessed." It is claimed to have been located on the White Island,

Hathor in Reeds

which was called Leuke or Leuce, a word that is very close to Luc, which means "light." In the apocryphal Book of Enoch, the prophet Enoch who walked the stars with God, speaks of proceeding to "the middle of the earth," where he beheld a "blessed land, happy and fertile." An angel shows him "the first and last secrets in heaven above, and in the depths of the earth: In the extremities of heaven, and in the foundations of it, and in the receptacle of the winds." Jesus also descended to what some believe to be the "inner earth" between his crucifixion and resurrection.

The Field of the Blessed resonates to the Christian ideal of the Kingdom of Heaven. They share the same message. Jesus urged us to "go within" to seek it, and to not stop seeking until we find the truth. Only then will we be free.

Those with a blessed heart, Jesus said, will see this kingdom. In addition, in the *Pistis Sophia* he is more direct, saying, "Cease not to seek day and night and remit not yourselves until ye find the purifying mysteries which will purify you and make you into a refined light, so that you will go on high and inherit the light of my kingdom." It appears that the wisdom taught to Enoch in the "inner earth" may have had something to do with transforming himself into a being of light preparatory to entering the dimension of the blessed.

THE AFTERLIFE JOURNEY

Among the primary source materials for the Greek and Roman tales about the Field of the Blessed, and I believe Jesus' statements, is the *Book of the Amduat* (or *Tuat*). This Egyptian text began appearing around 1500 BC. It describes the after-life journey of the initiated pharaoh to the Field of the Blessed (Aarru), the netherworld kingdom ruled by Osiris, where all the wishes of the deceased would be fulfilled.

The Egyptian Pyramid Texts, which provide instruction about the afterlife, are also loaded with references to the Field of the Blessed. Another Egyptian source is the Edfu Texts written in stone on the walls of the Temple of Horus, the Sun-god, at Edfu, Egypt, which was constructed around 250 BC, but whose sources are much older. The walls of this temple feature the story of the arrival of sages from the stars who created a civilization beside a Field of Reeds.

In Egypt, the papyrus reeds grow abundantly along the banks of the Nile. Intriguingly, *byblos* is the Greek word for "papyrus." Bible comes from byblos. Our English word "paper" is derived from the word "papyrus," an Egyptian word that originally meant "that which belongs to the house" (the bureaucracy of ancient Egypt). The Egyptians used the reed and triangular shape (when viewed in cross section) as a metaphor for many aspects of life. The pyramids at Giza, sometimes referred to as the Bible in Stone, are magnificent examples of this metaphor.

In Egyptian hieroglyphs, a rolled papyrus made from the papyrus reed is the symbol for knowledge. A roll of papyrus symbolized the unfolding of life itself. Correspondingly, writing utensils were originally made of reeds. Thoth, the Egyptian god of divine magic and alchemy, is shown writing with a reed pen. Hence, the reed simply and elegantly also symbolizes wisdom. Perhaps this is why reading is fundamental to acquiring wisdom.

The metaphor of the reed continues in the afterlife Field or Place of Reeds where it signifies the unfolding of life in a finer realm, along the heavenly Nile, the Milky Way. Interestingly, the Hopi, ancient inhabitants of America who now reside in northern Arizona, use the word *Songwuka*, literally "the big reed," for the Milky Way. This is strange. Bamboo grows in tropical areas, not in arid Arizona. Had the Hopi somehow heard the tales of the reed from tropical Egypt or Canaan, the land across the ocean or from elsewhere? From afar, our home galaxy is a whirling white or light island of stars in the ocean of life. Is the bright center of the Milky Way the Field of Reeds at the center of the heavenly Nile? Is our galaxy's black hole a gateway to another dimension?

Time and again we see paintings of priests and priestesses sailing on the waters of the heavenly Nile in the Blessed Field of Reeds. They are sailing the stars of the river of life, the Milky Way. The early 20th century British Egyptologist Wallis Budge explains, "The Egyptians . . . from the earliest days . . . depicted to themselves a material heaven wherein Isles of the Blessed were laved by the waters of the Nile . . . others again lived in imagination on the banks of the heavenly Nile, whereon they built cities; and it seems as if the Egyptians never succeeded in conceiving a heaven without a Nile."

The gods traverse the Field of the Blessed upon boats of eternity (which, by the way, precisely match the way modern science portrays a wormhole). Occasionally, they ascend and descend upon sky ropes, vines, and pillars. A key Egyptian symbol, the Djed pillar (also written TET),

Sailing the waters of the heavenly Nile, the Milky Way.

Raising the Djed pillar or Tower. In Egypt, the bundle of reeds is call a Djed, the ladder or stairway to heaven.

was originally made of papyrus reeds bundled together, and was connected to the mother goddess, Hathor, and to Osiris, the Lord of the Eternity and the Field of the Blessed. The raising of the Djed was a symbol of the king's ascent to the sky, the heavenly Nile, for it was thought of as the world pillar or ladder that connects the earthly realm with the heavenly Field of Reeds. As such, it was a multidimensional symbol. Its function suggests that a tether—a rope or cord that fastens two poles together—is also involved.

In the East the reed, which sprouted from the universal waters, stands for manifestation and equates with the lotus. It is the earliest stalk or tree of ascent. The Babel builders knew it well.

The Old Testament story of Moses parting the Red Sea (or properly the Reed Sea) with the Rod of God corresponds with the Egyptian ideas about the Field of Reeds and the Djed. As such, the story of parting of the Reed Sea is easily interpreted as an allegory for the opening of the Field or Dimension of the Blessed.

CANA

It is highly significant that Cana ("reedy") is the place where Jesus performed his first miracle, turning water into wine at a (his?) wedding feast, demonstrating his magical ability to interact with the other dimensional sacred reality . . . or to alter this one. In early Christian art Jesus, in the role of the Redeemer (phonetically reed-e-mer), is repeatedly shown performing this miracle, and all the others, with a rod or wand in his hand. What is this wand? Where did he get it? What is the rod made of? What happened to it? I've wondered about this for a very long time.

The reed symbol next reappears as a prominent tool in the crucifixion, first subtly, then overtly. After Pilate washed his hands of Jesus, the soldiers of the governor took Jesus into the common hall, and they stripped him, and put on him a purple robe, symbolic of royalty and sovereignty.

After putting the purple robe on Jesus, "they [had] platted a crown of thorns, they put [it] upon his head, and a reed in his right hand: and they bowed the knee before him, and mocked him, saying, Hail, King of the Jews!"

Next, "they took the reed and smote him on the head."

Finally, a sponge soaked in vinegar was put upon a "reed," and raised to Jesus' mouth. They said, "Let's see if Elias (in Hebrew *Eliahu* "Yahveh is God," also called Elijah) comes to save him." And Jesus gave up the ghost.

Like Enoch, Elias was "translated," so that he should not taste death. He became a starwalker. He was last seen talking with his spiritual son Eliseus on the hills of Moab when, "a fiery chariot, and fiery horses parted them both asunder, and Elias went up by a whirlwind into heaven." In effect, the Romans are saying, "let's see if Elijah comes out of the whirlwind to save him." It appears the whirlwind (symbol of a vortex) and the reeds (symbol of another dimension) are entwined symbols.

Based upon the spotlighting of the reed symbol in the Passion of Jesus it is clear to me now that his rod was likely a "reed" rod or wand that conducted the rays and radiations, the song of the Dimension of the Blessed. By portraying Jesus as a magician (or musician) with his reed wand, the early Church (AD 1st to 2nd century) returned to him his power symbol or tool, which was turned against him by the Romans. This "reed wand," I propose, is the Holy Grail.

Intriguingly, the Holy Grail tradition kept the memory of the blessed place alive. For instance, Avalon is sometimes referred to as the legendary location where Jesus visited the British Isles with

Jesus before his crucifixion, with his reed "scepter."

Joseph of Arimathea and was later the site of the first church in Britain. This church, known as the Wattle Church, was composed of reeds—a reed church.

Joseph of Arimathea revived the ancient tradition of symbolizing the Church by a reed.

One of the first of the Holy Grail romances was a poem called "The Tale of the Grail," written by the French poet Chrétien de Troyes around the year 1190. Curiously, introducing the book Chrétien says he got the story from an older book given to him by his patron. He refers to the Grail Castle as the White Castle. Another grail romance, now known as the "Didot Perceval," refers to it as "the White Castle in the White Town." Another anonymous grail author attempted to advance Chrétien's "Tale of the Grail" and stated that the White Town is in a region called "the White Land." Yet another grail tale written around the time of the 12th century, the Welsh story called "Peredur" adds the incredible detail that the White Land is an area situated in the "Old Marshes" or . . . Old Reeds.

The reed symbolism reappears in the word Canon-ization, the ultimate act of consciousness in the Christian tradition. This is when one becomes a saint, effectively dividing or setting oneself apart from the rest of humanity.

According to some writers, the origin of beatification (becoming a blessed one) and canonization in the Catholic Church is to be traced back to the ancient pagan apotheosis: Deification, the exaltation of men to the rank of gods, or god making. The apotheosized are translated, like Elijah, to heaven—presumably in a whirling vehicle—and become starwalkers.

In Acts 2:4, the apostles were recognized as canonized when a "flame of invisible light," a lamp, appeared on top of their heads (as it did on the Buddhist bodhisattvas). This flame streaming from their heads signified superintelligence and illumination.

Webster's says the word *candor*, honesty in expressing oneself, comes from *candere*, to shine. This is also the root of candle. In early Christian history, those who had received baptism were called illuminati and were given a lighted taper as a symbol of their spiritual enlightenment. It is easy to see why a lit candle symbolizes Christ, the light of the Field of Reeds, or the Dimension of the Blessed.

Whether spelled Canaan, Cana, Canon, Kanon, Kan, or Kenon this word-vibration refers ultimately to the most mystical of paths, the one leading to the Field of Reeds, the Dimension of the Blessed. In one of those ironic twists of history the word *canon* was applied to cannon, a weapon, and to an ecclesiastical law or code of laws established by a church council and to scriptures ratified (adopted as law) by the church. The books of the Bible officially accepted as Holy Scripture are known as the Canon.

Ironically (or perhaps not), in the collective consciousness of the 21st century, the Cana word-vibration is most closely associated with a space port. I speak, of course, of the Kennedy Space Center and Cape Canaveral (Spanish for "Cape of Canes or Reeds"), where many space shuttle launches have taken place. Though the place was named 400 years before NASA came along, "Canaveral" rings of its purpose: the connecting place to the blessed Field of Reeds. Humorously, its telephone area code is 321.

From the ancient to the modern world the reed place has meant the same thing. Now you know the rest of the story.

This article first appeared in *Atlantis Rising* #63 (May/June 2007).

19

ANCIENT WINGS OVER THE NILE

*Did the Saqqara Glider Merely Represent a Bird or Did
it Show Knowledge of the Principles of Flight?*

BY JOSEPH ROBERT JOCHMANS, LIT.D.

In 1891, the burial remains of a Ptolemaic minor official named Padi-
Imen (Amun) were unearthed at Saqqara, Egypt. Though the remains
dated to circa 200 BC, they were part of the general excavation findings
associated with the tomb of Queen Khuit, one of the wives of Pharaoh Teti
of the 6th dynasty, from two millennia earlier. As was the common practice
during the later Ptolemaic period, many of the tombs of former royal dignitaries were reused, which was the reason Padi-Imen's burial objects were
part of the Old Kingdom artifacts brought to light.

By 1898, the discovered artifacts had made their way to the Cairo
Museum. Among the Ptolemaic pieces was a curious winged object catalogued as Special Register No. 6347 (also designated with the number
33109). Within the context of today's technological mindset, we can
immediately see just by looking at it that it bears an uncanny resemblance
to a glider craft of some type. But because at the time of its discovery the
birth of modern aviation was still several years away—the Wright brothers'
first flight did not take place until 1903—the strange object was shelved
away among other miscellaneous items to gather dust, unrecognized for
what it really was.

In 1969, over seventy years later, Dr. Dowoud Kahlil Messiha—an
Egyptologist, medical doctor, and Professor of Anatomy for the Medical
Arts at Helwan University—was examining a particular museum display
in Room No. 22, labeled "bird figurines." The other contents of the display were clearly bird sculptures, but the Saqqara artifact was different. It
possessed characteristics not found on birds, yet which are part of modern aircraft design. Dr. Messiha, who was a model plane enthusiast and
member of the Egyptian Aeromodelers Club, immediately recognized the

Saqqara Glider

aircraft features and persuaded the Under Secretary of the Egyptian Ministry of Culture to form a committee in order to investigate the model. In the meetings of the committee in late 1970 and early 1971, the participating historians and aviation experts were so impressed with their findings that it was recommended that the model be placed in the Central Hall of the Cairo Museum as a temporary main exhibit. Afterward it was returned, and today it is still housed in Room No. 22, on the second floor.

The small craft is made of very light sycamore wood and weighs 39.12 grams, or 0.5 oz. The only markings on it are faint eyes painted on the nose and two red lines under the wings, in a similar fashion that decorations appear on modern aircraft. The eye dots—which were largely responsible for giving it the appearance of being a bird—are actually the ends of a very small obsidian bar that is fitted through the head and gives the craft an important balancing weight.

The model's wings are straight and aerodynamically shaped, with a span of 18.3 centimeters, or about 7.2 inches. Its pointed nose is 3.2 centimeters (1.5 inches) long. The body of the craft totals 14.2 centimeters (5.6 inches), tapered, terminating in a vertical tail fin. Dr. Messiha found evidence for a tail-wing piece that very likely had once been attached to the vertical tail precisely like the back tail on a modern plane. Also on the tail can faintly be seen a hieroglyph inscription which reads, "The gift of Amun," who was the Egyptian deity associated with the wind.

Dr. Messiha, interviewed in the May 18, 1972 *London Times*, made these comments on the ancient plane's shape and sophistication:

"It is the tail that is really the most interesting thing which distinguishes this model from all others that have been discovered. No bird can produce such a contortion at the rear of its body to assume anything that looks like the model. Furthermore, there is a groove under the fin for a tail-plane (crosspiece) which is missing. This is no toy model—it's too scientifically designed and it took a lot of skill to make it."

A full-scale version of the plane could have flown carrying heavy loads, but at low speeds, between 45 and 65 miles per hour. What is not known, however, is what the power source of the ancient craft was. Several engineers did note that the model makes a perfect glider as it is. In fact, it would have taken only the efforts of a small catapult to get a life-sized model in the air. Simply by using the rising heat currents off the Egyptian deserts on either side of the Nile, such a craft would have been able to stay in the air indefinitely with skilled maneuvering. The little model itself, even though over two thousand years old, will soar a short distance with only a slight jerk of the hand. As Dr. Messiha discovered, fully restored balsa replicas will travel even farther.

Just before the time period from which the little model came, a philosopher and friend of Plato, Archytas of Tarentum (circa 400–365 BC), is said to have successfully "set in motion a flying machine in the form of a wooden dove by means of compressed air."

The source of his construction plans and designs had been obtained from manuscripts, which eventually made their way into the Library of Alexandria, dating back to a period already considered ancient in his day.

The Saqqara sailplane has inherent within it design features that appear to have been standardized by the ancient Egyptians over a long period of time. Three relief figures from the Temple of Khonsu at Karnak, the earliest dating to the time of Ramses Ill or a thousand years before the Saqqara model was made, show the mastheads of royal ships possessing bird-like weathervanes, which look remarkably like the wooden glider, complete with fixed outstretched wings and vertical tail.

As modern free flight glider designer and builder Martin Gregorie pointed out, the intrinsic shaping of these ancient figurines, like that of the Saqqara model, would have made them excellent weathervanes, for they would have pointed directly and steadily into the wind and would not have veered from side to side.

Based on these reliefs, and on the Saqqara glider itself, creative modeler and aviation historian Paula Mercado has drawn detailed designs for a modern version of the ancient sailplane, which any small-scale glider enthusiast can build and successfully fly today.

Yet the question remains, what was the original Saqqara "bird" based upon? As Dr. Messiha noted, the ancient Egyptians always built scale models of everything they were familiar with in their daily lives and placed them in their tombs—model temples, ships, chariots, servants, and animals. Now that we have found a model plane, Dr. Messiha wondered if perhaps somewhere under the desert sands along the Nile there may yet be

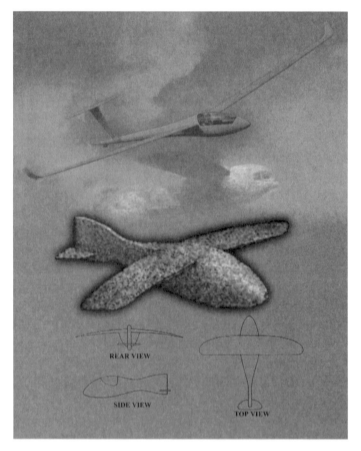

REAR VIEW

SIDE VIEW

TOP VIEW

Composite glider drawings based on the Saqqara glider.

unearthed the remains of life-sized gliders, after which the actual Saqqara sailplane was copied.

During my 25 trips to Egypt between 1981 and 1997, I had several opportunities to meet with Dr. Messiha and his family. He was kind enough to take time out from his busy medical practice and lecture engagements to speak to our tour groups on a number of occasions, even accompanying us to Saqqara and showing us where the model glider had been found.

Twice I was also invited into his home for dinner and to meet with a group of local intellectuals. On one of these private visits he showed me the balsa model of the Saqqara glider he had made and allowed me to toss it in a "test flight" across his living room. Messiha's model is roughly five times the size of the small glider in the Cairo Museum, to make it more airworthy, but I could plainly see that he had faithfully incorporated all the design features inherent in the ancient artifact.

Dr. Messiha told me that he was of the opinion that the model from the tomb was an artist's impression of something much larger that he had seen up close and in operation when he was alive. The small wooden object, when it was in pristine condition, probably did not fly very well. But that had not been its purpose. Its purpose, as far as the artist had been concerned, was to make a simple diminutive replica of something worthy enough to be a tomb offering for the afterlife. As Dr. Messiha noted, most of the design features inherent in the full scale craft it had been based upon were accurately artistically reproduced to the point that they are still clearly identifiable over two thousand years later.

Not long before he died in 1998, Dr. Messiha made arrangements for one of our tours to meet him in the Cairo Museum. He escorted us up to Room No. 22, which the museum guards temporarily closed off specially for our group. With the permission and under the supervision of a museum official who was a colleague of the doctor, the display case was opened; and for almost an hour, we were privileged to examine the Saqqara glider up close. Unfortunately, because of museum policy, we were not allowed to take any photographs or videotape, but I did take careful notes both of Dr. Messiha's observations and what I saw for myself.

The very first impression one gets when looking at the model is that it is no artist's expression of a bird. Unlike the other objects in the same display case in which the model is kept, there are no renditions of legs, feet, aviary-type wings-in-flight attitudes, pronounced beak, or artistic portrayal of feathers, drawn or carved.

There is a slight protrusion at the front suggesting a beak, but it is part of the overall aerodynamic design. No paint or change of coloration was made to accentuate a bird beak—instead it is an aerofoil feature that is an essential part of the fuselage.

There are no prominent holes anywhere on the body of the model— certainly not for holding feathers, or feet, or even a pole to swivel on as some have claimed if the object was once used as a weathervane. When I was handed the glider I carefully turned it over, because there are no published photographs showing its underside. I found no evidence of any holes where legs or feet were once attached, or any smaller holes into which feathers could have been inserted. The underbelly was relatively smooth, though worn with age. The only original significant indentation that I could see was in the center of the top of the wing, where the wing assemblage was attached to the main body.

There is, to be sure, a prominent circular indentation in the artifact's underside, but there is very good evidence that this was added soon after it had arrived in the Cairo Museum, toward the beginning of the last century. The shallow "hole" was deliberately set in place by the Museum's early restoration department so as to be able to mount the piece on an exhibit stand. Similar modern indentations can be observed on the bird figurines that share space with the Saqqara glider in its display case. Every one was an addition necessary for mounting and exhibition purposes.

Neither does the artifact have any artist's renderings of feathers. Skeptics have suggested that painted on feathers could have been worn off over time. But though I had the time to carefully examine practically every square millimeter of the model, I saw no images of feathers, or even flecks of paint indicating residue that would have been left behind had the model's surface been subjected to some kind of paint coating that had subsequently weathered away. The only painted images I could detect were the simple outlines of eyes, two lines under the wing, the inscription near the tail, and a catalog number added in modern times. The ancient markings, as Dr. Messiha pointed out to me, may have been placed on the model as an afterthought, part of an effort to make it into a religious relic, to better fit within a tomb setting. Or as other researchers have surmised, these may have mirrored actual designs seen by the artist on the original craft—part of the same type of decal decorations seen on modern planes today.

The claim is further made by skeptics that the model was made to resemble a falcon because it was meant to be a ceremonial object commonly used to represent one of the two main falcon-headed deities in ancient Egypt, either Horus or Ra-Harakhty.

Actually, this argument works in reverse. In Egyptian sacred iconography, the images of either Horus or Ra-Harakhty were invariably depicted with very specific symbols and accoutrements. Horus in his full form was always shown holding either an Ankh or Shen symbol, and wearing a Pshemty or royal double crown on his brow. Ra-Harakhty was never portrayed without a solar disc prominently placed on top of his head. Such features are totally lacking on the Saqqara model, and an inspection of its surfaces revealed no points where such important deific symbols were once attached. In fact, it is the striking absence of any traditional sacred markings that takes the model out of the realm of being a religious object and puts it instead squarely in the context of a technological artifact.

Horus

By far the two most unbird-like features are the model's wings and vertical tail. These are inherently linked with its aerodynamic body, which is certainly very bird-like yet radically different from any other ancient Egyptian statues of birds, particularly deified ones. One need only look at the bird figures exhibited in the same museum display case as the model to see the glaring differences. The figurine bodies were often slightly deformed to accentuate deific strength and power, while the wings were spread wide, feathers splayed, either in an attack or protective mode. And the tail was invariably fanned out horizontally when the figures were portrayed in flight. In contrast, the model's body is sleek yet aerodynamically true, the wings are tight and fixed to support airlift capacity, and the back tail is rigidly vertical. All these are distinctive features of a glider, not a bird.

Still other skeptics have dismissed the Saqqara model as having been nothing more than a child's toy. The unanswered question, however, is if this was only a toy, why does it contain such sophisticated design features? The examination of the model I made convinced me this was not any haphazard creation made on a whim by an ancient artist trying to mimic a bird in flight. Holding the glider in my hand, I got a strong sense of its inherent balance and design sophistication. Rather than being a mere plaything, I felt that, to the contrary, this was the end-product of a long series of intensive experiments performed by a multitude of serious researchers over a very long period of time, perhaps several generations. The model was primarily meant to be studied and appreciated as a learning tool.

One of the main criticisms against the Saqqara model being a glider is the apparent lack of a stabilizing tailwing. Some authors have mistakenly written that Dr. Messiha found such a tailwing, or that there is an obvious slot in the model's vertical tail where a tailwing was once attached. But Dr. Messiha assured me that neither was true.

However, as the doctor pointed out to me when we looked at the Saqqara glider together, the bottom edge of the vertical tail extending back into the main body is rough in appearance and to the touch, in contrast to the smoothness of the surfaces elsewhere. It is obvious another wood component that was once part of the original model extended out the back end from this point, and that it had subsequently broken off.

I also detected that the top of the vertical tail was flattened out of its natural contour, and there is the possibility something also was attached here in former times. In certain modern aircraft designs, in fact, the tailwing appears at the top of the vertical tail rather than at its base.

Looking from a purely design function point of view, the only logical component that would have been placed in either location would have been a tailwing, and that is precisely the one item that is missing. The majority of those model plane enthusiasts who have taken the time and effort to actually build and fly a replica of the Saqqara glider, and have added the lost tailwing in precisely the designated position where one very likely existed, find that the craft works very well and perfectly sails through the air over an extended distance.

Yet despite all that has been researched and observed about the Saqqara glider, there is an intransigence in the world of conservative thinking that refuses to even consider that flying was known in the ancient past. All that we are left with are "authoritative" statements such as this one, found in Wikipedia:

"No ancient Egyptian aircraft have ever been found, nor has any other evidence suggesting their existence come to light. As a result, the theory that the Saqqara Bird is a model of a flying machine is not accepted by mainstream Egyptologists and is generally regarded as pseudo-archaeology."

20

THE GREAT PYRAMID

Plumbing the Deeper Waters

BY FRANK JOSEPH

R eaders of *Atlantis Rising* are more familiar than most Americans
with the mind-boggling details of ancient Egypt's Great Pyramid.
But of all the theories used to explain its construction, one postulated by an American construction engineer, Edward Kunkel, in the early
1950s, is still compelling. He was intrigued with a passage in the *Histories*
(II, 25), by Herodotus, a travel-writer who visited the Giza Plateau and
personally investigated its monuments in the early 5th century BC. Kunkel
read that "the Pyramid was built in steps, battlement-wise, as it is called,
or, according to others, altar-wise. After laying the stones for the base, they
raised the remaining stones to their places by means of machines formed
of short wooden planks. The first machine raised them from the ground to
the top of the first step. On this there was another machine, which received
the stone upon its arrival, and conveyed it to the second step, whence a
third machine advanced it still higher."

Contemporary theorists, like the science-fiction author, L. Sprague de
Camp, took Herodotus' "machines" for hoists. "As nobody has found any
trace in Egyptian art, architecture or literature of anything like these hoisting machines, it is likely that they were merely the fantasy of some guide
or priest, recounted to the eminent Greek tourist in the hope of extracting
an extra obolos from him." But Kunkel looked beyond such deprecating
attitudes on the part of scientific dogmatists who presume to know better than original sources. To him, the "machines formed of short wooden
planks" described in the histories were not hoists, but sluice-gates, part
of a coffer dam. He postulated that stones were taken by raft from their
quarries down the Nile, and were brought through a canal which raised
them to the Giza Plateau by a series of locks, directly to the building site.
When the coffer dam was flooded, each block was literally floated to its
proper course. Once there, only four or six men were needed to quickly

and easily maneuver it into perfect position without risking damage. Upon each completed level, an extension of the coffer dam was built to service the next course, and so on toward the top.

If this was, in fact, the method used by the pyramid builders, only several hundred laborers actually engaged in placing the blocks for perhaps five to ten years would have been required to finish the job. Work requiring far greater effort was quarrying and transporting stones to the building site. For this huge task, a national effort, involving many thousands of laborers, was needed. Naturally, after completion, every trace of the coffer dam and its connecting canal with locks would have been eliminated, just as all machines today are removed from a building site as soon as their presence is no longer required. Kunkel's theory is credible, because it was evolved entirely within the context of Egyptian civilization.

Not even the most hide-bound conservative scholar denies that the Egyptians were outstanding irrigationists from the 1st dynasty. Their mastery of the Nile, upon which the country's prosperity depended, is universally recognized. Envisioning and constructing such a coffer dam were by no means beyond their experience. De Camp admits, "For pyramids built on low ground, the kings had canals dug from the Nile partway to the pyramid, so that the stones could be brought near the site." Originally, the Great Pyramid may itself have sat in a moat of some kind. A square depression or shallow indentation cut into the bedrock immediately surrounding its base might have been filled with water to serve as a reflecting pool. Indeed, a few Arab traditions refer to such a dramatizing feature, and some archaeologists speculate on its possibility.

Kunkel's theory cannot elucidate every aspect of the Great Pyramid's construction, but many believe it does offer the most convincing solution yet. His proposed coffer dam cannot explain how the uppermost stones were brought into place. The only device capable of fitting them would have been a powerful crane hauled up the side of the largely completed structure and mounted near the apex. Although hoisting stones to a height more than 400 feet would have required great skill; at least the blocks involved were the smallest and lightest used in the building. As de Camp pointed out, no evidence exists to show that the pyramid builders had such a crane. One was employed in Egypt, however, at the harbor-city of Alexandria. The largest known crane in the ancient world serviced freighters from all over the Mediterranean Sea. Erected for the Greek Ptolemies,

Edward Kunkel's drawing of how the Great Pyramid's stones might have been floated into place.

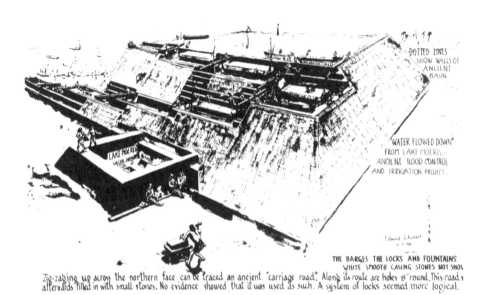

Kunkel's vision of a lock system which he believed could have been used to build the Great Pyramid.

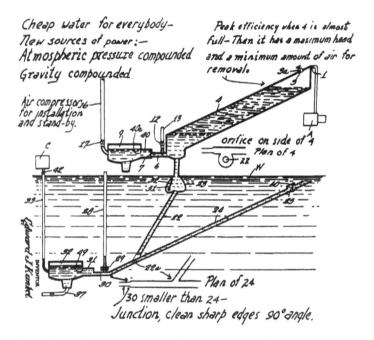

Edward Kunkel's 1959 patent based on his theory that the Great Pyramid was a pump.

who ruled Egypt after the death of Alexander the Great in the 4th century BC, the crane was so powerful it could lift the largest ship loaded with its cargo from the water and place it gently in dry-dock. It did not however, survive the fall of the Roman world, save in the record of rare coins. One such coin was especially minted for the Alexandrian crane operator, the highest paid manual laborer in classical times.

We do not know if such a machine was actually employed to complete the Great Pyramid, millennia earlier. The Ptolemies' crane may have been a descendant of similar "machines" developed thousands of years before to assist in the construction of Egypt's stupendous monuments. No remains of such a monstrous crane have so far been found, nor are likely to be, because it was never intended for permanence. Conventional Egyptologists have no trouble believing that super-barges were used to float many tons of stone blocks down the Nile, yet not a trace of even a single barge survived into modern times. In any case, the invention and use of such a crane, however splendid, pales in comparison with the monument itself. As a modern construction engineer once remarked, "whoever built the Great Pyramid could build anything!"

These mysterious construction engineers originally positioned the Pyramid as closely as possible to the absolute center of the world's landmass. This means that it sits at a unique location where the lines of latitude and longitude pass over more of the earth's surface than at any other place. Location and very form epitomize its identity as a geodetic symbol. As Alexander Braghine explained, "The summit of the pyramid is situated in 290 58' 51.22" of north latitude. This circumstance at first sight does not seem significant. The moment, however, we remember that the apparent position of the Polar Star is invariably 1' 8.78" out, owing to the phenomenon of atmospheric refraction, we see what was in the mind of the builder. If we add the value of the refraction, i.e. 1' 8.78" to 290 58' 51.22", we get exactly 300, and we realize that the mysterious builder of the pyramid, guiding himself by the Polar Star (or by a corresponding point in the constellation of Draconis), wished to center the pyramid upon the 13th parallel.

"This parallel is remarkable for the fact that it separates a maximum of the land of our planet from the maximum of the ocean surfaces. Apparently, the builder wished to record permanently the distribution of the continents and oceans of those days, and we can see that this distribution has remained almost the same until our own times" (237, 238). Physicist Michael Csuzdi seconded Braghine's explanation: "The six continents of the Earth markedly form a pentagonal pyramid. Africa is at the apex lines drawn from its center to the centers of the other continents are evenly spaced at 72 degrees. The other five centers are nearly on a common plane to form the pyramid's base line."

Incorporated in the dimensions of the Pyramid itself is a trio of key measurements with which we can calculate the size and shape of the Earth with accuracy. They correspond to the three most important planetary measurements defining Earth's circumference, polar radius, and equatorial bulge. From them may be precisely deduced the flattening at the poles and the irregularity of the equator, neither of which were rediscovered until the 18th century. The perimeter of the Great Pyramid's sockets equals a half-minute of equatorial longitude, or 1/43,200 the Earth's circumference. Its total original height equaled 1/43,200 the polar radius. Its original perimeter exactly equaled one half-minute of latitude at the equator, which means that its baselength represented the distance the Earth rotates in half of one second.

If the perimeter of the Great Pyramid was reduced to inches, it would express 36,524.2. This figure equals exactly one hundred times the number

of days in a year, or the number of days in a century. The baseline of the Great Pyramid is 500 cubits, or 750 Egyptian feet. This number corresponds precisely to the distance our planet travels in half-a-second of time at the equator, because the earth's circumference is 86,400 cubits, just as one 24-hour day is made up of 86,400 seconds. The ancient building's architectural accuracy in measuring our planet was not achieved again until satellite surveys from outer space, only 25 years ago.

Even the weight of the Great Pyramid incorporates profound knowledge of the Earth. Its six million tons equals one-quintillionth of the weight of our planet. If the pyramid's volume of 88 million cubic feet is multiplied by the average density of its stone, the result, expressed in ancient Egyptian units of measurement (known as "elbows"), will be 552. And 55.2 is the density of the Earth in its relation to water. Perhaps most incredible of all, multiplying the original height of the Great Pyramid by one billion produces 93,000,000—the average distance of our planet from the Sun, something only rediscovered in the 19th century.

Giza Death Star (2001) author, Joseph Farrell, observed how "the mean density of the Earth is approximately 5.7 times that of water at 68 degrees Fahrenheit at a barometric pressure of 30 pounds per inch. In the King's Chamber, all the stone courses have 23 or more stones, except the fifth course, which contains only seven. Thus, encoded in the fifth course of the King's Chamber is the mean density of the Earth." Moreover, the Great Pyramid's interior is a constant 68 degrees Fahrenheit, the average temperature of our planet. Farrell goes on to point out that the pyramid's original height of 5,449 inches equals the average height of land on the Earth above sea-level.

The Great Pyramid's four sides face the cardinal points of the compass, less than 1/10th of a degree from true north and south, and within 2/60th of a degree from true east and west, a precision modern construction engineers were incapable of laying out until little more than 100 years ago. Each of the four faces of the Great Pyramid, with their almost imperceptible indentations, represents a curved quarter of the northern hemisphere, a perfect spherical quadrant of 90 degrees. David Davidson, a structural engineer from Leeds, Yorkshire, proved that slight indentations on each of the pyramid's four sides calculated the solar year (the exact time between equinoxes), the anomalistic year (the time needed for the Earth to return to the point nearest the Sun, the perihelion), and the sidereal year (the time it takes for a star to reappear at the same spot in the sky).

The side of the base of the Great Pyramid measures 9,131.416 inches, a figure corresponding to the number of days contained in 25 years. This allots to each sidereal year of 365.25664 days, just a 30 second difference from the sidereal year ascertained by 20th century astronomers. Moreover, this same measurement virtually equals 1/480th of one equatorial degree. Braghine remarks (240), "At this rate, the total length of the equator line would come to 24903.86181 miles, which quantity is only 1.5 miles more than the measurement adopted by modern science. If we divide the length of the equator, as given by the pyramid, by pi, we will get the diameter of our planet equal to 7,927.1 miles, which quantity is only 0.5 miles longer than the measurement calculated by the modern astronomer, Sir James Jeans."

Theorists, armchair or otherwise, are free to imagine any number of propositions to explain the Great Pyramid's method of construction. It was nonetheless indisputably designed as a geodetic structure. In other words, its interior and exterior dimensions are measurements of our planet.

This article first appeared in *Atlantis Rising* #56 (March/April 2006).

21

WALLIS BUDGE GETS THE LAST WORD

Surprising New Evidence Supports
the Venerable British Linguist

BY LAIRD SCRANTON

Sir Ernest Alfred Thompson Wallis Budge was a late 19th century British linguist and historian who came to be a leading authority on ancient Egyptian culture, artifacts, and language. As a student he was fortunate to serve as an assistant to pioneer Egyptologist Samuel Birch, which enabled him to study Egyptian and Assyrian antiquities extensively at the British Museum in London. Well versed in many different ancient languages including Hebrew, Greek, and Coptic, Budge was also a prolific writer. He later studied Egyptian hieroglyphs and eventually authored a well-known dictionary (1920) of the Egyptian hieroglyphic language.

Wallis Budge

Budge held the unpopular view that the ancient Egyptian religion was fundamentally similar to modern religions found in North-Central and East Africa. Since his death in 1934, many of Budge's views—along with his dictionary—have fallen into general disfavor among traditional Egyptologists.

Questions about how to properly read and translate Egyptian hieroglyphs date at least from the 4th century BC, some three thousand years after the rise of Egyptian culture and long beyond the high point of classical ancient Egyptian culture. Serge Sauneron writes in *The Priests of Ancient Egypt* (1960) that the principles of Egyptian hieroglyphic writing had remained remarkably consistent throughout those many centuries, and that knowledgeable priests from later eras remained quite able to read inscriptions from any earlier period. Then, for reasons unknown—by around 400 BC—use of the language subsided, and knowledge of the intricacies of the Egyptian hieroglyphic system of writing was lost.

Many of the words and concepts expressed by Egyptian hieroglyphic symbols—especially those of ancient cosmology (the term cosmology refers to a culture's concept of how the universe and humanity were created)—are known to date from pre-dynastic times, from before the 1st dynasty in Egypt and prior to the first appearance of written language. For example, it is known based on surviving drawings and artifacts that the Egyptian god Amen and the great Egyptian Mother Goddess Neith (or Net) were worshipped by various hunter tribes that preceded ancient Egypt. Likewise it is inferred—based on word forms that survive among the Berbers, who are thought to be descended from these tribes—that key Egyptian religious words also existed in similar form prior to dynastic Egypt.

As much as we have been able to learn over the years about the Egyptian hieroglyphs, there are still aspects of the language that remain fundamentally enigmatic. For example, no one knows with absolute certainty how any given Egyptian hieroglyphic word was pronounced. Despite this uncertainty, one key point of disagreement between Budge and most modern Egyptologists lies with the question of how to pronounce various glyphs. The problem of pronunciation begins with the fact that—like other ancient languages such as ancient Hebrew—Egyptian hieroglyphic words were formed without the use of written vowels; so the reader is left to infer which vowel sounds to insert before, after, or between on-going strings of consonants. In cases where Egyptian glyphs are used to write a word phonetically— say, to record the name of a Pharaoh or a foreign dignitary—we are often able to gain insights into the likely pronunciation of a glyph simply based on its position in relation to the known pronunciation of the person's name. But these interpretations, too, can be subject to disagreement when we consider how differently people of various modern-day cultures often pronounce the same name; so—even here—there may still be room for argument about proper pronunciation.

Likewise, there are suggestions that the Egyptian glyphs could not have been primarily intended for use as phonetic characters in the first place. Most modern languages require characters to represent upwards of 40 different phonetic sounds. If we are to see the Egyptian hieroglyphs primarily as phonetic placeholders comparable to the letters in a modern alphabet, how do we explain the need to invent more than 4,000 glyphs to represent those sounds? Likewise, if the main purpose of a glyph was to define for us how to pronounce a word, how is it that the Egyptian scribes could have justified categorically omitting written vowel sounds—sounds that are arguably essential to the correct pronunciation of a word and whose presence would so greatly facilitate the reading of a word?

Over the centuries, there were many unsuccessful attempts to translate Egyptian hieroglyphs. Thomas Young—the famous English polymath whose efforts to interpret the Egyptian glyphs in the early 1800's laid a foundation for Champollion's later successful efforts to translate the Rosetta Stone—felt strongly that there was a conceptual element to the Egyptian hieroglyphs, that each glyph carried a fundamental association with a concept and was meant to represent an object, idea, or action. Champollion is reported to have shared similar beliefs and is said to have harbored lingering doubts about the purely phonetic nature of the language that caused him to delay publication of his translation of the Rosetta Stone for several months. His eventual translation offered a view of the language that—like most modern languages—was essentially letter-and-word based. In any given inscription, several Egyptian glyphs were grouped together like alphabetic letters to form words, which Champollion then correlated to words in matching inscriptions written in two other languages. From this perspective, words came to be seen as the carriers of meaning, just as they are in most modern languages. Other glyphs were interpreted as determinatives—glyphs whose presence within or following a word was meant to establish context or emphasize some particular aspect of meaning.

For example, the purpose of three vertical lines at the end of a word was seen as a way to indicate a plural number. The purpose of other trailing characters was more difficult to explain. Not uncommonly, an Egyptian word exhibits an unpronounced trailing glyph whose image may bear an apparent relationship to the meaning of the word in which it is written—for example, a word meaning "table" might be followed by a picture of a table as its final glyph. Traditionally, these glyphs are understood as having been "drawn into the word" for emphasis.

Although Budge's dictionary remains the one that is perhaps the most accessible to English-speaking researchers of Egyptian hieroglyphs, traditional modern-day Egyptologists often prefer a dictionary that is written in German called the *Aegyptisches Worterbuch*. Use of the German language can pose a potential obstacle to any researcher who is not familiar with German in much the same way that the French dictionary of the Dogon language may to anyone who is not well-versed in French. Traditional Egyptologists have described Budge's dictionary as being out-of-date and somewhat unreliable. Some cite problems with Budge's scholarship. Others go so far as to assert that Budge was—in truth—only marginally able to read Egyptian hieroglyphic words. Given all of this, one can understand why Budge's dictionary is often characterized as being so very flawed as to be virtually useless to the study of Egyptian hieroglyphs. In practice, what this means to the casual student of Egyptian hieroglyphs is that they are frequently cautioned not rely on Budge's dictionary as a basis for comparisons to other languages, since—in the traditional view—no trustworthy match can reasonably be made if it is founded on Budge's fundamentally flawed representation of Egyptian hieroglyphic words.

It is within this context that we must consider the words of Dogon cosmology and how they might relate to ancient Egyptian words. The Dogon are a modern-day African tribe who share many civic and religious customs with ancient Egypt, including many aspects of cosmology. Officially, the Dogon language has not been considered to bear any direct relationship to the Egyptian hieroglyphic language; so—in the eyes of traditional Egyptologists—has not been a candidate for comparisons to ancient Egyptian words. In practice, the Dogon language is comprised of upwards of thirty discreet word groups that can be seen as having been adopted from several different languages. Consequently, the Dogon language has historically been characterized by linguists as technically unclassifiable. My contention is that the words of Dogon cosmology—along with many of its myths, symbols, rituals, and traditions—are fundamentally ancient Egyptian in nature; and I have devoted several books to the task of highlighting the many specific points of commonality between Dogon and Egyptian cosmological words. The Dogon are a living culture with a vibrant tradition of knowledgeable priests who place a high value on purity of language and who retain a clear sense of meaning as it relates to their own cosmological words and symbols.

In theory, each Dogon cosmological word can be seen as a kind of package of meaning. Each has a well-defined pronunciation. Each carries at least two distinct meanings that exhibit what I call a "logical disconnect," such that a person cannot reasonably infer one meaning simply by knowing the other.

Dogon Cliff Dwellings in Mali

(For example, the Dogon creator-god Amma—a likely counterpart to the Egyptian Amen—is described as a "hidden god," but his name can also mean "to grasp, hold firm, or establish.") Each word is associated with a cosmological drawing, which may bear a close resemblance to a written Egyptian glyph. Each is used in a specific context within Dogon cosmology, and some may carry direct associations with a mythical storyline, character, or deity. Consequently, when we compare this kind of Dogon word to a word from some other culture, what we are really doing is attempting to align an entire set of related values with a set of likely counterparts in that second culture. Therefore, when we find a match, we know that it is not merely a casual match but rather one that is based on multiple confirming aspects of commonality.

As an important aspect of my studies of Dogon and Egyptian cosmology, and using Budge's dictionary as a reference, I have made it my goal to trace each key Dogon cosmological word to a likely ancient Egyptian counterpart. When I began my Dogon/Egyptian studies, I considered it to be fortuitous that I had studied German both in high school and in college, and was at least marginally equipped to navigate a German-language Egyptian dictionary. My eventual choice to adopt Budge's dictionary as a preferred tool for aligning Dogon and Egyptian words came out of a gradual realization that Budge's word-entries were friendlier to African word forms than those in the preferred *Worterbuch*. From a conceptual standpoint, what this statement means is that if you were looking for definitions of archaic English words like *bodkin* or *fardles*, it is easy to see that you would be better served to work with a Shakespearean dictionary than with the latest Collegiate dictionary. As a practical matter, African words can be difficult to align to likely Egyptian counterparts when using a dictionary like the *Worterbuch*, in part arguably because of the changes in pronunciation that have been adopted since Budge wrote his dictionary. For example, the African terms Amma/Amen—words that are central to African and Egyptian cosmology—could go unmatched because they appear in the *Worterbuch* under the pronunciation of "Imn." (Virtually every culture with claim to a relationship to ancient Egypt except Ethiopia—either before, contemporaneous with, or after the Egyptian civilization—pronounced the word Amma or Amen.) The net effect of such differences on a researcher of African language is somewhat like what happened during World War II when French Patriots rearranged local street signs in order to confound the invading German troops.

Over time what I have found in Budge's dictionary are word entries that are typically pronounced like the Dogon words, that carry the same logically-disconnected meanings, and that are often written using glyphs that compare favorably to the associated Dogon cosmological drawing. Typically the Egyptian word can be shown to be used in the same cosmological context as its likely Dogon counterpart, or in association with a comparable deity, myth, or mythological character. Eventually I was able to demonstrate that Budge's dictionary documents a close Egyptian match for nearly every Dogon cosmological word. This strikes me as a truly amazing accomplishment, since the comparisons are based on a dictionary that—in the view of traditional Egyptologists—must be fundamentally flawed, and should be incapable of producing such matches.

Simple logic dictates that Budge's dictionary cannot be both grossly incorrect AND in predictive agreement with the well-defined body of Dogon cosmological words. One could argue that the apparent agreement of any single word comparison could be the product of mere coincidence; however, my books present not random single words, but rather a large discreet body of related words—the words of Dogon cosmology—each of which can be shown to be in substantial agreement with word entries in Budge's dictionary. My contention is that these word comparisons constitute independent corroboration of Budge's cosmological word entries. Whatever Budge's dictionary may or may not be, careful comparisons to the Dogon show that it cannot be very far off the mark when it comes to its presentation of Egyptian words of cosmology.

I argue that Dogon cosmology preserves for us an approximate pronunciation for each of these words (subject to the kinds of changes in pronunciation that would be typical for any word that may have been passed down from generation to generation) that is in substantial agreement with Budge, so—given the many other Dogon/Egyptian cultural parallels—is within the realm of believability for ancient Egypt. Likewise, in most cases Dogon cosmology preserves a precise definition for each term, each of which can be shown to be consonant with definitions presented for the corresponding words in Budge's dictionary. The sheer number of cosmological words precludes any credible suggestion of simple coincidence.

Each Dogon word "package" provides enough distinct points of correspondence with its Egyptian counterpart as to constitute a definitive match, albeit not strictly on the terms of a traditional linguist. It is important to recognize that I am not proposing that words in one cosmology were passed between cultures through traditional contacts, but rather that both cultures appear to have adopted comparable words from a common, pre-existing cosmology. Likewise, I argue that if we can show (based on the mythic position, role, actions, icons and relationships) that a goddess in culture A correlates to a similar goddess in culture B, by the same argument their similar names must also bear a legitimate correlative relationship.

Although it has never been my goal to try to rehabilitate Budge's dictionary, it would be fair to say that Dogon cosmology provides us with a body of new evidence that seems to consistently uphold Budge's outlook on the Egyptian hieroglyphic language. Likewise, it appears to support his belief that modern tribal religions in Africa may hold important clues for us about the true nature of ancient Egyptian religions—clues that, although they may have been overlooked or neglected in the past, now surely deserve careful examination.

This article first appeared in *Atlantis Rising* #79 (January/February 2010).

PART FIVE

ENDANGERED PLANET

Lightning storm

22

WEATHER GOES TO WAR

U.N. Rules Notwithstanding, Could the Military
Application of Environmental Science Be with Us Now?

BY JERRY E. SMITH

MARK TWAIN IS OFTEN QUOTED, "Everyone talks about the weather, but no one does anything about it." Well, maybe Twain was wrong, about the second part anyway. Researcher Jerry E. Smith thinks so and argues accordingly in a new book *Weather Warfare,* 2006, from Adventures Unlimited Press. Following are some of his arguments. —Ed.

ankind has always had a keen interest in the weather. Through out human history we have seen the effects of weather on crops, and the loss of life and property through the violence of storms. In ancient times, people made sacrifice to the gods in a crude attempt at influencing the weather. In many parts of the world today people still conduct elaborate rituals for rain and fertility.

Modern interest in making rain for profit and/or the public good began, surprisingly enough, following the American Civil War.

Over the next 80 years Congress maintained an on-again, off-again interest in funding such research. One notable expenditure occurred in 1967 when the U.S. Senate passed the Magnusson Bill authorizing the Secretary of Commerce to accelerate programs of applied research, development, and experimentation in weather and climate modification. That bill allocated $12 million, $30 million, and $40 million over the next three years, respectively. Expenditures were projected to be $149 million annually by 1970.

It can be argued that by the beginning of the 1970s, portions of the U.S. government and military viewed weather and climate modification research as having transitioned from the "basic research" stage to the "operational" stage. Experiments were occurring—or had occurred—in 22 countries, including Argentina, Australia, Canada, Iran, Israel, Kenya, Italy,

France, South Africa, Congo, and the U.S.S.R. Airborne seeding programs were undertaken to combat drought in the Philippines, Okinawa, Africa, and Texas. Fog clearing had become a standard operation at airports, as had hailstorm abatement, which had been proven successful in several parts of the world. Forest fire control had been carried out in Alaska and watershed seeding was widely practiced, while lake storm snow redistribution was under extensive investigation. By 1973, there were over 700 scientists and engineers in the U.S. whose major occupation was environmental modification (EnMod).

And then it all changed. In 1978 the United States became a signatory to the "United Nations Convention on the Prohibition of Military or Any Other Hostile Use of Environmental Modification Techniques" (EnMod Convention for short). The EnMod Convention prohibits the use of techniques that would have widespread, long-lasting, or severe effects through deliberate manipulation of natural processes and cause such phenomena as earthquakes, tidal waves, and changes in climate and weather patterns.

Could it be that the U.S. government said, "Oh gee, we can't do that any more" and just gave up on military EnMod—or did the whole program go "black"?

PROJECT POPEYE

The American military-industrial-academic complex early on recognized the importance of weather as a weapon. After the great battles of the Civil War it was noted that rains seemed to follow. One general even patented an idea for making rain from this observation, but it would take nearly 80 years for a technology to be developed that was GI friendly. The Battle for Britain was partially won because Allied forces successfully used a fog-dispersal system known as FIDO to enable aircraft to takeoff and land under otherwise debilitating fog conditions. Cold fogs were similarly dissipated during the Korean War. Cloud seeding became a weapon in Vietnam under "Project Popeye."

Project Popeye is a now exposed and proven conspiracy on the part of the military to circumvent the laws of humanity in time of war using environmental modification as a weapon—and to keep this secret the Secretary of Defense was forced to lie to Congress!

Originally conducted as a pilot program in 1966, Project Popeye was an attempt to extend the monsoon season in Southeast Asia with the goal of slowing traffic on the Ho Chi Minh Trail by seeding clouds above it in hopes of producing impassable mud. Over the course of the program, silver iodide was dispersed from C-130s, F4 Phantoms, and the Douglas A-1E Skyraider (a single engine, propeller-driven fighter-bomber), into clouds over portions of the trail winding from North Vietnam through Laos and Cambodia into South Vietnam. Positive results from the initial test led to continued operations from 1967 through 1972.

Some scientists believe that it did hamper North Vietnamese operations, even though the effectiveness of this program is still in dispute. In 1978, after the efforts at cloud seeding in Vietnam produced mixed results, the U.S. Air Force declared its position to be that "weather modification has little utility as a weapon of war."

SECRET WEATHER WARS?

After events like the Christmas 2004 Asian tsunami and 2005's record-shattering Atlantic hurricane season, many people have wondered just how "natural" those natural disasters were. Has "weather control" really become a key element of national strategy?

In the post-EnMod U.S. of the 21st century, weather control is an activity mainly confined to local governments and privately owned commercial enterprises ("civilian contractors") like Weather Modification, Inc. (WMI) of Fargo, North Dakota. WMI provides services to universities, governmental agencies, and private sector entities across the country and around the world. These services include hail suppression in Argentina, snowpack augmentation in Idaho, and cloud seeding in Nevada. Interestingly, one of the senior scientists at WMI went on Art Bell's "Coast To Coast" AM radio show in 2005 to "out" himself as having been one of the scientists involved in Operation Popeye!

Intentional hostile control of the weather and other environmental processes is collectively called geophysical warfare. Dr. Gordon J. F. MacDonald wrote, "The key to geophysical warfare is the identification of environmental instabilities to which the addition of a small amount of energy would release vastly greater amounts of energy." This was in "Geophysical Warfare: How to Wreck the Environment," a chapter he contributed to Nigel Calder's 1968 book, *Unless Peace Comes: A Scientific Forecast of New Weapons.*

In the 1960s, MacDonald was a distinguished geophysicist and climatologist. He was Associate Director of the Institute of Geophysics and

Planetary Physics at the University of California, Los Angeles (UCLA). He was a member of the President's Science Advisory Committee and the President's Council on Environmental Quality, as well as being a senior member of NASA's first Physics Committee. He was also a member of the Council on Foreign Relations and one of the JASONs, a military think tank at the top of the military-industrial-academic pyramid.

Dr. MacDonald wrote many articles on future weapons. In "Space," an article for the book *Toward the Year 2018*, released in 1968, he elaborated on the possibilities of geophysical warfare writing, "technology will make available to the leaders of the major nations a variety of techniques for conducting secret warfare . . . techniques of weather modification could be employed to produce prolonged periods of drought or storm, thereby weakening a nation's capacity and forcing it to accept the demands of the competitor." Elsewhere he wrote, "Such a secret war need never be declared or even known by the affected population. It would go on for years with only the security forces involved being aware of it. The years of drought and storm would be attributed to unkindly nature and only after a nation was thoroughly drained would an armed takeover be attempted." He warned that these geophysical weapons systems, should they in fact be developed, would produce long-term upsets in the climate.

Business Week magazine reported on October 24, 2005, "China has 35,000 people engaged in weather management, and it spends $40 million a year on alleviating droughts or stemming hail that would damage crops." North Korea, downwind of China, has been ravaged by droughts for a decade. It is entirely possible that China has been intentionally stealing North Korea's rain so as to force North Korea to follow. Reports from North Korea make not just the nation's dictator, Kim Jong-Un, but the whole country sound crazy. Could their seeming mass insanity be induced?

HAARP

One much discussed project that embodies both civilian and military geophysical applications is the High-frequency Active Auroral Research Program (HAARP). Although HAARP proponents claim it is nothing more than a simple civilian research station designed to investigate the properties of the upper atmosphere, few investigators buy that explanation.

HAARP does have the appearance of a civilian project with open access and the work being done by civilian scientists. However, the project is

The HAARP array (U.S. Air Force)

managed by a joint U.S. Air Force and Navy committee and is funded out of the Department of Defense (DoD) budget. Most recently the heart of the program, the Ionospheric Research Instrument (IRI), was completed by one of the world's largest defense contractors working under the direction of the Defense Advanced Research Projects Agency (DARPA), a top research and development organization for the DoD. DARPA manages and directs selected basic and applied R&D projects for the DoD pursuing research and technology "where risk and payoff are both very high and where success may provide dramatic advances for traditional military roles and missions."

Under construction since 1990, the HAARP IRI is a field of antennas on the ground in southeastern Alaska. The facility was probably completed late in 2005 with the announcement of same added to the DARPA website in March of 2006. It is now the world's largest radio frequency (RF) broadcaster, with an effective radiated power of 3.6 million watts—over 72,000 times more powerful than the largest single AM radio station in the United States (50,000 watts). The IRI uses a unique patented ability to focus the RF energy generated by the field, injecting it into a spot at the very top of the atmosphere in a region called the ionosphere. This heats the thin atmosphere of the ionospheric region by several thousand degrees. HAARP, then, is a type of device called an ionospheric heater. This heating allows scientists to do a number of things with the ionosphere. Controlling and directing the processes and forces of the ionosphere is called "ionospheric enhancement."

An early HAARP document stated, "The heart of the program will be the development of a unique ionospheric heating capability to conduct the pioneering experiments required to adequately assess the potential for exploiting ionospheric enhancement technology for DoD purposes."

What might those DoD purposes be? Something about winning wars, eh? How might those purposes be achieved? What technologies will be needed to win the wars of the future? Researchers trying to answer those questions have come up with a vast number of possibilities, most bordering on science fiction. But then again, good science fiction is about recognizing the problems of the future, and suggesting solutions to them before they happen.

On March 23, 1983, President Ronald Reagan called upon "the scientific community in our country, those who gave us nuclear weapons, to turn their great talents now to the cause of mankind and world peace, to give us the means of rendering these nuclear weapons impotent and obsolete." This quest for the creation of a technology, of a weapon or weapons system that would make atomic war impossible, was officially named the Strategic Defense Initiative (SDI). The press lost no time in dubbing it Star Wars after the George Lucas movie franchise.

That Initiative sent the United States military-industrial-academic complex on the greatest and costliest weapons hunt in human history. Thousands of ideas were floated, hundreds of those were funded. While much SDI research has since been officially abandoned, some ideas are still being actively pursued to this day.

Not all of these ongoing developmental programs are taking place in laboratories of the military and its contractors. Some of these ideas involve technologies or applications that, as weapons, some argue, violate international treaties—others, the use of which might be repugnant to the ethical and moral values of the majority of Americans. In an effort to avoid public outcry (and international condemnation) some of these programs have been disguised as civilian science. One of those may be HAARP.

As Dr. Bernard Eastlund, the putative inventor of HAARP put it, "The boundary between science fiction and science comes with: can you actually make the thing that you're proposing?"

The APTI patents that HAARP is probably based on openly discuss manipulating the weather by moving the jet stream and using other techniques to create floods and droughts at will. These patents also describe a way to raise the ionosphere, sending it out into space as an electrically charged plasma capable of destroying anything electronic (like an incoming ICBM or a spy satellite) passing through it. HAARP certainly looks like a ground-based Star Wars weapons system, a "relic" of the Cold War. But unlike most such relics this one is up and running and now fully funded.

Getting back to Dr. MacDonald: Among the coming "advances" he wrote about were manipulation or control over the weather and climate, including destructive use of ocean waves and melting or destabilizing of the polar ice caps; intentional ozone depletion; triggering earthquakes; and control of the human brain by utilizing the earth's energy fields. Today the polar ice caps are indeed melting and holes in the ozone layer are growing. Could these be the handiwork of advanced weapons? What about earthquakes and mind control? Are we, the private citizens of the world, in the crosshairs of bizarre, unthinkable weapons?

Studies of the effects of natural electromagnetic fields on animal and human biology date to as far back as 1935, and possibly even earlier. One such study successfully correlated the occurrences of solar-generated magnetic storms with increases in the incidence of such things as deaths from myocardial infarction, mental hospital admission, and automobile accidents. Russian studies of animals and humans experimentally exposed to electromagnetic fields found that such exposures induce hypermotility (excessive movement; especially excessive motility of the gastrointestinal tract) and impairment of conditioned reflexes. These would therefore be of keen interest to the behavioral scientist (mind controllers) as well as to the climatologist.

Dr. MacDonald commented on the possible use of the destructive effects of electromagnetic fields in the environment on human health and performance. He said that weapons systems could be developed that would increase the intensity of the electromagnetic field oscillating in the spherical-shaped cavity between the Earth and the ionosphere, and that these weapons could be used to "seriously impair brain performance in very large populations in selected regions over an extended period."

Could HAARP, or another similar antenna elsewhere, be the source of North Korea's madness? Could Kim Jong-Un be a true Manchurian candidate? And if so, whose?

This article first appeared in *Atlantis Rising* #65 (September/October 2007), and has been updated to reflect current events.

23

GLOBAL COOLING

Is Mars Sending Us a Message about Planetary Geriatrics?

BY SUSAN MARTINEZ, PH.D.

With great expectations hinging on NASA's latest exploration of Mars—the Phoenix lander touching down smoothly on the Red Planet's northern ice plains on May 25, 2008—scientists had been holding their breath for signs of ancient water and life on that barren world. Could success for the $457 million-dollar mission—the first to study Mars' arctic plains— depend on finding, under polar ice, organic chemicals or perhaps "nanofossils"?

Back in 2004 when Mars was last making news, NASA having landed a rover on the Red Planet, one MIT engineering student floated the idea of "terraforming" Mars by melting her polar caps to make her warm, wet, and habitable once again. The quixotic sci-fi scheme is reminiscent of those miraculous wrinkle creams that inevitably pop up when you go online. Most of us, though, will have to settle for growing old gracefully and getting a laugh out of the latest crackpot scheme to reverse aging or bring the dead back to life. In such matters, I think of the eternal truth of Hindu theology, which posits a holy trinity composed of Brahma, Vishnu, and Shiva. These great deities in turn resolve into creator, sustainer, destroyer. And finally they represent birth, life, and death.

If planets are living things, they too, it seems, must have a natural lifespan, ending inexorably in dust and decay. But Western science and sensibility, enamored of unlimited growth, has been loathe to admit death and dissolution. Indeed, when the first dinosaurs were exhumed early in the 19th century, the very idea of species extinction was not only brand new, it was repugnant. It was horrible. "It is contrary to the common course of providence to suffer any of his creatures to be annihilated," said Quaker naturalist P. Collinson.

At the time of the first dinosaur discovery, the world of extinct life was an unknown, still buried in the past. "Geologic time," as it is called, was just being discovered. Although the first dinosaur ("the Great Fossil Lizard of Stones-field" at Sussex, UK, 1822) was much celebrated, the "overgrown lizard" triggered instant debate and controversy. How could a species have vanished from the good earth? Soon it would be known that "a staggering number" of other creatures, as well as plants, sang their death song to the dawning tertiary.

Shiva, or the "destroyer," as the ancient world dubbed the force-pulling-down, was nothing sinister (quite the contrary), but simply the inevitable vanishment or dissolution of all material substance. And while the sages of old knew all about the birth and death of worlds once they fulfilled their labor, we moderns seem to have forgotten that all stories have a beginning, middle, and end; instead, our "sages" would inject the patently geriatric Red Planet with their version of new life; or would interpret her moribund frigidity (-40 degrees F on a typical summer's day) as the result of being "currently in the grip of an ice age"; or would account for her Stygian, tomblike "drought" as "some change in the planet's atmosphere . . . causing water to vaporize." Or titillate the mind with recondite (and so far inconclusive) studies into "possible life on Mars."

The Red Planet, well into her dotage, is not a potential piece of real estate, nor is it likely to be making a comeback any time soon. She will, in all likelihood, get only colder and drier.

She's history, it appears.

Neither is our Mother Earth—Mars' "sister planet"—a youngster. Three things are seen to happen in the life of a world—any world. Slowing, drying, and cooling, from day one.

The proto-world, we are told, began as a seething ball of liquid fire, boiling and roiling, whirling and swirling. Earth was still a twisting turbulent vortex of friction, gas clouds in rapid rotation, slowly but surely condensing particles in solution. It would take, the argument goes, almost a billion years for the newborn world to produce the first shred of life. The molten Earth, after all, before we can go for a walk in the park, must turn down the lights, slow down, cool down, and solidify (form a crust). And from that time forth, "there is ever a trifling loss toward perpetual coldness and darkness," or as the sages of science thought they knew a hundred years ago, "a constant heat loss from a once fiery earth."

Planet Mars, senior citizen of our little solar system, has lost most of her warmth; deep cold grips the Red Planet in her senescence. As Professor Robert Jastrow concluded, "Not only has Mars been wet; it has also been warm in the past. . . . Mars was slowed down many hundreds of millions years ago when the planet's water supply diminished and the temperature dropped."

Going out like a candle in the firmament, Mars appears tectonically exhausted and makes a somewhat elliptical orbit—both apparent signs of slackening and old age. Her inner moon, Phobos, has one-twentieth the brightness of our own Earth moon. Frigid and dark, Mars has also lost most of her atmosphere and gravity; her magnetic field dissipating, she is a dry, cold, and lifeless world that has seen better days. Features of fluvial erosion whisper hoarsely of once-extensive waterways and vibrant landscape. Today she is a desert—"dull as beans"—with huge ice caps (dry ice).

As our elder sister, could Mars—"once wetter, warmer, and more friendly to life"—teach us something about the passage into planetary extinction? The tiny planet (with about half the diameter of Earth) is held in an atmosphere 200 times thinner than ours. The gravity of Mars is less than half that of Earth. If the Presidential pledge of 2004 pledge to put man on Mars is ever fulfilled, we will tip the scales there at 40 percent of our true weight. Arroyos and dry channels, floodplains and lake beds, readily suggest a land once filled with crater lakes, rivers, streams, meanders, and rushing waters. Today only high winds course over her deathlike surface. She is a windblown, pockmarked desert.

Yet, despite her obviously advanced age and deterioration—perfectly natural for a venerable but worn-out old world—some scientists would have us think her landscape "bizarre, alien." No, there is nothing bizarre or unnatural about it, unless we are still in the mindset of early Victorian England, which refused to come to terms with the bald facts of extinction when faced with the enormous but bygone "fossil lizards." Even more disingenuous is science's vain hope to discover "where Mars' ancient water went."

Could it have gone the same road as its light and heat, its atmosphere and gravity, its plasticity and zoology, its velocity and magnetism? Will its younger sister, planet Earth, follow by "rapidly giving off its life force and its moisture, rapidly growing old"? As Dr. Paul Sylvester has painfully observed, "4.5 billion years after its birth, Earth is fueling far fewer major tectonic events. In island arcs like Japan and the Aleutians, new continental crust is . . . piling up [only] at a geriatric pace. Like Venus and Mars, Earth is on its way to becoming a dead planet; the heyday of its continents is long gone. You just don't get as much production of crust anymore. . . . It's kind of sad."

Vulcanic crust-building, mountain-raising, in my view, are all the handiwork of a vibrant, growing world. Mars, in her glory, raised the most majestic mountains in the solar system. Her volcanoes are quiet now, like Olympus Mons—15 miles high! And there is no way of separating her current repose, her quietude, from her played-out atmosphere, which exerts less than 1 percent of the pressure that pummels Earth's surface. And there is no way of separating it from her flagging magnetic field. Could these be but the inevitable symptoms of old age? Could the enfeebling process be equally evident here on planet Earth?

Artist's rendering of the Phoenix Lander on the arctic plains of Mars. (Art by Corby Waste, Jet Propulsion Laboratory, NASA)

"At this very moment, the Earth's magnetic field strength is decreasing," wrote John White in his book, *Pole Shift* (1988). And it has done so at every moment of its existence. The deep decay of Earth's magnetic field, verified by space satellites, is witnessed also by "erratic" rocks and boulders, silent record-keepers of our planet's early field, which "we now know" was a supercharged dynamo, bristling with energy, electric storms, monumental surges, tumultuous winds. Some of these rocks register ten times the magnetism of other rocks in situ; some have a hundred times the expected magnetic charge.

And as this great gestalt of planetary aging unfolds, abating field strength is inevitably accompanied by a slowing of pace. Could the planet begin like a wild spinning top and then, over the aeons, simply spin out?

But none of these decrements is an isolated—or even unexpected— event. Rather, cooling and drying are the normal companions of the slowing orb, though each does dwindle in an exquisitely, infinitesimally, gradual manner. Infant Earth spun jauntily on her axis in just 14 hours, losing two milliseconds per century. No, the calculus of Earth's axial velocity cannot be separated from her dwindling warmth, moisture, atmosphere, or radiance.

They are all aspects of the same thing.

Conventional astronomy tells us that the entire universe is cooling down. "The further back you go, the higher the temperature of the universe," says physicist James Trefil.

If this is true, it is the same for Mars and Earth. Conventional science tells us until the end of the Cretaceous Period, planet Earth had no ice caps at the poles. Nor was there any continental ice until the Cretaceous/ Tertiary boundary, at which time the great herds of dinosaurs declined and departed forever. Smaller animals, though, managed to escape the Klimasturz of the cretaceous mass extinctions. They burrowed, they hibernated, they survived. Such a strategy was not available, so the theory goes, to the giant saurians whose vast bulk alone had once been sufficient to retain body heat. But now it would be their undoing. It took the dinosaurs a long time—perhaps a million years it is believed—to check out; the loss of two or three degrees of blood heat was their probable downfall. Ice, at the time, was just beginning to accumulate at the poles.

Later, the pleistocene mastodon, saber-tooth tiger, giant ground sloth, and other near-mythical beasts, met their end, in all likelihood, by a critical drop in temperature. The woolly mammoths, according to some new research using ancient DNA, were not killed off by hunters but by the results of "a lengthy cooling trend [in which] dry conditions dominated."

Cooling.

Drying.

Slowing.

Notwithstanding the arguments of those who believe Earth's history has been replete with catastrophic interruptions that have often altered the predictable course of evolution, the ruling gradualist school of conventional science has postulated a world ruled by inexorable processes of decay and disintegration without exception, albeit also without certainty.

"Quite honestly," said science writer Donald Goldsmith, "our understanding of how planets generate and maintain magnetic fields is as uncertain as our knowledge of how life began."

Although the existence of ancient life on Mars "remains a mystery," every possible condition favorable to biological life appears to have once existed on our sister planet. And though scientists cannot prove it, many nonetheless are convinced "that Mars once teemed with life." As we crack that cosmic egg, as that possibility becomes indeed a probability, as our naivete is replaced with wisdom and certainty, the living universe comes into view. We are not alone.

"If it happened . . . twice here in our own backyard," says writer Nick Bostrom, speaking metaphorically of life on these two sibling planets, "it must have happened millions of times across the galaxy." Anything less, I dare say, smacks of geocentric blindness. But perversely, NASA seems to be pushing the notion that life on Mars is anything but likely. To the contrary, though, we could and should assume a multiplicity of worlds, a plethora of living experiments—successes and failures—near and far in the infinite cosmos.

Since there is a greater chance of finding organisms beneath the polar caps of Mars than at her frozen surface, the Phoenix lander, equipped with a robotic arm, was programmed to dig under the permafrost in search of ancient water. On July 31, 2008, NASA announced that Phoenix confirmed the presence of water ice on Mars. We are further surprised by the news that Mars' polar caps are not made of water, but of frozen carbon dioxide—dry ice. Moreover, without vegetation (trees and plants) to absorb ambient CO_2, most of the atmosphere of Mars (and Venus for that matter) is also composed of carbon dioxide.

Phoenix Lander's solar panel and robotic arm scoop, taken June 10, 2008. (Picture, University of Arizona, NASA)

Now what do we make of this nasty "greenhouse gas" showing up in spades on frozen Mars?

It seems that while carbon dioxide causes warming in the lower atmosphere, in the upper atmosphere it can have a cooling effect.

As a waste product of burning fossil fuels (coal, oil, wood, gas), poor old carbon dioxide has been made the villain of so-called global warming, even accused of the heinous and dastardly act of melting the glaciers! And while we are taught to fear its ominous increase in the air, as well as the devastating "heat waves," it will trigger, a sober look at this trace gas quickly reveals that:

1) Regardless of fluctuations, CO_2 makes up less than 1 percent of the air we breathe.

2) In the past 50 years, "during the 20 years with the highest carbon dioxide levels, temperatures have decreased."

3) But most importantly, consider the folly of demonizing carbon dioxide and the proliferation of other myths in the name of alleged global warming. If rising temperatures are really due to increased levels of CO_2 (a "heat-trapping" gas), then how come frigid Mars is 95 percent carbon dioxide? Could the simple fact that CO_2 is emitted from the Earth each spring mean that gas is far more likely an effect, not a cause, of warming?

Could global warming be nothing but hot air?

This article first appeared in *Atlantis Rising* #71 (September/October 2008).

24

AN ANGRY PLANET?

What Do Today's Headlines Mean?

BY STEVEN SORA

Might it be that we, the people of planet Earth, have recently become the guests who overstayed our welcome? Over-population, pollution of air, land and sea, destruction of the ozone layer, and finally the threat to the oxygen balance in the atmosphere, it seems, have long tried the patience of a living planet. Mother Earth may not be happy with the bad behavior of her children. In fact, she might be downright angry.

Tsunamis, hurricanes of biblical proportion, flooded cities, Mad-Cow Disease, Avian flu, AIDS and melting ice caps do not bode well for the near future. And, it turns out, this may not be the first time mankind has paid a heavy price for its home on Earth.

Plato's tale of Atlantis depicts the visit of the Greek lawmaker Solon to the priests at Sais in Egypt. There the wise Solon is admonished by the priests, "Oh Solon, Solon, you Hellenes are but children." When Solon asks why they would say that, he is told of the numerous catastrophes recorded in their archive, of which the Greeks know nothing. Worldwide conflagrations, floods survived only by those who fled to the mountains, pestilence that claimed whole cities.

In terms of geology, major climactic changes, the movement of tectonic plates, seas that turn into deserts, and plains that turn into oceans take long periods of time. They do, however, happen. But now we must: Are we entering a critical phase—an accelerated phase—in the process?

Politics aside, few can disagree that planet Earth is heating up and that this appears to be creating problems. Hurricanes Katrina, Rita, and Wilma escalated to Category Five levels because of one thing: water temperature. The sea surface temperatures of the Gulf of Mexico rose from an average 80 degrees F to a torrid 90 degrees by the summer of 2006. To a hurricane, warm water is fuel, and the destructive force of both Katrina and Rita reached epic levels because of it.

The warm Gulf waters, however, are just a small part of the global picture. Five years ago, we began to see the first breakdown of the mega icebergs. From Greenland to Antarctica, icebergs the size of Rhode Island, 1,000 square miles, began breaking off shelf ice and heading out to sea. Recently, one such iceberg was the size of Jamaica. This 4,000 square mile monster began floating to a warmer climate. It was named B15 and before it began to break up, it blocked access to the sea near the Ross Ice Shelf and was responsible for the deaths of millions of penguins.

In Alaska, the Columbia glacier is melting at a rate of one mile every two years. While it doesn't sound alarming, it and other melting glaciers are causing the permafrost that covers much of the state to turn to mush. Roads crack and become broken, telephone poles tilt and fall, and even buildings twist as underground ice melts. Fairbanks has had a summer that included three weeks of temperature over 80 degrees F.

It doesn't help the tourist industry either as cruise ships cannot get close to this fantastic glacier: a sea of broken ice keeps them away. Once beautiful forests sink into newly formed swamps, creating a phenomenon called the "drunken forest." Half of Alaska's white spruce may be gone in 15 years.

The western Arctic is at times 25 degrees higher in temperature than the average of the last hundred years. This has caused salmon to swim farther out to sea and species of flora and fauna to disappear, or appear. For the first time in modern history, mosquitoes are able to survive in polar regions. Immigrant spruce bark beetles have invaded the taiga of Siberia, which is also losing its forest cover as the warmer air stunts tree growth.

In Greenland, the Arctic sea ice has diminished by nearly 400,000 square miles in 30 years. The Sermeq glacier was shrinking at a rate of four miles per year in 1967, and is now shrinking at twice that rate. Native Inuit people have a shortened fishing and sealing season. The survival of polar bears, dependant upon the sea ice for breeding and foraging, is already in danger. In Northern Finland, a newer species of plantlife has found the far north more habitable—and it has thus become invasive to the plant species native to that area. This is leading to suffocation of the plants that reindeer feed on.

Ancient texts are replete with descriptions of horrific destruction from heat and fire. The blame is generally put on God, who destroys cities like Sodom and Gomorrah for their sinfulness. The destruction is also credited to gods whose weapons have the power to scorch the universe. The Mahabarata of ancient India recalls when such a war "rained down death." "The heavens cried out, the Earth bellowed an answer. Lightning flashed forth, fire flamed upward." Such hellish scenarios are seen in fires in the west where overuse of water combined with dry climate and extended heat waves burn thousands of acres in places like Southern California. Even without fire, heat alone has taken its toll. A summer heat wave in 1995 took the lives of 700 Americans, mostly in Chicago. In 2003, a European heat wave claimed the lives of 10,000, mostly elderly French citizens.

The Maya have suggested that the world was already destroyed four times. Fire, flood, and attacks by jaguars have all brought an end to the world and a new beginning. We are now, however, at the end of the fifth world. Each is measured in *baktuns* Our civilization, it was predicted, would end at the end of the thirteenth baktun—the winter solstice, December 23, 2012. This epoch, the thirteenth baktun, started on August 13, 3114 BC with the rising of Venus. The Maya left us with this date, but it seems like it indicated the *beginning* of the end. Perhaps it actually serves as a warning.

Those alarmed by global warming point to the dramatic increase in carbon dioxide in the atmosphere. This level was steady until 1850 when the industrial age began. Between 1950 and 2005 the rapid increase in carbon levels was sharp and steady. And it is getting worse. The further growth will come from the NICs, the "Newly Industrialized Countries," where gas and oil fuel transportation for millions who did not have access to automobiles before.

While it may be easy to blame the American consumer's addiction to fossil fuels and fluorocarbons, it is not the only reason the Earth is warming up. Every day more roads are built, more buildings erected, and concrete and asphalt cover more of the earth's surface. From the Amazon to the coast of China, a worldwide explosion of construction is matched only by the population growth. Asphalt retains heat and causes the temperature to rise.

Cities have their own weather caused by artificial means. Concrete, asphalt, and brick take the heat of the Sun and retain it longer. They become storage units that only gradually give up their heat. The sun's heat is only half of the story. Waste heat, from auto emissions, central heating, industry, and power stations, add to the mix. They create a dome of heat that hovers over a city. The city of Philadelphia can typically exceed the local highs by ten degrees. The effect of a city's heat can stretch ten to fifteen miles outside the city.

Some cities even get larger increases in annual rainfall than areas just outside the city. But in winter, these areas experience snow-melt faster than the suburbs. Great American population centers are increasingly dwarfed as new population centers like Beijing, Shanghai, Manila, Mexico City, Mumbai, Dhaka, and Tokyo grow.

It just may be that in addition to millions of square miles of asphalt, there is one other component to a changing earth. Us.

In 1650, Mother Earth hosted an estimated 470 million people. She now has to contend with 7.4 *billion* crowding her surface. Population experts expect the current annual growth rate of 1.5 percent to slow to 1.1 percent, but even if such a huge reduction does take place they estimate that 9 billion people will cling to the Earth's surface before 2050. Some believe that could be a problem.

There is a growing theory that the Earth, or Gaia, is a living thing. The argument of biology against geology is not accepted by most, but has its merits. The Gaia Hypothesis is a belief that the planet has a physical and biologic process that requires a self-regulating system to keep a balance. All living things contain their vital organs at the core, their expendable organs at the surface. People live on that expendable surface and on occasion become redundant.

A Greek epic poem, "The Kypria," said "There was a time when thousands upon thousands of men encumbered the broad bosom of the Earth." To lighten her burden, Zeus created war that "he might make a void in the race of man." Man was upsetting the balance.

People, animals, plantlife, lakes, and oceans all exhibit this need for balance in order to survive. High acidity in a lake, too many toxins ingested by plants, harmful pollution surrounding man, all can create an imbalance that leads to illness and death. We can either correct the problem or suffer the consequences.

Nine billion people burning more gasoline, emitting more carbon monoxide, may be more than a living planet can handle. It may be a problem the Earth has to solve to survive. At some point, like a snake shedding an old skin, Mother Earth may need to shuck off the accumulated hide of cement, brick, and asphalt, along with some of the billions that crowd her surface. Tsunamis, floods, earthquakes, disease, and killer hurricanes may not be the worst of what's to come.

To be reborn, the planet might relive its first billion years, a time when, it is believed, the surface had hellish volcanic upheavals, burning constantly, with hydrogen consuming oxygen to produce the water, which then gave life. In this period, living things hid under water from the Sun until they assisted in creating an atmosphere by consuming excess oxygen and stabilizing its level.

Scientists that debate the Gaia Hypothesis say the world may have had four catastrophes that might have been total destruction. Geologists, even those who do not agree with the idea of a "living" Earth, agree that as many as one hundred catastrophes might have happened that eliminated 90 percent of Earth's living things.

If this is true, we might take comfort from the fact that it occurred in a 4.5 billion year period that both modern science and the Brahmin calendar agree is the age of the Earth. This means a near-total catastrophe occurs on average, every 45 million years. But before we get too comfortable, we must consider that the all-critical oxygen balance is now being threatened. Can a global catastrophe be in store?

National Geographic was considered to be taking an alarmist position when it highlighted the dangers of rising water levels and specifically the threat to New Orleans in 2005. The warning became a reality. Scientists now predict at the current rate of melting polar ice, the world's sea level could rise by 23 feet before 2100. Rising water levels do not happen gradually; instead they happen in fits and starts. What global catastrophe caused the Black Sea to go from fresh water to saltwater? We can only guess or accept tales of Noah to explain. The breaching of the levees after Hurricane Katrina in New Orleans is a modern example.

Flooding due to rising sea levels is one threat. With most of the world's largest cities bordering oceans, the effect of a large rise in sea levels can be catastrophic. Cities from New York to Miami are built at sea level. Scores of smaller cities from Atlantic City to St. Augustine hide behind a thin barrier that can disappear overnight. The maps of sand bars off the coast of Massachusetts' Cape Cod change nearly every summer. The same might happen to North Carolina's Outer Banks by mid-century.

It could be much worse. The Sanskrit Mahabharata describes a split in the Earth causing the drowning of sixty million people in one night. The Mayan land of Mu was said to suffer two upheavals in one night before it disappeared. Atlantis suffered a similar fate. Genesis has the springs of the abyss breaking through to flood the earth. The Celtic tales are similarly dramatic with The City of the Y's and the forests of Cornwall becoming submerged as a result of floods.

The world has no shortage of historical flood stories. In 2004, the Asian tsunami added a new story to modern mythology claiming over 200,000 lives and leaving possibly 100,000 people unaccounted for.

Sumerian texts blame Indra, a god whose name meant "storm," for massive loss of life. The Hittites blamed Teshub, meaning "windy storm," for the same. The evil Seth was "Typhon" in Greek, meaning "fierce wind." Such wind-caused catastrophes left cities in desolation according to the Lamentation Texts of the Sumerians. And when such storms passed, they left sickness and contamination; exactly what happened in a post-Katrina New Orleans. Not understanding cholera and plague, the ancients believed such invisible death was brought by ghosts who stayed beyond the destruction.

"When it enters a house, its appearance is unknown" says one text. Before it leaves "mouths were drenched in blood . . . the face was made pale"—death and desolation, courtesy of angry gods.

Storms, floods, and any catastrophe that forces many to move, causes and spreads disease as well. Plague in the 14th century caused many major cities to lose 20 to 40 percent of their populations. In smaller places, like Trapani on Sicily, the plague left no survivors at all. Thus, desolation was as complete as in Sumerian texts which described the horror. "No one treads the highways, no one seeks out the roads."

This article first appeared in *Atlantis Rising* #55 (January/February 2006), and has been updated to reflect current events.

PART SIX

NATURAL ORDER REVEALED

Earth in honeycomb

25

IS OUR PLANET A CRYSTAL?

A Broken Web of Power May be
Our Legacy from the Distant Past

BY JOSEPH ROBERT JOCHMANS, LIT.D.

I s there, flowing across the world, a single planetary energy system, long
forgotten to modern humanity? And here and there along the energy
pathways, did a prehistoric global civilization once tap into its power
by building vast transmission and receiving stations, using various forms
of monumental architecture?

Have today's historians been so out of touch with the obvious interconnections of all of these remains that they have tried to explain the silent
sentinel ruins as nothing more than "primitive" construction projects having little meaning or purpose beyond localized superstitious needs?

Were such mysterious sites as Stonehenge in England, or Machu Picchu in Peru, or the Pyramids of the Sun and Moon near Mexico City, or the
megaliths of Malta, or the stone heads of Easter Island, or Serpent Mound
in Ohio—or thousands upon thousands of other structures scattered
across the globe—simply a matter of chance arrangement or design? Have
the modern theories, whatever they may be, fallen far short of explaining
what really once was?

Is it true that these great monumental edifices were deliberately fixed
into the geometric configuration of an "enchanted" energy landscape? And
did they together create a gigantic, intricate, web-like pattern, the meaning
and purpose of which has defied the explanation of the most scholarly of
modern archaeologists and historians? What is the missing element that
interlinks everything into a single fabric and weave, of which the prehistoric linear patterns among the silent structures are but the threads?

Is there a universal energy source, once known but lost to us today,
which springs from the Earth? Was it distributed along the sacred lines
and pathways and broadcast out of the temples situated at the focal points?
Is this the mythic hidden "power" of magic and healing at one time shared

by everyone, in a forgotten golden age in the distant past? How was such a system lost, and can it be understood and restored again today?

Several leading, modern researchers in the fields of ancient mysteries and Earth energies have gleaned from ancient sources what may be new answers to these questions regarding the true nature of the planet and its power systems, as well as how these have effected not only climatic and geologic changes in the Earth, but also significant physical-emotional-mental-spiritual transformations among peoples and nations.

What is also being realized is that ongoing shifts and alterations in personal and planetary energy fields have subtle yet profound influences on world events. Only as we can learn more concerning Earth energies—how they were once used and can be rediscovered again today—will we find an important key to the potential directions of the future.

MEMORIES OF A BROKEN WEB OF POWER

Among the world's ancient and modern indigenous peoples are very similar traditions of Earth energy patterns and how they were once utilized. In England, alignments among standing stones and stone circles are called leys, along which flowed the life force that fertilized the landscape. In Ireland they are remembered as fairy paths, and in Germany as holy lines. The Greeks knew them as the Sacred Roads of Hermes, while the ancient Egyptians regarded them as the Pathways of Mim.

The Chinese today still measure the Lung Mei or "dragon currents," which affect the balance of the land, as practiced through the ancient art of feng shui. Much as the application of acupuncture needles in Chinese medicine helps the flow of Chi or life force in the human body, so the placement of pagodas, stones, trees, temples, and houses in the environment is regarded as a way to "heal" the Earth.

Likewise, the Native Australians still go on walkabouts or pilgrimages down their dream paths, crisscrossing the desert in an effort to seasonally reenergize the life centers of the region. They work with boards called Turingas, which map out the dream lines; by meditating on them, they are able to predict the approach of storms and the location of game animals as they interact with the line systems.

The ancient Polynesians spoke of using the *te lapa*, or "lines of light," flowing in the ocean as a method of navigation. The stone heads of Easter Island and the sacred Ahu platforms of Hawaii were positioned to receive their mane or life power along aka threads from over the watery horizons.

When the Spanish conquistadors entered Peru in the 16 century, they found the entire Inca Empire organized around *wacas,* or sacred centers, situated along ceque lines, which all converged at the Coriconcha or Temple of the Sun in ancient Cuzco. Similarly, the Maya of the Yucatan interconnected their pyramid sanctuaries by means of *sacbes,* or raised white roadways, that were built in dead straight segments through the jungle swamps.

In Western North America, medicine wheels and kiva circles are often found in linear arrangements, and in the Midwest and East coastal regions the Mound Builders left many of their great earthen works in alignments covering large areas. In New England, mysterious stone chamber sites also fit into linear patterns; many Native American shamans today speak of energies—called Orenda, Manitou, and by other names—which flow through the Earth to promote healing.

Not only were local terrestrial powers tapped into around the world, but many ancient and modern traditions recognize that these local patterns were part of a much larger energy configuration called the Earth's Crystal Grid.

SPOTTED FAWNS AND SPLITTING CONTINENTS

In North America, the Elders of the Hopi nation say that the Earth's surface is like the back of a spotted fawn. As the fawn grows, the spots move and change number. Similarly, every time the Earth Mother "sings a new song" or enters a new vibrational shift, her power centers also change to a new configuration, interconnected by a more complex sacred geometry.

In the 1970s, several students of inventor Buckminster Fuller performed a series of experiments that were later repeated by other researchers and taken to new levels. The experiments involved submerging a balloon in a liquid medium filled with blue dye and subjecting the balloon and liquid to a certain frequency of vibration. The result was the dye collected at specific points on the surface of the balloon, and thin lines formed joining the points in geometric arrangements. When the frequency was turned higher, the original dye points first quickly dissolved and then a greater number of dye points began to slowly form, joined by lines in a more complex configuration.

It is now believed that the Earth also has its own energy centers, much like the human body has chakras and acupuncture points. Like the growing fawn or the balloon subjected to a higher frequency, when the Earth peri-odically moves into a higher energy state, so the overall planetary energy patterns shift into new crystal-like forms. This is a global phenomenon which appears to have been going on for a very long period of time.

A study of map projections and worldwide geological patterns con-ducted in 1976 by Athelstan Spilhaus, consultant for the National Ocean-ographic and Atmospheric Administration (NOAA), revealed that when the super continent Pangaea first broke apart approximately 220 million years ago, forming the rudiments of our modern day continental masses, the breakup occurred along equidistant lines forming the edges and points of a tetrahedron. This is a geometric shape composed of four equilateral triangles, the first and simplest of the Sacred Solids of Plato.

Based on the research of Hanshou Liu of the Goddard Space Flight Center, who analyzed stress lines in the Earth caused by polar and land movements over the last 200 million years, Spilhaus found that what was next outlined in the planetary structure was a combination cube and octahedron. A cube is composed of six squares, and the octahedron has eight triangles arranged like two Egyptian pyramids end to end, or in the configuration of a flourite crystal. These constitute the next two higher Platonic solids beyond the tetrahedron. The Earth's crystalline evolution did not end there, however, but has moved into two even more complex Platonic forms.

A KEY TO NATURE AND ANCIENT MYSTERIES

In the 1970s, three Russians—historian Nikolai Goncharov, construction engineer Vyacheslav Morozov, and electronics specialist Valery Makarov—announced in the science journal for the Soviet Academy of Science, Chemistry and Life, their discovery of a geometric grid pattern that appears to interlink a wide number of natural phenomena into a single planetary system. Their work was based on the findings of American researcher Ivan T. Sanderson who identified what he called twelve "vile vortexes" or elec-tromagnetic energy disturbances located equidistant over the surface of the globe; the so-called Bermuda Triangle near the Caribbean, and the Devil's Sea off Japan being two of these. What the three Russians found was an underlying framework linking these centers into a dual crystal struc-ture, a combination between an icosahedron and a dodecahedron. Not surprisingly, these happen to be the fourth and fifth solids in the Platonic series, which were projected outward by the Earth for over the last million years or so. The icosahedron is composed of 20 triangles forming a ball, and the dodecahedron is made up of 12 pentagons as its sides. When these two are distributed over the surface of the globe, their lines and node points closely delineate the following planetary elements:

1. High and low barometric pressure areas in the Earth's atmosphere, where storms originate and move along the crystal lattices.

2. The center points for major ocean currents and whirlpools.

3. Areas of highest and lowest solar and electric influx, along with regions of highest and lowest geo-magnetic gauss strength.

4. Points of magnetic/electric anomaly, which serve as gateways into other dimensions.

5. Major planetary fracture zones, where the tectonic plates come together and create seismic and volcanic activities.

6. Major concentrations of ores and petroleum.

7. Planetary hotspots where the internal magma surges closest to the surface.

8. Migration routes of land, air, and sea creatures.

9. Locations of major life breeding grounds and genetic pool regions, where new species have originated.

10. Concentrations of human population centers, both past and present.

11. Birthplaces for human religions, philosophies, sciences, arts, and architectural forms.

This last point is most significant, for it includes the location of most of the major ancient monuments either directly at or clustered around each of the node points of the Earth's crystal grid, including: the Great Pyramid at Giza in Egypt, the ruins of Great Zimbabwe in central Africa, the cultural center of Mohenjo Daro on the Indus river in Pakistan, the Shensi Pyramids in China, the Kunoonda stone circle complex in Australia, the

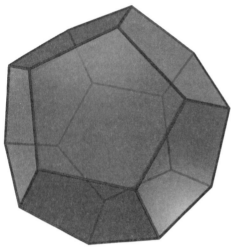
Dodecahedron

ruins of Nan Madol on the Caroline Island of Pohnpei, the stone heads of Easter Island, Machu Plcchu in Peru, the Pyramids of the Sun and Moon at Teotihuacan in Mexico, the Hopi Four Corners area in the American Southwest, and many more. Fully 3,300 separate ancient monuments or sacred complexes have been found directly associated with the Icosa-Dodeca grid configuration.

Many of these same structures are also related to the more localized linear energy patterns. It would appear that the planetary crystal grid lines form the main arteries of power, while the local extensions are like capillaries running off the main system which bring the "flow" of life force into smaller regions.

That the ancients were very familiar with the Earth's crystal grid can be seen in their literature and in their remains. Plato, in describing how the planet appeared from space, stated that it looked like a ball sewn together with twelve pieces of cloth. These would be the twelve pentagons of the Dodeca, which also forms the framework for the Icosa grid as well. Gold objects found in the Khmer ruins in Southeast Asia and among Druidic remains in France, in addition to stone balls unearthed from the Neolithic period in Scotland, were all shaped to show the geometric progression of the crystal grid from tetrahedron to dodecahedron and were used as teaching tools for the Initiates to understand the evolution of the planetary energy systems.

THE NEXT CRYSTAL EVOLUTION

Within the last few years, researchers around the world have been seeing that a dramatic shift has been taking place in the natural phenomena of the planet. Earthquakes are occurring where there have not been quakes before. Volcanic activity is increasing worldwide. Weather patterns and climates are in major flux, with a rise in the number of floods in some areas and droughts in others. Migration routes are changing, with birds nesting in new places; and dolphins and whales are increasingly beaching themselves as if lost or looking for new routes. Most significantly, the geomagnetic field of the planet has been steadily dropping, while the Schumann Resonance, or overall global frequency, is increasing.

Like the dye points on the balloon, a change of frequency means the old centers and the old crystal grid are dissolving, and a new crystal energy structure is in formation.

Beyond the Platonic series of solids is another form being geometrically generated out of the old Icosa-Dodeca crystal. If you take an icosahedron and join together with lines every other point inside the form, you create 12 pentacles or five-pointed stars. If you extend the outer edges of the icosahedron and join these node points together, you create a second group of 12 pentacles or stars. This becomes the seed crystal that gives birth to a new crystalline form called a double penta-dodecahedron composed of 12 double pentacles equally spaced across the surface of the globe.

In one of his prophetic visions of the future, the apostle John, writing in the Book of Revelation, described the coming New Jerusalem as "having the light like the light unto a crystal," and being "as long as it is wide as it is high," or geometric in shape. He described it as having "crowns" or node points, and indicated that its structure would be based on "a golden measure" or the golden mean proportion of 1 to 1.617. Significantly, the only geometric figure that is composed entirely of golden mean proportions is a five-pointed star, the pentacle. What the prophet may have been portraying is the future New Earth with the new Penta-Dodeca crystal energy grid in place. The "twelve gemstones" and "twelve

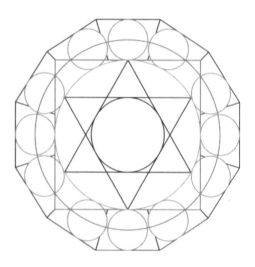

A diagram of the "New Jerusalem," from the Book of Revelations. The sacred geometric structure is based on the abstract geometric relationships explained in John Michell's book *City of Revelation*.

gates" of the New Jerusalem would be the 12 double pentacle faces of the Penta-Dodeca crystal form.

Because the bio-electrical field of the human brain is intricately related to the geomagnetic field of the Earth, any energy shifts in the planet could cause corresponding transformations in the consciousness of humanity as a whole. Is the present spiritual awakening occurring among humankind around the world tied into the transition from one planetary crystal energy form to another? Are prophesied "Earth changes" not something to be feared but simply sign posts for both personal and planetary changes now happening, linked with the Earth's crystalline metamorphosis? Will the apostle John's vision of a coming world of universal peace and tranquility be our eventual gift once the Earth's crystal transformations are completed? These are questions only the future will answer.

This article first appeared in *Atlantis Rising* #78 (November/December 2009), and has been excerpted and edited from the report, "The Earth's Crystal Grid: Re Discovering Gaia as a Living Evolving Energy Structure."

A Matter of Gravity

We May Feel It but Do We Know What It is?

BY PETER BROS

The noted American astronomer Halton Arp jumped through all the hoops of big bang theory and discovered one of its major flaws, that objects from the same source have drastically different red shifts, and thus the big bang was a big bust. Instead of having the big bang community confirm and celebrate his discovery, it ostracized him, denying him telescope time, space in scientific journals, and speaker time at conventions. When others within the big bang community started coming up with the same results, they were provided with similar treatment.

D. L. Dotson shares a charming story that relates to mass gravity in "Dirac's Equation and the Sea of Negative Energy," in issue #43 of *Infinite Energy Magazine*. Dotson says he was questioning his professors on the fact that the conservation of mass and energy could never be violated. This author had long since come to the conclusion that the real reason for the conservation of mass and energy law is that mathematical equations, the source of empirical science, have to be limited, and thus mass and energy have to be limited.

But Dotson didn't realize that empirical science has to ignore reality to exist, and pointed out to his professor that something called "pair production"—where a proton creates an electron-positron pair with energy balanced—didn't account for the spin of the electron that was needed to stabilize the result. Where, Dotson wanted to know, did the energy that produced the spin come from?

"We regard spin angular momentum as an inherent property of the electron and positron, not as a violation of conservation," his professor replied.

"But," Dotson insisted, "if it is real energy, where does it come from?"

"Inherent property means we don't talk about it," his professor replied, "and you won't either if you want to pass this course."

Nicolaus Copernicus (Jan Matejko painting, Nicholaus Copernicus Museum, Frombork)

Dotson was later told his attitude was disrupting the class and there was no chance of his completing a graduate program in physics. He, like me, switched to a language major, but became a professional land surveyor.

This is much the same reaction I received when questioning that gravity is a property of mass. When empirical science needs to limit the terms of its equations, it blocks off reality by saying the speed of light can't be exceeded, or that energy can neither be created nor destroyed, or that the planets are moving in straight lines as a result of being born in a swirling mass of gas, the straight-line motion being altered by gravity and that the elusive gravity responsible for altering the straight-line motion of the planets, and for causing objects to drop, is the property of the matter that makes up the condensing gas, the matter that is the planets.

Saying that a dynamic force results from being a static property is middle-age religious authoritarianism, not science, but because everything is learned by rote, and because everyone's living depends on that rote learning, no one can question the learning, lest it endanger the income it produces. Anyone—if inside the scientific community living off the rote learning—questioning the rote learning is ostracized and then if they continue to get publicity, they are demonized. Those questioning the rote learning from outside the community are simply ignored.

Allow me to comment on the baseless notion of gravity as a property of matter, a subject that the scientific community will not discuss in public (after all, when the Boeing Company starts to expend millions based on Russian Scientist Eugene Podkletnov's anti-gravity experiments, the scientific community can only mumble). Why would anyone spend money on something that has been proven impossible? As an independent researcher, I have remained free to trace the mistake that led to our ignorance of gravity, and the mistake is one as simple as misapplying the universal "time-equals-rate-times-distance" formula.

We are all familiar with the story of Copernicus, and how his sun-centered solar system led to a century of controversy. Before Copernicus, everyone thought the Earth was the center of the universe—much like today, everyone thinks gravity is a property of matter. Tycho Brahe was one of the most famous supporters of the Earth as the center of the universe. Brahe spent his lifetime plotting the courses of the Moon and the planets and he had this data recorded carefully in journals for anyone who could make sense out of it.

Tycho Brahe

But, of course, making sense out of what we see is what we do as human beings, and Brahe had no intention of failing to interpret his data. Among the data he collected was a very interesting fact. The Moon and the planets, especially Mars, appeared to speed up in the summer and slow down in the winter.

Now, this is accepted as rote learning today, but think about it. The Earth is a pretty good size, as is the Moon and, say, Jupiter or Saturn. According to Brahe's measurements, which are just as valid today as they were the day he made them, the Moon and the planets were speeding up and slowing down. But it's a pretty ridiculous notion that something the size of the Moon or the planets could speed up or slow down.

What would make them do so?

Well, that wasn't important. The important thing was, and is, that's what they do, so who's to question our measurable reality?

Brahe spent most of his life carrying out his measurements, and then along came Johan Kepler, a person who liked to create order out of chaos. He wormed his way into becoming Brahe's assistant, but he had one real big disagreement with his boss. Kepler was not a pre-Copernican believer in the Earth-centered universe but rather believed that the planets orbited a stationary Sun in the center of the solar system.

No one knows what bitter arguments this led to between boss and employee, but Joshua Gilder and Anne-Lee Gildar give more than a hint of the friction that must have existed in their book *Heavenly Intrigue: Johannes Kepler, Tycho Brahe, and the Murder Behind One of History's Greatest Scientific*

Discoveries, published by Doubleday in 2004. The Gildars show, through the exhumation of Brahe and the testing of his mustache hairs, how he was poisoned twice, and how that poisoning was carried out by Kepler to get control of Brahe's 40 years of observations for his own use.

Kepler used Brahe's data to create his famous law, that the planets sweep out equal areas in equal times. This law meant that as the planets speed up, they move closer to the Sun, and as they move away from the Sun, they slow down. This gives us a sort of rubber band picture of planetary motion in which the planets are attracted to the Sun, pass around it and then, as they travel away from the Sun, slow down until the Sun starts to pull them in again.

This is another rote-learned law that is immutable and as ridiculous as the idea that the planets speed up and slow down in the first place. The Sun is only .025 off center, which means nothing, but that comets fall toward it, and in any event, the planets would be falling toward the Sun during each half of their orbits and away from the Sun during the other half; so if the Sun did have the effect of causing the planets to speed up and slow down, it would be equal on both sides of the orbit and wouldn't result in the uniform speeding up and slowing down that the rubber band effect implies.

Newton was able to use Brahe's orbital velocity observations, which showed a different constant that applied to orbits around each planet and the Sun to produce a theoretical property of matter he called gravity. He then made the assertion that planets were uniformly made up of identical particles of matter so that he could compute a planet's gravity by volume.

Using the resulting gravity, he created a formula that showed that the Moon would be going in a straight line but for the force of the Earth and Moon's gravity. The equation didn't balance, but because it produced an explanation for planetary motion and a reason why we, on a planet that was rotating at a thousand miles an hour, weren't hurtled off into the darkness of space, was accepted as gospel, Newton was deified, his pronouncements made dogma, and so-called Celestial Mechanics was born.

The result has been a lock on gravity, removing it from the table of rational consideration, effectively crippling our technology. Newton had ascribed the straight-line motion to God, but 18th century rationalist Pierre-Simon Laplace produced the swirling mass of gas, and the stupidity of computing gravity by volume was reversed so that the motion of the planets was used to compute the unprovable nature of the volume, whether it was iron or gas, using the assumption of proportional gravity.

In short, Brahe's simple observation that the Moon and the planets speed up and slow down is the basis for our present-day belief, similar to the once-held belief that the Earth was at the center of the universe, that gravity is a property of something—and if you question it, leave the room, preferably by the window.

Brahe was a true believer in the Earth being the center of the universe. With the Earth at the center of the universe, it was stationary. The Sun went around it, the Moon went around it, and the planets went around it. But no matter what motion occurred around the Earth, the Earth didn't move one iota in any direction.

As he began his timing measurements, he was steeped in ignorance about the real nature of the solar system. He had a picture of the solar system that was about as backward as you can get, although our present-day view of solar system motion adds ridiculous to backward. He was creating an explanation for an observation out of total ignorance, and that observation has been translated into the rote learning we teach in our most advanced lecture halls today.

With Earth motionless, Brahe measured the passage of the Moon in summer and measured the time it takes to pass across the sky. He did the same in winter and found it was a longer period.

He then did the same thing for the known planets and found the same thing. The planets move faster in the summer than they do in the winter. In technical terms, winter is the point the Earth is closest to the Sun (the winter solstice), and summer is the point the Earth is furthest from the Sun (the summer solstice). So the Moon and planets were moving faster between the winter and summer solstices, than they were moving between the summer and winter solstices.

What could be the reason for this?

Brahe went back to his basic education: time equals rate times distance. For the time to vary, the formula required that either the distance varied or the rate varied. Under the mistaken impression that the Earth was stationary at the center of the universe, Brahe concluded that it couldn't possibly be distance that was causing the change. That left rate. The rate was changing, causing the change in time. The Moon and the planets were speeding up in the summer and slowing down in the winter.

When Kepler "inherited" Brahe's figures, he put the Sun stationary in the center of the solar system with the Earth moving around it. However, this didn't lead him to question Brahe's throwing out of distance as a possible reason for the change in time. Kepler was capable of ordering the chaos of Brahe's figures, but he wasn't about to question Brahe's unfounded and ignorant conclusion made on the basis of his Earth-centered beliefs.

Let's pretend we are Brahe, and instead of being ignorant of the movement of the Earth, or even today, ignorant of the movement of the Sun, we go to our time-equals-rate-times-distance formula and say, well, it's pretty far-fetched to believe that something as big as the Moon is slowing down and speeding up, so how could it be distance that is affecting the change in time?

Well, we would answer, if the Earth is moving, then when it is moving forward in its orbit, and the Moon is moving in the direction opposite that movement. The Moon would travel a shorter distance than it would when the Moon was moving in the same direction as the Earth. Then, the Moon would have to travel not only the half the distance of its orbit, it would have to travel the distance the Earth had traveled to make up that distance, too. So the distance the Moon travels away from the direction of the Earth's motion is shorter than when it traveled in the direction of the Earth's motion.

But this is not the motion that Brahe measured. His measurements were made over successive months in both the winter and the summer and the measurements applied to the planets as well. The change in the Moon's distance, which occurs each month, is too short to measure unless you are looking for it. But successive monthly measurements and planetary measurements that produce the same result suggest that the Sun is the culprit, that it is moving forward in its orbit; and thus, when its components are moving from the winter to the summer solstice, they have a shorter distance to go than when they move between the summer and winter solstice because those solstices are moving as the Sun moves.

As enlightened observers rather than ignorant concluders, we could then say, so the Sun is moving and in doing so it is dragging the planets along with it. Its direction of movement is toward the winter solstice so that's why the planets pass closest to the Sun in the winter and reach their furthest point from the Sun in the summer. The time variance is the result of components traveling a shorter distance in the summer than they do when they are playing catch-up in winter.

Unfortunately, rote learning today does not even consider this a possibility because, with Celestial Mechanics resting on Kepler's Laws, if the Sun is moving, then Newton's mass gravity is what it really is, a fantasy.

Empirical science has no way to control the concepts it attaches to the terms of its mathematical equations. It uses those equations to predict possible facts, which are, of course, always found, and then says the facts turn its concepts into facts. Facts that disagree with the concepts, which are now facts, are ignored.

No wonder we live in ignorance about the forces that move the objects around us, assigning the motion of the galaxies to a historical big bang, the motion of the planets to a swirling mass of gas, and the most dynamic force in our existence, gravity, as a property, which in the words of Dotson's professor, "Inherent property means we don't talk about it and you won't either if you want to pass this course."

This article first appeared in *Atlantis Rising* #56 (March/April 2006).

27

POWER FROM THE NIGHTSIDE

*Could Earth Itself Be Trying to Provide the
Clean Abundant Energy We Need?*

BY SUSAN B. MARTINEZ, PH.D.

Mobil and Exxon won't like it. Neither will the nuclear power industry. Even solar power enthusiasts may frown in disbelief. But give them time. All new ideas, especially those that reverse conventional wisdom (180 degrees exactly), fall on deaf ears, unwilling ears.

Take polar energy, for example: that glorious spectacle of colored lights painting the night sky of the northern and southern latitudes. Auroral readings taken in the Van Allen Belt are on the order of 3 million megawatts. That's four times the power used in the U.S. at peak (summer) demand!

Can atmospheric conditions be used as power? Some think so.

Alaskans have begun to investigate the possibility of harnessing energy from those stunning nocturnal displays, known to us as aurora borealis, to the Maoris as Burning-of-the-sky, and to Europeans as Merry Dancers, shimmering, swaying and waltzing across the firmament with dazzling grace and ineffable beauty. Yet, chances of tapping this almost occult power are slim, barring a revised (really, reversed) view of terrestrial mechanics; we need to know where auroras come from before launching the intriguing business of capturing their energy for the use of mankind. And, if Ray Palmer, a founding editor of *Fate* magazine, was right, those flickering fireworks of the polar skies originate, not from the heavens above, but from the very bowels of the Earth. "Our recent ISIS satellite [ca. 1970]," commented Palmer, "has just confirmed ... that the energy that causes the northern lights flows upward from the north pole, rather than downward from outer space (from the sun) as previously held by scientists." Ray's use of the label "previously" was optimistic; for today's science stronghold, stubbornly ignoring its own findings, would have us believe that our cascading, gliding auroras are triggered by the far-off Sun. And here's the explanation, the science-speak, that makes it so—Entrapment: Solar particles that "get trapped in our planet's magnetic field" bump into atmospheric gases, causing them to glow.

But can it be?—given the perfectly well-known fact that gases of Earth's atmosphere occur only in molecular form, while auroral wavelengths are frequently atomic—that is to say, atomic nitrogen, atomic oxygen, and so forth. Where does this atomic energy come from if, as scientists have observed, ordinary energy from the Sun cannot radiate these lines, that is, these auroral rays?

With science to the rescue, a new kind of "high energy particle" (from the Sun) is quickly postulated to fit the bill. And the explanation becomes: Solar Wind. Conveniently, the fancied solar wind (invented in 1958), is also assigned the difficult task of pushing the auroras toward the Earth's polar regions (missing all other latitudes), thus killing two birds with one stone; for how else may we account for the fact that a "donut" of light (auroral ring) favors the poles, as pictured by satellite images over the Arctic and Antarctica? And why would the solar wind perform this prodigy only at night? Let's just stand this thing on its head and see how right Ray Palmer may have been. Let's change the direction of this auroral energy and suffer it to emerge, nightly, from the center of the earth. This powerful current, the

An Aurora Borealis lights the northern sky

Earth's own motor or dynamo, thus completes its round trip by emerging from "the northern pole . . . in flames of fire, which are called borealis."

Picture it: the Earth-body breathes in by day, and out by night; the north pole, nicely dented (no one knows why), serving as the primary vent, the chute, for Earth's powerful effluvium. And what is aurora, then, but her own beautiful aura?

Careful observers, like William Corliss, have quietly admitted that "some auroras may record the slow discharge of terrestrial electricity to the upper atmosphere."

And so it is: away from the Earth to the atmosphere, gushing, shooting outward and loaded with bolts of free and clean energy. Such currents, Corliss goes on to observe, "that create auroral displays are accompanied by similar currents in the Earth's crust." In fact, the same researcher is struck by "puzzling observations linking auroras to . . . earthquakes and mountaintop glows."

Yet, not so puzzling once the terrestrial origin of the Merry Dancers is allowed; and, too, once the various "vents," (secondary vents) are identified. Especially on dark nights, the Brown Mountain Lights of North Carolina rise brilliantly over the ridge like "a bursting skyrocket." Interesting that the area is seismically active; just as British studies show "a clear connection between these light displays and the presence of fault lines"— giving us our "vents." The Brown Mountain Lights, just like auroras with their famous split-second changes, "suddenly wink out." The phenomenon, generally known as the Andes Glow—occurring also in the Alps, Rockies, and so forth—involves bright flashes of colored light emitted from mountain peaks and shot high into the sky at great speed, sometimes seen hundreds of miles off.

Striking is the family resemblance between auroras, earthquake lights, Andes Glow, airglow, reykir, marine phosphorescence, volcanic glow, spontaneous Earth fires, spooklights, and will-o'-the-wisps.

The poles are by no means the only path of escape for the boundless energy which, after sunset, surges through the heart of the planet on its way back to the atmospheric dynamo (vortex) from whence it came. Ruptures deep in the Earth give us volcanoes and earthquakes, the latter—in Chile, Japan, China, California—at times filling the sky with "earthquake lights" discharged from the depths. Tall blue flames, just before the great San Francisco quake of 1906, played over foothills and marshland. Such wastelands, swamps (and even graveyards) produce phenomena intriguingly similar to auroras.

Yet, the most prevalent of marshland lights—will-o'-the-wisps—are so strange and mysterious that "serious scientific studies are non-existent." These playful phosphorescent flames, small armies of which magically erupt at night over swampy land, command the self-same descriptions as the floating auroras. The "soft eerie light" of will-o'-the-wisps compares readily with the ethereal curtains and supple draperies of the northern lights. The "ghostlike quality" of the swampland flames matches the "ghostly veils" of auroras. If will-o'-the-wisps prance and hop, auroras are Merry Dancers. If will-o'-the-wisps change colors instantaneously and disappear in a flash ("like a cinder"), auroras do the same. Appearing just a few feet off the ground, these small but bright pyrotechnics of the marshlands are nocturnal only, and they are of the earth—like Andes Glow, spooklights, "money lights," "fairy lights," airglow, ginseng glow, and assorted terraqueous luminosities—all of which manifest only at night. What is that "special Earth vitality" that, according to the Chinese, makes ginseng glow at night? (That's how hunters find ginseng.) And what exactly is the energy that enables vegetable growth to take place mostly at night?

We could have none of these "marvels" if the Earth itself did not possess a specifically nocturnal energy as yet undreamed of by the science of man, the cabal that would repudiate the well-known ghost lights of various locales, attributing them to some dull, prosaic cause, such as refraction from headlights (even though the phenomena predate the invention of automobiles); or blame it on natural gas (even when these marsh flames burn cold); or invoke that old standby—collective hallucination! Yet the enigmatic earthlights are real, and their spectral quality faultlessly imitates the gliding auroras—mobile and shape-shifting, "blinding" (Esperanza Light), "dancing in the dark" (Marfa Lights of Texas), color-changing (Summerville Light of South Carolina), and "blinking out" (Ozark Spooklight, near Joplin, Missouri). Arising from the ground, our ghost lights, witnessed constantly by thousands, are strictly nocturnal, like auroras, and speak the language of Earth's effluvium in their every tour de force. Only nature's nightside can produce these spectacular visions which, like Puck, the British hobgoblin, emerge only at night. They are not freaks of nature; they are part of nature, part of the same grand plan that gives us day and night, and they are endowed with all the idiosyncrasies of the northern lights, which are spewed in lavish array from the planet's primary vents—the poles.

Everything that spouts from the nightside Earth is marked by the same implacable force that thrusts auroras high in the sky, like volcanic ash that is propelled 20 miles into the stratosphere. We recognize in these prodigious earth-lights the familiar pigments—greens, yellows, blues, reds—of the colorful auroras. The sulfur/ozone smell of auroras is also perfectly analogous to that of waterspouts, earthquakes, volcanoes, surprising beach flames, and mud fires. Too, the vast and wondrous rotating wheels of light, perfectly geometrical and witnessed by astonished observers on the seas, are identical to auroral wheels. These marine wheels, enormous and accompanied by "swishing sounds," have been sighted in the East Indian Archipelago and "bear an intriguing resemblance to the sounds reported during low-level auroras," according to Corliss, who adds that the luminous marine waves "emulate the auroral fogs." No one knows why these radiant mists should occur mainly in the Indian Ocean. But given a major seismic chain running under those waters (and hundreds of volcanoes in Southeast Asia), is it any wonder that the hidden forces of the Earth erupt there? (This is the same area of the disastrous tsunamis of 2004.)

Dame Science remains silent on the subject of that awesome power. Nonetheless, the vortexyan powerhouse that envelops the Earth, and the polar outcropping that is its nightside, are "very close indeed to our atomic energy." The extraordinary heat of the interior of volcanic fountains—over 2,000 degrees F—also bespeaks atomic energy, as does the piezoelectric effect of earthquakes. The incandescence and rocket speed of ghostlights and mysterious fireballs also suggest a rarefied power. Indeed, the blue glow so frequently associated with earthlights may be traced to the chemistry of atomic nitrogen, as are the blue auroras. And if auroral wavelengths correspond to oxygen in its atomic form, so does night airglow—that soft, faint light which, absent moonlight, is brighter than all the starlight together. Does airglow come from the upper atmosphere, as science teaches? Perhaps it is the planet's gentle and diffuse outbreath, quietly oozing out the Earth from dusk to dawn. A "fictional" view of inner Earth, envisioned by the prophetic Jules Verne in his *Journey to the Center of the Earth*, pictures our planet's interior "lit up like day . . . the illuminating power . . . flickering [and] evidently electric;

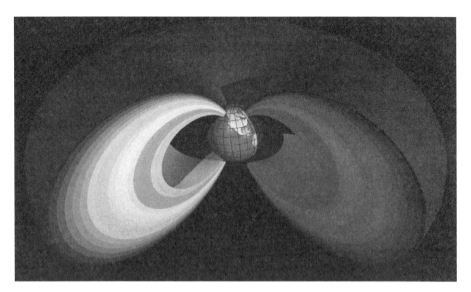

The Van Allen Radiation Belt

something in the nature of the aurora borealis . . . light[ing] up the whole of the ocean cavern." His ideas, far in advance of the times, were one part imagination and one part ear to the ground. When a 13th century Norseman speculated that auroras "radiate at night the light which has [been] absorbed by day"; when Scandinavian folklore insists that auroras originate from the depths of the sea; when Eskimos tell of auroras so low they have killed people—shall we dismiss their folk science as superstition?

Though many have dreamed of drawing power (free energy) from the Earth's magnetic envelope, precious few have warmed to the secret of the northern lights. And with auroras romanticized as "a breath from beyond this planet," commentary on the auroras flip-flops from sentimental doggerel to scientific dogma. In fact, the "solar wind" theory bogs when we take a look at the Van Allen Belt where the northern lights are supposedly manufactured by solar radiation. But—have a look—the belt girdles the Earth like a donut, straddling every latitude except the poles (where the Earth's vent-stream cuts its own swath into the atmosphere). If the northern lights were rained down to Earth from the "Aurora Factory in the Sky" (Van Allen Belt), they would not cover the poles but would head for the equator and mid-latitudes. But they don't. What is the sciencespeak that will emasculate this obvious fact?—The chimerical solar wind is supposedly empowered by something called "Alfven waves" which "accelerate particles down from space," nicely accounting for the fact that auroral rays are actually "more intense as [they] converge near Earth"! And "fade away rather gradually" into the atmosphere. But NASA has it the other way around! Filmed at Antarctica, their footages show "the aurora emanating from an orifice in the continent . . . spouting out from the opening [and] shooting up luminous streamers . . . directed toward the zenith." Indeed, physicists, led by the giant Karl Gauss, recognize the magnetic nature of the Earth's interior, arguing that the Earth's force field is in fact generated by electric currents in the interior.

So why haven't we connected the dots?

Madame Science, for her own reasons, prefers to remain mum on the simple question of why auroras are nocturnal. Why can't they, like rainbows, occur at any time? Do Alfven waves/solar wind sleep by day? Or—was Ray Palmer right after all, in calling our attention to that nocturnal energy that "flows upward from the north pole"?

Have you ever wondered why most earthquakes and volcanic eruptions occur at night or in early morning? Now you know.

What about the 24-hour delay between "solar flares" (read: vortexyan surges) and exceptionally large auroral displays?

Now you know, for that same energy must first pass through the Earth in the nightwatches before streaming out the polar vents. And it has nothing to do with the Sun.

The natural Earth receives her energy by day and discharges her powerful magnetic flux by night. Is this "anomalous"? (and therefore beneath the purview of science)? Shall we banish these lights, sounds, motions, smells, flames, surges, and commotions of our dynamic planet to the siberia of scholarship, to do time with other rogues and mavericks of "fringe" science? In place of a thousand and one "sophisticated" explanations of Dame Science, a few, very few, principles will surely underlie the great panorama of Earth's mysteries.

Geysers are tapped to heat the Icelandic city of Reykjavik.

Volcanoes, which release the energy of atom bombs, have proven an immense source of cheap power.

Huge (natural) steambath galleries heat the towns of Antarctica with hot underground water.

And the auroras, one of the wonders of the world—the great light-show in the sky—may yet prove a greater wonder when their awesome power is tapped for the good of mankind.

The force of the vortex [roughly, geomagnetic field] is toward its own center, but turns at the center and escapes outward at the north pole—as one may draw a line from the east to the center of the Earth, then in a right angle due north, which would be the current of the vortex.

This article first appeared in *Atlantis Rising* #64 (July/August 2007).

28

SOUND AS THE SCULPTOR OF LIFE

*Exploring the Science of Cymatics
and the Secrets of Creation*

BY JEFF VOLK

Perhaps because it is invisible, less attention has been paid to the sea of sound constantly flowing around and through us than to the denser objects with which we routinely interact. To those of us for whom "seeing is believing," Cymatics, the science of wave phenomena, can be a portal into this invisible world and its myriad effects on matter, mind, and emotions.

The long and illustrious lineage of scientific inquiry into the physics of sound can be traced back to Pythagoras, but we will focus here on more recent explorations into the effects that sound has upon matter. However, a brief summary of the last three centuries of acoustic research will help to highlight a few of the pioneers who blazed the trail so that Cymatics could emerge as a distinct discipline in the 1950s.

SAND FORMS, SOUND FORMS

On July 8, 1680, the English experimental philosopher, Robert Hooke, broke the visible sound barrier when he spread flour on a small glass plate and passed a violin bow along the edge of the plate. As he continued, he noticed that the flour, rather than just flying off the plate, configured itself into an oval shape, which re-oriented itself along the surface, depending on how he bowed the plate.

About 100 years later this phenomenon was rediscovered by the German physicist, Ernst F. F. Chladni, known as the "Father of Acoustics," who laid the foundations for the study of the physics of sound. Chladni devoted much of his experimentation to the phenomenon of resonance. In the manner of Hooke's experiments, he spread fine sand on a suspended steel plate and then bowed the edge of the plate. Intricate patterns formed as the sand migrated away from areas of greatest vibration and settled along the nodal lines, or the areas of minimal vibration within the plate. He made extensive drawings of these patterns, which came to be known as Chladni figures.

His demonstrations to scientists and socialites in laboratories and salons throughout Europe were so impressive that eventually word reached Napoleon, who paid him a princely fee for a court presentation.

In 1831, the great experimental scientist, Michael Fara-

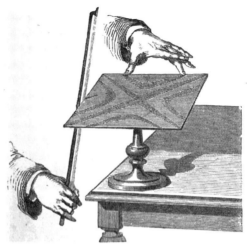

Illustration from an 1879 textbook on acoustics showing how vibrations from a violin bow create the sand figures of nodal lines called Chladni figures.

day, published a paper describing his observations of geometric "nodal forms" appearing in granular solids under the effect of vibration. Although he was fascinated by these phenomena, he soon moved on to other areas (like electromagnetism) as he could find no practical application for them. But it was not only royalty and men of letters who found this so fascinating. In 1885, an American, Margaret Watts Hughes, a singer and "devout Congregationalist," began experimenting with the "eidophone," a small, saxophone-like instrument with a membrane spread tightly over the bell, upon which she spread various powders and liquids. By singing long, sustained tones into this device, she was able to create finely detailed images mirroring the brachiated structure of plants and flowing water, as well as the amazingly complex forms of flower petals.

Jumping ahead to the 1960s, in the small town of Dornach in the foothills of the Swiss Alps, Dr. Hans Jenny constructed a similar device, which he called a tonoscope, to transform the human voice into visual "sound figures." Jenny's association with the Waldorf school system, which specialized in educating physically impaired children, led him to employ this "toy" to teach deaf children to speak. Although a deaf child might not be able to hear the difference between a properly pronounced "oh" and a guttural, poorly articulated "uhh," using the tonoscope they could see the difference!

Although this very simple device was similar to the one created by Ms. Hughes over half a century earlier, Jenny did not stop there. He went on to hook up a frequency generator and amplifier to differently shaped steel plates, animating lycopodium powder (a fine, spherical powder, highly responsive to vibration) as well as a variety of denser pastes and liquids.

This enabled him a much greater degree of control over the parameters of the phenomena, including the ability to repeat specific patterns at will. He, too, was able to produce a variety of structures similar to those found in the natural world. The resulting patterns and flow forms he observed were extensively documented in films and books compiling over 14 years of detailed research. Jenny coined the term "Cymatics" (*Kymatics* in German) from the Greek to *kyma* (pertaining to waves), delving deeply into an area of scientific inquiry that had only been superficially explored at the level of effect.

One might well wonder, what is so interesting about watching a mass of powder moving around a plate? Perhaps it depends on your ability to discern patterns, not just in the sand, but in the interplay of sound—the animating principle of vibration, interacting with substance—the dense matter that gives form to these dynamic structures.

It was his analysis of these patterns and his profound insights into their universality that set Jenny apart from previous researchers. Truly a Renaissance man, he was a medical doctor, a fine artist (painter) and musician, an astute observer of nature and a philosopher of science in the Goethean tradition. He was also an Anthroposophist, having personally studied with Rudolf Steiner. So, needless to say, his perspective was vast! Jenny went so far as to say that wherever one fixes one's gaze, in whatever field of observation, be it astronomy, geology, orology (the study of wave movements within the Earth) or in the life sciences, biology, cytology (cell development), anatomy, physiology, embryology—one may observe the principles of Cymatics at play.

Hidden within the physical formations of standing-wave patterns, Jenny perceived and documented specific processes manifesting through

Hans Jenny

the energetic impulse (oscillations) of sound frequencies interacting with matter. For example, he was able to show empirically how certain frequencies within the audible range could create fluid forms, not only in liquids, but also in powders and even viscous pastes. What's more, this previously inert matter, animated by sound, could assume a circulatory motion and would often create life-like, flowing forms, analogous to organs of the body or to complex, living organisms. Viewing his films, one can easily imagine how life forms could evolve from the primordial, energetic matrix, organized by the orderly pulsations of sound.

EFFECTS WITH WATER

Another generative aspect of sound was brought to light in these experiments—the creation of a turbulent field that further "sensitizes" the material to other, more subtle influences. Experiments were done projecting sound into a variety of gases and liquids, but perhaps the most revealing were his experiments with water.

A little over 15 years ago, I arranged to film an exhibition in Zurich where some of Dr Jenny's original equipment was reassembled to demonstrate a few of the experiments he had done some three decades earlier. We placed a small sample of water onto a lens with a containment ring around it to keep the water in place and then positioned a light beneath the lens, which projected through the water and reflected off a mirror and onto a screen. When we set the lens vibrating with an audible frequency the water began to reflect

Strobe image of vibrating water viewed from above.

back and forth on the lens, forming an oscillating dynamic of hills and valleys—and voila! the pattern of sound-induced, standing waves became visible as a luminous image.

As the water is subjected to gradually increasing frequencies, the complexity of the patterns increases with the increasing pitch of the exciting tone. At a critical pitch the entire structure dissolves into chaos, only to reconfigure into a higher order of complexity, as the tone continues to ascend.

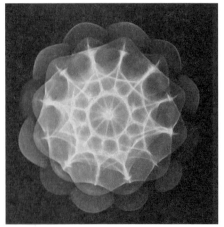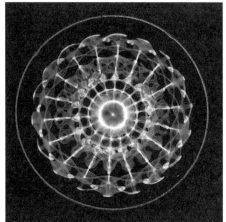

Samples of light refracting through a small sample of water (about 1.5 cm in diameter) under the influence of vibration..

This process of chaos and re-integration is seen throughout nature, from the valence fields of electrons within the atom (the Periodic Table of Elements), to complex weather patterns, to intricate, physiological processes within our bodies that allow us to function in homeostasis within an ever-changing sea of vibrations (our environment). It also serves as a "living metaphor" for the process of evolution occurring at all levels of creation, from the physical to the subtlest domains of consciousness—and its implications are equally vast.

Chaos: a necessary phase—Acceptance: a personal choice

Jenny's work was truly ground-breaking; he was a forerunner of chaos theory and complexity science and his experimental method now provides a solid foundation for the therapeutic application of sound and music. It is interesting that, although Jenny was a medical doctor, he purposely steered clear of taking the leap into what we now call sound healing. I have no doubt that Dr. Jenny was aware of these implications of his work. Rather he chose to focus on the empirical aspect of observable phenomena, so as to provide an indisputable body of objectively verifiable research that would establish a foundation for further experimentation.

For me, personally, viewing these phenomena objectively allowed for a deeper understanding of just how this process of "disintegration and re-configuration at a higher order of coherence" constantly plays out in my own life. "We live in a vast ocean of sound": in other words, we are perpetually bathed in a plethora of energetic currents, which invite—nay, compel—us to flow along with them! Our choice lies in selecting which of these currents we will merge with and what forms we will animate through our vital forces of acceptance and will. Whatever our situation—be it a healing crisis or some other life challenge that we no longer can ignore—something is flowing into our awareness urging us to incorporate a greater point of view. The way we identify with our situation—the stories we tell ourselves about it and how we feel about ourselves—absolutely determines how we navigate our experience. We can either get caught up in the turmoil by accepting a reality that has yet to evolve to a more coherent state, or we can relax in the knowledge (perhaps faith, at this point) that a lovely, harmonic form is just waiting for us to enter into resonance with (embody) it.

ECHOES OF LIGHT AND WATER

As I was compiling Jenny's work for the new edition of my book *Cymatics*, I was unaware that there were two contemporary researchers who were carrying on similar experiments independently, one in the UK and the other in Germany.

Acoustic engineer and long-time UK Cymatic researcher, John Reid, has developed an electro-acoustic device enabling one to visualize the voice, music, and other sound sources. We will be working together to bring these instruments into the hands of researchers, musicians, therapists, and especially children, to further evoke the awe and wonder that arises spontaneously as creation takes shape right before your eyes. One of these new CymaScopes was recently installed at Explora, a children's science museum in Albuquerque, New Mexico.

Within a few months of the publication of the new edition of *Cymatics*, Alexander Lauterwasser's book, *Wasser Klang Bilder* (*Water Sound Images*) was published in Switzerland. His expertise as a photographer as well as his use of 21st century technology allowed him to capture precise and spectacular, standing-wave patterns in water. (Is it fate or destiny that a man whose name translates as "Loud Water" would be drawn to this kind of work?) Lauterwasser has clearly elevated Cymatic phenomena into the realm of photographic artistry.

One of the many things he documented was the phenomenon of different wave patterns created by various musical instruments.

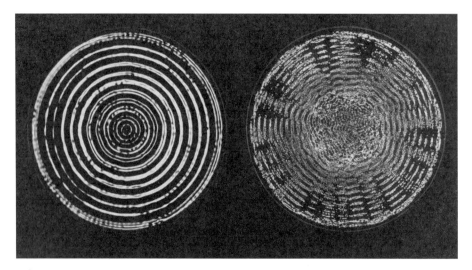

Left: water sound image of a monochord. Right: monochord with overtone singing.

A small sample of water is contained within a petri dish and lit from above, highlighting the wave crests. The first image is a simple tone, almost a pure sine wave, generated by plucking a single string, a monochord. This sets up a very basic, resonance pattern in the water as it is excited by the (electronically amplified) pulsation of air generated by the oscillating motion of the string. The concentric ring pattern is the result of the water moving outward and striking the boundary of the dish, then reflecting back in upon itself and repeating this over and over as long as the tone is maintained. In another image you can still distinguish the monochord's "sound-print" amidst the greater complexity added by the overtones of the voice.

It is interesting to consider the effect that these multiple-frequency impulses would have on the tissues of the physical body, much less the highly responsive and dynamic "tissues" of the psyche. British osteopath, Peter Guy Manners, compiled a large body of research over several decades to discern specific frequency commutations that would effectively treat various physical and emotional conditions.

How Cymatherapy works

All matter exists at specific densities or, looked at another way, at different rates of vibration. Therefore, each individual particle or collection of particles will have its own unique, resonant frequency. This is why you can make a wine glass or a crystal bowl sing so brilliantly when you excite them within the narrow range of their natural, resonant frequency. For several years medical scientists have been using this principle to break up kidney stones and, more recently, to excite the individual cancerous cells within a tumor to the extent that they rupture, thus destroying the tumor.

Because every person's anatomy is different, the same organ or tissue in your body will have a slightly different resonant frequency from mine, but within a very narrow range. Manners solved this problem by using a tone consisting of an overlay of five frequencies, producing a harmonic of the tissue. Five seemed to be the "magic number," creating a frequency signature precise enough to stimulate the targeted bone, organ, or muscle tissue, while at the same time enabling one generic setting to work effectively, despite individual variations.

Why five frequencies? Various theories have been put forth including that it relates to the Chinese theory of the five elements, which are themselves based on the esoteric principles of the five platonic solids. A more biological interpretation might be that these frequencies are somehow related to the five main stages of the cell renewal process. Suffice it to say that this particular patterning of five audible, sound frequencies has been shown to effectively correspond with the given tissue throughout a broad population over several decades of clinical research and therapeutic application.

Atlanta-based Cymatherapy International is continuing Manners' research and development in the U.S., with its thoroughly revamped, therapeutic device, the Cyma 1000.

The implications of this research into the field of sound therapy are vast, and there are many yet unimagined applications that await our creative investigation. Even a rudimentary knowledge of the generative process of sound is immensely enlightening to anyone who makes music, especially for therapeutic purposes.

This article appeared in *Atlantis Rising* #69 (May/June 2008), and is reprinted with permission from *Caduceus* magazine.

PART SEVEN

CHALLENGING THE CONVENTIONAL WISDOM

29

INDEPENDENT THINKING
IN THE ACADEMIC WORLD

*Reflecting on the Professional Perils of
Challenging Conventional Wisdom*

BY ROBERT M. SCHOCH, PH.D.

As regular readers of *Atlantis Rising* know, I have found myself butt-
ing heads with mainstream academics more than once. Perhaps
most famously, or infamously, for two decades I have advocated the
position that the Great Sphinx of Egypt traces its origins back thousands
of years earlier than the standard Egyptological date of circa 2500 BC (as
recounted in various issues of *Atlantis Rising*, including most recently AR
#s 76 and 78). An older Sphinx overturns the classical view of when and
where civilization and high culture arose. Not only is the Great Sphinx
older than conventional wisdoms holds, but so, too, is the oldest portion
of the Great Pyramid (see my 2005 book *Pyramid Quest*).

Further enraging my traditional colleagues, I contend that climatic
changes, earthquakes, volcanic eruptions, and bombardments by comets
may have destroyed some ancient civilizations catastrophically (*Voices of
the Rocks*, 1999). Still further countering establishment views, I believe
ancient peoples were not totally isolated from one another but were in
contact across the continents and across the oceans, with the concomitant exchange of ideas and even material goods, thousands of years before
Columbus (*Voyages of the Pyramid Builders*, 2003). In my opinion, the evidence points to a primordial civilization, which arose toward the end of
the last ice age (with earlier precursors) and subsequently spread around
the globe.

My unconventional thinking on ancient history is bad enough, but
much to the chagrin of some of my academic colleagues, I have delved into
various "esoteric" and "occult" studies, seriously researching such taboo

subjects as parapsychology and psychical research (*The Parapsychology Revolution*, 2008, as well as my articles in AR #s 66, 67, 68, 71, 73).

Schooled to be a mainstream academic scientist (Ph.D. in geology and geophysics, 1983), I am now a full-time tenured faculty member at Boston University. I started out with a conventional career, studying fossils and rocks from the period of about 65 to 40 million years ago, so how did I become sidetracked? Where did I "go wrong"? Why challenge orthodoxy? Why make life difficult for myself?

I never set out to question traditional notions. Trained as a natural historian, my desire is to make sense of the world as a whole. I am not satisfied with simply understanding a little piece in detail (many scientists are extreme specialists, and even I have my specialties). Between my theosophist grandmother (she taught me to question everything, including the things she taught me) and a graduate education that encouraged true inquiry, open-minded consideration of the unconventional comes naturally to me. I remember well the private advice I was given by a senior Yale professor while still a fledgling graduate student: If you want a satisfying intellectual career with the potential to discover something significant, then study important, cutting-edge, possibly unconventional, subjects, even if such a path is difficult and controversial. Of course, he warned, such a strategy is a genuine gamble, potentially risking one's career and with it one's mental, emotional, and physical health and well-being!

As science historians Juan Miguel Campanario and Brian Martin (in the 2008 book edited by M. L. Corredoira and C. C. Perelman, *Against the Tide*) have pointed out, there are different strategies one can pursue as a scientist (or as an academic scholar more generally). Most scientists build their career by accepting, and working within, the existing paradigm of the time, adding to the overall picture with carefully sifted bits of data and perhaps elaborating and tweaking slightly existing theories. The work they do is neither highly original nor spectacular, but in terms of peer acceptance and likelihood of success (whether measured in terms of contributions to the paradigm, or more honestly, promotion and upward mobility in terms of jobs and salaries), it is a good, conservative, approach. Such a path, herding with the scientific pack, generally results in a stable career, moderate prestige, and the material benefits that go with being a well-paid industrial or academic scientist.

On the other hand, we can consider the "scientific risk-takers," those who pursue speculative or unusual ideas, do not dismiss anomalous data, and end up questioning the reigning paradigm. The stakes are high. If the dissident succeeds in having a new idea or theory accepted by the mainstream, the rewards in terms of prestige (which may result in funding, jobs, or other material benefits) can be enormous. However, the odds are stacked against the true innovator, and such a path is difficult, to say the least. Not only, one can argue, is there a high probability that the theory or ideas espoused by the innovator are false in an absolute sense, but even if there is something to them, there is an incredible prejudice against new ideas among status quo scientists. As the Nobel Prize winning physicist Max Planck (1858–1947), one of the founders of quantum mechanics, famously asserted, "A new scientific truth does not triumph by convincing its opponents and making them see the light, but rather because its opponents eventually die and a new generation grows up that is familiar with it."

Among my academic colleagues, at informal university gatherings for instance, I often find that I must be extremely careful as to how much I reveal concerning my interest in either paranormal phenomena or anomalies of ancient history. A scientist or scholar who seriously studies the idea of a primordial civilization in the deep recesses of the past (before civilization is supposed to have originated), or researches paranormal phenomena like telepathy, may be branded as a crank, quack, charlatan, or pseudoscientist. To be labeled a pseudoscientist is probably the most disparaging epithet one can receive (and, for good measure, there are numerous variations on the "pseudo-" theme, such as pseudoarchaeologist, pseudobiologist, pseudophysicist, pseudohistorian, and so on). This may be simple name calling, but in the academic world it can hurt (a person labeled as a pseudoscientist may be turned down for funding requests and denied promotions and raises), at least in the short-term. Regarding the long-term, I am a firm believer that the data and truth will prevail, and this is what keeps me going. Concerning the bitterness of in-fighting among academics, I learned my lesson well many years ago, at a Boston University faculty-staff Christmastime gathering.

It was back in the early 1990s. During the holiday party, a faculty member with the archaeology department accosted me concerning my work on the Great Sphinx. I had never met her before, though she had previously attacked me in the local press. Suddenly she appeared before me, face-to-face, as I was attempting to enjoy the hors d'oeuvres. She loudly spouted out a diatribe, virtually spitting in my face, accusing me of falsifying data and results, and called me a pseudoscientist. Then quickly, before I could respond, she disappeared back into the crowd. It was all quite disconcerting, and I even felt a bit threatened. Clearly, she had prepared her statement, ready to be delivered in a staccato voice, if she happened to run into me. She did not want to open a dialogue on the subject. She did not care to learn about my evidence or analyses. I was the enemy as far as she was concerned, and that was that! I later learned that she and her colleagues in archaeology were doing everything they could to make trouble for me behind the scenes, attempting to prevent me from any salary raises and spreading rumors in the Egyptian press (which I believe they thought I would never get wind of) that I was not a member of the Boston University faculty, though I had already received tenure, as they knew. These are classic tactics attempting to marginalize someone who dares to challenge the dominant paradigm. The goal is to generally make life miserable for the dissenter with the hope that the challenge to the status quo will quietly disappear.

I have found that my ideas and theories, whether concerning the Great Sphinx and the origin of high culture or topics related to the paranormal, generally receive a fairer and more considered hearing at academic conferences overseas than in my home turf. Certainly I do not intend to compare myself to the great visionaries of the past, but more than once the biblical words have come to my mind, "a prophet has no honor in his own country" (from John 4:44). In my moments of melancholy and academic loneliness, I reflect on Isaiah, the prophet crying in the wilderness. (For the record, I do not consider myself aligned with any particular religion, but I certainly am familiar with Judeo-Christian traditions.) It is difficult to pursue one's research with little financial support (big grants are not generally awarded to pursue alternative thinking) and few, if any, sympathetic academic colleagues. Always being on the defensive, always feeling under attack, is draining.

People who consider it their duty to maintain the status quo often attempt to dismiss ideas and data that counter their limited worldview with overly simplistic, patronizing remarks. One of their favorite mantras is along the lines that "extraordinary claims require extraordinary evidence." This is an assertion that may sound superficially profound but does not hold up under careful and logical scrutiny as, when typically applied by the debunkers, it presupposes what is extraordinary in terms of claims and then sets an evidential standard that precludes the possibility of the claim being validated, no matter what the evidence. To give an extreme example, the 19th century physicist Hermann von Helmholtz declared that no amount of evidence, not even the evidence of his own senses, could ever convince him that telepathy is real since he knew that it was impossible. Talk about close-minded!

Certain topics are, it seems, simply taboo in "respectable" scientific and scholarly circles. One such subject is extraterrestrial intelligent alien contact with Earth. To even raise such a notion in anything other than a humorous or downright mocking context is seen as a reason to question one's scientific competence, if not one's sanity. It is a call to arms. When the late psychiatrist and tenured Harvard University professor John E. Mack, M.D., had the temerity to seriously investigate possible alien encounters and abduction phenomena in the early 1990s, he was not only openly ridiculed but also investigated by a special committee reporting to the Dean of the Harvard Medical School. Ultimately it was determined that Mack had the right to study whatever subjects he pleased, but certainly such an investigation was extremely unsettling, if not blatant harassment.

The late Harvard professor John Mack

Yet when it comes to a subject like alien contact, is it necessarily downright ridiculous on the face of it? The late astronomer Tom Van Flandern did not think so. I first met Dr. Van Flandern at a conference where he and I were invited presenters. We both received our Ph.D.s from Yale, his in astronomy, and for many years he worked at the U.S. Naval Observatory, Washington, D.C. He and I had some extremely interesting discussions. He was a scientist who truly believed in following the evidence, as he interpreted it, and he propounded some very unorthodox ideas when it came to cosmology and the origin of the solar system. He also felt that there was evidence supporting the notion of a former civilization on Mars (such as the so-called "Face on Mars").

Concerning the topic of possible extraterrestrial contact with humans, Van Flandern did not dismiss the idea. In fact, he applied the scientific principle known as Occam's Razor to the issue; that is, the simplest hypothesis is to be preferred. In this vein he wrote (Van Flandern, in *Against the Tide*), "Occam's Razor argues that the single hypothesis of earlier contact with extraterrestrials to explain the wonders of the ancient world and the remarkable agreement among ancient texts in speaking of visitations by 'the gods' should be preferred to the multitude of separate and ad hoc explanations others have offered. If mainstream science were not so preoccupied with avoiding extraordinary hypotheses, it would surely be agreed by most parties that the evidence, severely lacking though it is, mildly favors the extraterrestrial visitation hypothesis over most others. However, it cannot be argued that the evidence is anything approaching compelling, especially since it is all indirect (*i.e.,* no definite extraterrestrial artifacts have been found)."

Let me be clear that I am not here advocating the reality of extraterrestrials or alien intervention in human affairs, either in the present or distant past. However, there is nothing unscientific *per se* about discussing such possibilities, and indeed simple contact with extraterrestrials need not break any generally accepted laws of nature, such as the law of gravitational attraction between objects with mass. Aliens, for all we know, might play by the same laws of physics as we do. There are other subjects that, arguably, go beyond the known laws of nature, at least as generally understood today. Such subjects are therefore variously referred to as para- this or para- that (paranormal, parascience, paraphysics, parapsychology) or relegated to the preternatural or supernatural (I consider them all "natural" in the sense that we may not yet understand all the truths of nature). Just like possible alien contact, these para-subjects are generally taboo among orthodox scientists. A good case in point of such a taboo subject, as already mentioned above, is the possibility of telepathic communication between individuals.

There is plenty of solid evidence for telepathy (direct mind-to-mind communication), both experimental and anecdotal, and related paranormal and parapsychological phenomena; yet when it comes to serious discussion of these subjects, most academics dismiss them out of hand. Worse still, many academics (most of whom have no firsthand knowledge of the field and are not aware of the serious research in parapsychology) have a strong emotional aversion to the topic. These feelings are all too often transferred to the paranormal researcher, and anyone showing an interest in the subject may find himself or herself ostracized and marginalized, looked down upon and made fun of, and dismissed without a fair hearing. As philosopher and parapsychologist Dr. Stephen E. Braude (professor of philosophy at the University of Maryland, Baltimore County) has written, "it still amazes me that when I so much as raise the subject of parapsychology to my academic colleagues, I often find nothing but stiff body language, sarcasm, and (perhaps most surprising of all) sometimes even *outrage* [italics in the original]. Not exactly the way you'd expect truth-seekers to respond to serious and thoughtful empirical and philosophical investigation" (p. xvi of Braude's book *The Gold Leaf Lady and Other Parapsychological Investigations*, 2007). I have had the same types of experiences.

Long ago I decided to join the genuine truth-seekers. I do my best to follow this sometimes lonely path, no matter how difficult the journey and despite the personal consequences. It is now too late to turn back. I am at peace with my decision.

This article first appeared in *Atlantis Rising* #80 (March/April 2010).

30

WHY CAN'T SCIENCE SEE THE LIGHT?

*Evidence Aside, There May Be
Deeper Forces at Work Here*

BY MICHAEL E. TYMN

In an early review of Dr. Raymond Moody's 1975 best-selling book, *Life After Life*, the late Dr. Elisabeth Kübler-Ross wrote, "It is research like Dr. Moody presents in his book that will enlighten many and will confirm what we have been taught for two thousand years—that there is life after death." And, at *Amazon.com*, the product description of this still-popular book, which has sold over 13 million copies, reads, "the extraordinary stories presented here provide evidence that there is life after physical death."

Moody's groundbreaking book created a new area of science called "near-death studies" and a number of other scientists added to Moody's research of the phenomenon that came to be known as the "near-death experience," or more simply as the NDE. Generally, there are six characteristic associated with the NDE:

1. Seeing things from outside the body as in observing one's surgical operations from above or viewing an accident scene from outside the accident.
2. A feeling that one is in a tunnel and that he or she is proceeding through that tunnel toward a light at the end of the tunnel.
3. Being greeted by deceased relative or friends who act as a guide, by an angel, or by a Being of Light, and then receiving some kind of orientation relative to the person's situation.
4. A life review in which the person sees every instant or highlights of her or his life flash in front of her/him.
5. Being told by the Being of Light, the "angel," guide or relative that he/she must return to the body, then usually protesting it.
6. A complete transformation in the person's outlook, generally moving from a materialistic outlook to a spiritual one.

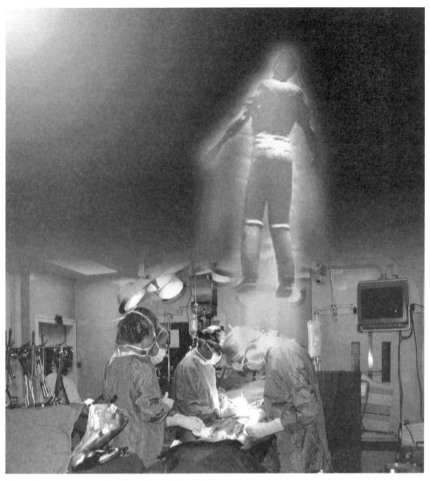

An artist's concept of a Near-Death Experience

Rarely did the researchers find any one person who experienced all of the characteristics, but there were enough reports of each one that they could recognize a definite pattern.

The NDE, *per se*, falls short of proving life after death. What it does is offer evidence that we do in fact, as St. Paul told us, have two bodies—a physical one and a spiritual one, the spiritual body separating from the physical body at the time of death. In effect, the NDE is an out-of-body experience (OBE). Many people have reported having OBEs without having suffered the physical trauma, such as a serious accident, often associated with NDEs. And while OBEs do not usually produce the tunnel effect, the life review, and the other end-of-life characteristics associated with the NDE, those people who have experienced an OBE, what some call "astral travel," report leaving their physical bodies, "seeing" with non-physical eyes, and visiting other realms of existence. A number of experiencers have reported seeing a cord connecting the two bodies. This is apparently what the Bible refers to as the "silver cord": "Remember him—before the silver cord is severed, or the golden bowl is broken; before the pitcher is shattered at the spring, or the wheel broken at the well, and the dust returns to the ground it came from, and the spirit returns to God who gave it" (Ecclesiastes 12:6-7).

It is believed to be the severance of this cord, the etheric counterpart of the umbilical cord, that results in actual physical death. Thus, the NDEr who returns to physical life after being out of body has not had the cord severed.

The early NDE research gave hope to many people who needed more than the blind faith offered by religion that consciousness lives on after physical death, or, to put it another way, that we are not all marching toward the abyss of nothingness or total extinction. It restored the meaning to life that science had taken away. Moreover, the lessons coming from the NDE, especially the life review, provided a more intelligent and just meaning than that offered by orthodox religion, suggesting that we judge ourselves and take a station in the next life based upon the spiritual body built here. But mainstream science wanted nothing to do with the resurrection of such superstitious thinking. It rejected, refuted, repudiated, and resisted the research, claiming that science had already cleansed the world of such infantile ideas.

Chief among the arguments advanced by the scientific fundamentalists is the oxygen deprivation theory. In the January 29, 2007 issue of *Time*, Steven Pinker, a Harvard psychology professor, proclaimed that the NDE is "not the eyewitness report of a soul parting company from the body but symptoms of oxygen starvation in the eyes and brain." However, Pinker did not explain how or why it is that brains are programmed to have such common and unusual hallucinations. One would think that the hallucinations brought on by oxygen starvation would be as diverse as dreams or hallucinations triggered by drugs.

Somewhat related to the oxygen deprivation theory is the dying brain theory, which holds that the tunnel effect is caused by increased levels of carbon dioxide in the blood or by an otherwise collapsing brain.

Skeptical researchers have also suggested that NDE "hallucinations" are caused by anesthesia, medication, or drugs, by mental instability, by religious expectations, by cultural expectations, or by overhearing medical personnel as the person is going in and out of consciousness. Moreover, the whole NDE phenomenon has been publicized enough that it is difficult to know now if someone reporting such an experience has been preconditioned to imagine it.

The spiritual camp of the NDE has offered the "Pam Reynolds case" as convincing evidence. During August 1991, Reynolds (a pseudonym to protect patient privacy) was operated on for a giant basilar artery aneurysm. Her body temperature was lowered to 60 degrees, her brain waves flattened, her heart stopped, her breathing stopped, and the blood drained from her. By medical standards, she was "dead." And yet, she later recalled watching parts of the surgery from above. She recalled seeing a particular kind of surgical instrument and hearing a comment that certain vessels were too small to handle the flow of blood. She further remembered being met by some deceased relatives after going down a dark shaft. An uncle took her back through the tunnel as it was not yet her time to cross over. However, the skeptics argue that she must have been hallucinating before or after the part of the surgery during which she was clinically "dead." As for seeing the surgical instrument (she had surgical patches over her eyes) she may have noticed it before the procedure started or have seen a similar one on a television program involving a surgical procedure on the brain and that picture was buried in her subconscious. The comment about her blood vessels may have been overheard before she was clinically "dead," even though she was under anesthesia. The spiritual camp counters with the contention that one does not have to be clinically dead to have an out-of-body experience, but there are enough question marks connected with the case that it is not as convincing now as originally thought.

Another convincing case offered by the spiritual camp involved a hospital patient reporting that she left her body during a 1977 surgery and soared above the hospital. She remembered seeing a tennis shoe on a third-floor ledge. She described it as dark blue, well worn, and scuffed on the left side where the little toe would go and the shoelace was caught under the heel. An investigator located the shoe and found it just as described by the patient. The investigator claimed that the shoe could not have been seen from where the patient entered the hospital or from any other location in the hospital except for the window right above the ledge, where the patient had never been. However, 17 years later, some skeptical researchers determined the exact spot where the shoe was found, placed a test shoe on the ledge, and went outside to the hospital emergency entrance to determine if they could see it. They reported having no difficulty seeing the shoe, although they apparently made no mention as to whether they could see enough detail to include the fact that it was a left foot shoe, blue in color, worn on the left side, and with the shoelace tucked under the heel. Perhaps the patient had a pair of binoculars as she was wheeled in after suffering a heart attack. Then again, maybe the investigator exaggerated the story. Another "could have."

Perhaps even more convincing that the "Pam Reynolds" or the "shoe on a ledge" case are those of people blind from birth being able to "see" physical objects during a NDE. In their 1999 book, *Mindsight*, researchers Kenneth Ring and Sharon Cooper documented 31 cases of blind people having NDEs, 14 of them having been blind from birth. However, the skeptics point out that the blind "experiencers" were found only after a notice was placed in various publications for blind organizations asking for respondents. Thus, the theory is that they had heard about such experiences and had unconsciously generated a fantasy that conformed to the stories they had heard.

And so it goes with every NDE story. There is always a "could-a," "would-a," "should-a" or "might-a" connected with it, and, of course, there is no way of replicating the experience, a key element in scientific validation. No doubt most of the researchers coming up with theories to counter the spiritual implications of the NDE are sincere and honest scientists who are in search of the truth, but the debunkers—often closed-minded journalists and bloggers pretending to be skeptics—make the most of the ammunition they receive to completely muddy up the waters and leave the public completely befuddled.

Indeed, even Dr. Moody seems uncertain these days. In his 1988 book, *The Light Beyond*, he wrote, "In the absence of firm scientific proof, people frequently ask me what I believe: Are NDEs evidence of life after life? My answer is 'Yes'."

Here, Moody was clearly making the distinction between proof and evidence. Evidence adds up to proof, but little, if anything, in science is proved with absolute certainty. Even biological evolution, clearly accepted by mainstream science, is not proved with absolute certainty. Put to the courts, it might meet the "beyond a reasonable doubt" standard of criminal law and would in all probability meet the "preponderance of evidence" standard of civil law, but to any discerning, open-minded person it is not proved with absolute certainty.

In the foreword of *Induced After-Death Communication* (2005), book, Moody goes even further, stating that "Life after death is not yet a scientific issue," and then saying "it is too early for science to tackle the biggest of the big questions of existence and humankind's ultimate mystery." He also says that it is to the author's credit that he does not present his work as scientific "evidence" of life after death.

Raymond Moody

Thus, Moody, at one point, seems to have accepted life after death with reasonable certainty, but in 2005 he didn't think science was ready to even tackle the subject.

Several other prominent researchers who once appeared to have accepted the NDE as evidence of life after death have taken a step back, probably from peer pressure, saying their continuing interest in the NDE has nothing to do with life after death but with enriching this lifetime.

So what is the person on the street—the one who was able to see a meaning in life by the early NDE research—to make of all this conflict and controversy? As Dr. Neal Grossman, a professor of philosophy at the University of Illinois at Chicago, related to me in an interview last year, "the evidence for an afterlife is sufficiently strong and compelling that an unbiased person ought to conclude that materialism is a false theory." Grossman believes the evidence is largely ignored because our current culture would not survive if the implications of the research were taken seriously, primarily because of the ego-driven materialism that exists in the world today.

"Academics and scientists matriculate in an environment . . . or paradigm, if you will . . . that ridicules the concept of an afterlife," Grossman added. "So it is psychologically difficult for them to take seriously the idea that there could be hard evidence for something they have been ridiculing all their professional lives. Using myself as an example, in the 25 years or so that I've been looking into these matters, not once has a colleague ever asked me why I am interested in it and take it seriously. On the contrary, they take my interest in these matters as evidence that I've 'lost it' or 'gone off the deep end'."

Grossman agrees with Dr. Kenneth Ring, the NDE researcher earlier, that the NDE is, in a way, subversive to the "American Dream," since the primary lesson of the NDE is that we are here to seek knowledge and to grow in our ability to give and receive love. This objective conflicts with the goals of fame, riches, and hedonistic pleasures prevalent today.

I recently discussed the resistance of academia, where most NDE research is funded, to survival evidence, including mediumship and reincarnation, with Dr. Stafford Betty, professor of religious studies at California State University, Bakersfield, another maverick educator. His observations have been much the same as Grossman's. "My atheistic friends resist even the slightest whiff of an argument for an afterlife," Betty told me. "I have not seen more closed minds. Why is this? Why would anyone resist such good news—the kind of news strongly supported by serious, in-depth research on the NDE, for example? I think I know. It is not so much that my hard-bitten friends hate the thought of living beyond death; what they hate is religion. And they associate religion with the afterlife. It doesn't matter how hard you try to convince them that the contemporary case for afterlife is not based on sacred texts, but on empirical studies conducted by well-credentialed social scientists or doctors. It doesn't matter. Their minds are set. Also, the older generation (in their seventies and eighties) grew up hearing that the only things that were real were material. Changing their minds on that score would threaten their very identity. So they bravely move toward death, trying not to think about it, and gritting their teeth when they have to. I think the young are less invested in metaphysical materialism than the elderly. Their minds are slightly more open, if only because of the barrage of Hollywood films set in an afterlife."

Concomitant with the issue of life after death is that of the meaning of this life. Dr. Dennis Ford deals with the question extensively in his 2007 book, *The Search for Meaning: A Short History*. He points out that science is driven by a control motive that leads to empiricism, which in turn leads to naturalism. He observes, "The awareness that science fosters is ultimately alienating, to the extent that it reduces the colorful world we had thought ourselves to be living in to a mechanistic world of cold, hard, indifferent facts."

In effect, science—the fundamentalist variety that opposes NDE research—gives us a meaningless and soulless world, one in which we can function only if we don't look for meaning and are successful in repressing the idea of death. Until we can overcome fundamentalism in science, as well as fundamentalism in religion, we appear destined to live in a world of moral decadence, egocentricity, intolerance, hatred, hypocrisy, disorder, flux, strife, chaos, and fear.

This article first appeared in *Atlantis Rising* #70 (July/August 2008).

31

BIG SCIENCE ON TRIAL

The News Has Not Been Good Lately for the World's Research Establishment

BY MARTIN RUGGLES

Late in November of 2009, a hacker broke through the computer security system of the Climate Research Unit (CRU) at the University of East Anglia in Norwich, England, and copied over 3,000 pages of email and computer code, which were shortly disseminated across the Internet. Revealed in the documents was what climate warming skeptics soon trumpeted as a shocking picture of scientific fraud and deceit of enormous significance. The ensuing internet/science tsunami was, and continues to be, of near biblical proportions. And while global warming alarmists have attempted to downplay the incident, it has been dubbed by others as "climategate," and/or the "CRU-tape letters." Many believe that the curiously unsuccessful outcome to the December 2009 Copenhagen Climate Summit could have been the scandal's first real feedback.

As of this writing, the identity of the hacker remains a mystery, but suspicion points to an inside job. If it is indeed the work of some conscious-stricken employee within the CRU, he or she may be protected from prosecution by Britain's whistleblower laws.

The CRU has become, along with NASA, one of the most influential organizations in the ongoing debate over man-made global warming. Its studies and numbers provide the primary basis for most of the pronouncements of the United Nations Intergovernmental Panel on Climate Change (IPCC) which is currently leading the charge for sweeping changes to the economies of the world, all aimed at countering the perceived threat from so-called anthropocentric global warming.

In the hacked files is advice on how the scientists can avoid complying with Freedom of Information Act (FOIA) requirements for release of temperature data supporting their conclusions (Britain's FOIA—more stringent than America's—makes it a crime to deny a legitimate request for the data underlying a decision from a government funded agency). Included are discussions of how to manipulate the peer review process to exclude skeptics. There is also the admission of "a travesty," the failure of CRU's computer models to account for an apparent worldwide decline in temperatures, which, since 1998, has inconveniently defied all predictions of the climate change lobby.

While most of the focus, as of this writing, has been on the emails, more potentially incriminating are other elements now slowly coming to light. Computer code included with the stolen documents is revealing many of the underlying assumptions used to construct the all-important models that provide the basis for alarm bells spurring the warming debate. While the revelations may not directly disprove the hypothesis of man-made global warming, they certainly cast considerable doubt on the integrity of the science involved, including the iconic and widely publicized "hockey stick" graph, created by world-famed climatologist Michael Mann, a Penn State University professor, which purports to show a steep and unprecedented rise in world temperatures. (Mann is one of the authorities whose motives have been thrown into sharp question by the CRU exposures).

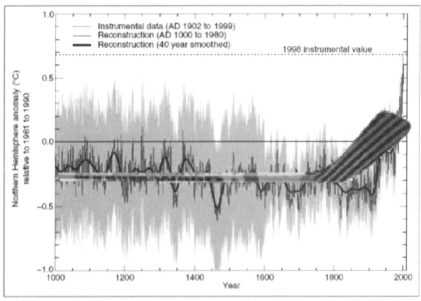

Figure 5: Millennial Northern Hemisphere (NH) temperature reconstruction (blue – tree rings, corals, ice cores, and historical records) and instrumental data (red) from AD 1000 to 1999. Smoother version of NH series (black), and two standard error limits (gray shaded) are shown. [Based on Figure 2.20]

The "hockey stick" of global warming

Within days of the revelations, CRU director Phil Jones had stepped down to make way for a University of East Anglia investigation of professional misconduct, but the process will certainly not end there. After all, vast sums of money are at stake, if not the very survival of many of the world's largest economies. And while the draconian measures that have been proposed might be worthwhile to help stave off a looming planetary eco-catastrophe, they can hardly be justified if the underlying science itself is in doubt. Major investigations—including, hopefully, independent ones—of the central arguments for and against man-made global warming are now being demanded.

The details of the entire affair are widely available on the Internet, and it seems only a matter of time until the story becomes common knowledge (it may even be reported on the—thus far reluctant—major TV news networks). Already the reaction in print media and the Internet blogosphere is scathing. *The Atlantic Monthly*'s widely respected blogger Clive Crook— though his initial writing was that nothing in the CRU dump surprised him much—soon changed his tune. Within days he was writing, "The closed-mindedness of these supposed men of science, their willingness to go to any lengths to defend a preconceived message, is surprising even to me. The stink of intellectual corruption is overpowering."

British *Guardian* columnist George Monbiot, who had previously been one of the most outspoken defenders of the warming hypothesis, wrote on November 23, "It's no use pretending that this isn't a major blow. The emails . . . could scarcely be more damaging. . . . I'm dismayed and deeply shaken by them. . . . I was too trusting of some of those who provided the evidence I championed. I would have been a better journalist if I had investigated their claims more closely."

ALTERNATIVE SCIENCE

For those in the alternative science community, the implications of Climategate are even more profound. One of the most troubling aspects of the case has to do with the peer review system itself, on which the big science establishment bases its legitimacy.

In theory the idea sounds fine: scientists look at a particular phenomenon, come up with some kind of explanation (hopefully a convincing one), do experiments to test their hypothesis, and then submit to other scientists (peers) to see if they can obtain the same results. If the hypothesis holds up, everything is published and then other scientists get to take a crack at the idea. To keep favoritism and politics out of it, the process is supposed to be anonymous so that no one need fear retribution or expect any particular reward. That is the way the system is supposed work, but does it?

As columnist Mark Steyn wrote for *National Review* online, "The trouble with outsourcing your marbles to the peer-reviewed set is that, if you take away one single thing from the leaked (CRU) documents, it's that the global warm-mongers have wholly corrupted the 'peer-review' process."

The "peer review process," however, was in trouble long before Climategate.

When Richard Sternberg, editor of the scientific journal *Proceedings of the Biological Society of Washington*, decided in 2004 to publish a paper making the case for "Intelligent Design" he had no idea what he was in for. Despite scrupulous attention to correct peer review procedures, Sternberg, who holds two Ph.D.'s in biology, was accused of being a shoddy scientist and a Bible thumper and of taking money under the table from fundamentalists. "I was basically run out of here," he recalls. The U.S. Office of Special Counsel, an independent agency whose job it is to protect federal officials from reprisals, found that senior scientists with the Smithsonian's National Museum of Natural History did indeed retaliate against Sternberg for running the article.

According to the *Washington Post*, the Special Counsel investigators examined email traffic from the scientists and noted that "retaliation came in many forms . . . misinformation was disseminated through the Smithsonian Institution and to outside sources. The allegations against you were later determined to be false." James McVay, the principal legal adviser in the Office of Special Counsel, wrote to Sternberg, "The rumor mill became so infected that one of your colleagues had to circulate [your résumé] simply to dispel the rumor that you were not a scientist."

The Sternberg controversy publicly exposed a common tactic of the mainstream science camp (epitomized by organizations like Csicop)—the use of *ad hominem* attacks have nothing to do with the merits of the arguments presented. Frequently heard is the accusation that Intelligent Design advocates are closet creationists masquerading as scientists.

A similar tactic used by global warming activists is to call those who question the validity of their arguments "deniers," thus equating them with holocaust "deniers." One use of the word involves an unproven theory

RICHARD STERNBERG, PH.D
FEDERAL SCIENTIST

Richard Sternberg on camera, and under attack.

and the other, a thoroughly documented historical event (the murder of 6 million Jews in WWII), but the distinction gets lost in the fray.

The usual claim made by the establishment in such disputes is that the matter is already settled, which is another way of saying, "don't argue with us we know best." In the global warming debate, such is emphatically not the case. Richard S. Lindzen, professor of meteorology (climate science) at Massachusetts Institute of Technology, for one, says in a November 30 piece for the *Wall Street Journal*, "climate science isn't settled. Confident predictions of catastrophe are unwarranted." Even the BBC recently expressed doubt over whether the facts can support the main contentions of the global warming alarmists. Is the sunspot cycle, for example, the real source of much of the warming we might have experienced? Such authoritative views have done little, however, to stem the widespread clamor that the debate is over, global warming is accelerating, human activity is the primary cause, and any questioning of the merits of that claim is at the planet's peril.

Over the last few years, *Atlantis Rising* has championed any number of unpopular causes in which, it was clear, that mainstream science had refused to play fair. Perhaps the best example is "cold fusion" which, since 1989 when it was originally unveiled by Stanley Pons and Martin Fleichmann at the University of Utah, has been scorned by the establishment as junk science. The two pioneer scientists, though, have now been clearly vindicated.

In March of 2009, almost exactly 20 years after the original press conference, the American Chemical Society, a leader in mainstream science's peer review process, announced to the world that researchers are now reporting "compelling new scientific evidence for the existence of low energy nuclear reactions (LENR)," the process once called "cold fusion." A newly released study from the U.S. Navy's Space and Naval Warfare

Systems Center (SPAWAR) in San Diego, CA, now for the first time finds the production of "highly energetic neutrons" from a LENR device. Such neutrons are considered to be the sure sign of a nuclear fusion reaction.

Another area where *Atlantis Rising* has questioned the conventional scientific consensus is over whether advanced civilization on Earth could have existed before the last ice age, something that orthodox archaeology hotly deputes and keeps out of its debates. But recent dramatic discoveries at Göbekli Tepe in Turkey are now widely acknowledged to be a "challenge to conventional history," and that characterization could well prove to be a major understatement.

Carbon dated at twelve thousand years old, Göbekli Tepe offers incontrovertible evidence for advanced human activity at a time when our ancestors are said to have been still at the hunter-gatherer stage—thousands of years earlier than we have been told was possible.

In the mid 1990s, when maverick Egyptologist John Anthony West and Boston University Geologist Dr. Robert Schoch announced that water weathering proved the Great Sphinx of Egypt was thousands of years older than traditionally believed, they were greeted with derision from conventional Egyptologists. And despite evidence widely accepted by professional geologists, the orthodox archaeologists have continued to deny the possibility of the Sphinx's greater antiquity.

Among the many other under-reported stories covered in these pages has been the work of Rupert Sheldrake, whose book, *A New Science of Life* (1981), containing his theory of morphic resonance, was declared by John Maddox, editor of the prestigious peer reviewed journal *Nature*, to be a book "that should be burned." Now Phillip Stevens, a Masters candidate at London's Imperial College, has based his dissertation on Sheldrake's treatment at the hands of the science establishment.

Rupert Sheldrake

Phillips, though personally skeptical of Sheldrake's theories, found, to his surprise, that despite an unblemished academic record and a research fellowship at the Royal Society, Sheldrake was unfairly subjected to public scorn from colleagues for publishing his theory. Phillips also found that skeptics like Dr. Richard Wiseman had failed to use the normal scientific procedures that scientists usually follow when collaborating and reporting their results. Wiseman had actually repeated many of Sheldrake's experimental results, a fact which was conveniently omitted in his published condemnation of Sheldrake's work.

Similarly hostile receptions have greeted the work of Sam Parnia on near-death experience, Dean Radin on psi phenomena, and others.

But so much for the way big science expresses its disapproval. How is it doing when it comes to approval? Not very well there either, it seems.

Take the case of Jan Hendrik Schön, a young German scientist whose star, reportedly, had already risen. After being credited with a number of amazing discoveries—including plastic transistors, new superconductors, microscopic molecular switches, and more—the 32-year-old researcher at Bell Labs was the toast of big science around the world and considered one of the hottest researchers on the planet. But he was, it turns out, a fake. His peers and the scientific journals (including *Science*) who published his bogus work had been completely fooled.

The Schön case, we learn though, is not that unusual. South Korean cloning pioneer Hwang Woo-Suk, for example, recently made international headlines when it was discovered that he was faking data. Now, according to the journal *Public Library of Science*, a review of 21 scientific misconduct surveys of the period from 1986 to 2005, more than two-thirds of researchers said they knew of colleagues who had committed "questionable" practices and one in seven said that included inventing findings. Of course, very few scientists, just two percent, admitted to having faked results themselves. The most common area of fraud appears to be in medical research, which is seen as evidence for the effect of commercial pressure.

It is not, however, just the gross violations such as falsification, plagiarism, and fabrication that are of concern. According to a study authored by Raymond De Vries, an associate professor of medical education and a member of the Bioethics Program at the University of Michigan in Ann Arbor, scientific misbehavior seems to be endemic today. The study was published in April 2009 in the premier issue of the *Journal of Empirical Research on Human Research Ethics.*

De Vries says that intense competition between scientists these days is causing them to worry about things they shouldn't be thinking about, like how their data will be interpreted, not just its integrity. In other words, they are thinking about whether their research will lead to conclusions their peers might not like. Other issues also mentioned by the study include the increasing number of rules that scientists are supposed to follow, and questions of how to deal with the growing competition for the rewards in a shrinking pie.

The study collected its data primarily from six focus groups with a total of 51 researchers gathered from the top U.S. research universities. The groups were asked to discuss misconduct that the participants had either practiced or witnessed. "After the focus groups," said De Vries, "we felt like we had been at a confessional. We didn't intend this, but the focus groups became a place where people could unburden themselves."

From the intelligent design of Richard Sternberg, to the cold fusion of Pons and Fleischmann, from West's and Schoch's greater antiquity of the Sphinx to the morphic resonance of Rupert Sheldrake, the same conflict, it seems, plays out over and over in scientific debate. Witness the heliocentric solar system of Galileo or the catastrophism of Immanuel Velikovsky. Some, like writer Thomas Kuhn (*The Structure of Scientific Revolutions*, 1962), have perceived a recurring pattern in which the ideas that are unthinkable to one generation become the orthodoxy of the next.

If, however, we want to be free right now from the tyranny that certain elites would seek to impose on the public mind, we will have to learn to do our own thinking. The first step in that process could very well be to remember that many who claim to know what they are talking about may, in fact, only *believe*. And although they may feel quite passionate on the matter, the rest of us will need to hear something much better than their preachments before converting to their faith.

In the trial of the soul described in the afterworld of the ancient Egyptians, the heart of the deceased—symbolic of his virtue, moral character, and earthly deeds—was laid on a set of scales before Osiris and weighed against a single feather representing *maat*, the divine law. If the scales balanced, the deceased was allowed to pass into heaven.

Will today's big science make the cut? You be the judge.

This article first appeared in *Atlantis Rising* #80 (March/April 2010).

Contributing authors

PETER BROS (deceased 2006) had long challenged the current, splintered concepts of empirical science and spent his life studying the nature of physical reality and humanity's place in the universe. He is the author of the 9 volume *Copernican Series* and *Let's Talk Flying Saucers: How Crackpot Ideas Are Blinding Us to Reality and Leading Us to Extinction*.

JOHN CHAMBERS is the critically acclaimed author of *Conversations with Eternity: The Forgotten Masterpiece of Victor Hugo* and *The Secret Life of Genius: How 24 Great Men and Women Were Touched by Spiritual Worlds*. He lives in Redding, California. (*newpara.com/johnchambers.htm*)

DAVID HATCHER CHILDRESS, known to his many fans as the real-life Indiana Jones, is author or coauthor of over 20 books. He has appeared on Fox-TV's *Sightings and Encounters*, two NBC-TV specials, *The Conspiracy Zone*, and segments for the Discovery Channel, A&E, The Sci-Fi Channel, The Travel Channel and others. (*adventuresunlimitedpress.com*)

WILLIAM HENRY is an author, investigative mythologist, regular guest presenter on *Ancient Aliens*, and star of Arcanum TV. He is the author of *The Secret of Sion, Mary Magdalene the Illuminator: The Woman Who Enlightened Christ, Cloak of the Illuminati*, among many others.(*williamhenry.net*)

FRANK JOSEPH is a leading scholar on ancient mysteries, and the editor-in-chief of *Ancient American* magazine. He is the author of many books, including *Atlantis and 2012, The Destruction of Atlantis, The Lost Civilization of Lemuria, Survivors of Atlantis*, and *The Lost Treasure of King Juba*. He lives in Minnesota. (*ancientamerican.com*)

LEN KASTEN has written numerous articles for *Atlantis Rising*. While in the Air Force, Kasten experienced a UFO encounter that transformed his life. Since then, he has been deeply involved in UFO research, life after death, sacred geometry, Atlantis, and related subjects. He brings his extensive metaphysical background to he writing of *The Secret History of Extraterrestrials*, which provides the reader with a depth of understanding of UFO phenomena not otherwise readily available. (*et-secrethistory.com*)

JOHN KETTLER is a former military aerospace intelligence analyst with a life-long interest in the "black world" of covert and special ops, government secrets and coverups, world-wide conspiracies, UFOs, ETs, secret technology and much more. He spent years working on defense projects for Hughes Aircraft and Rockwell. Kettler was a frequent contributor to *Atlantis Rising* magazine for more than a decade. (*johnkettler.com*)

GLENN KREISBERG, editor of the "Author of the Month" page at *GrahamHancock.com,* is a professional radio frequency spectrum engineer, writer, researcher, and licensed outdoor guide and currently serves as the vice president of the New England Antiquities Research Association. The author of numerous articles and papers, including *Lithic Mysteries of the Northeast*, he is the founder and editor of the alternative science and history website *ASHnews.org.*

JOSEPH ROBERT JOCHMANS (deceased 2013) was an American researcher with a special interest in ancient mysteries. Jochmans is credited as the researcher for Rene Noorbergen's 1977 book *Secrets of the Lost Races*, as well as a number of other books by Noorbergen. Jochmans was a frequent contributor to *Atlantis Rising Maginine,* with a particular interest and focus on the subject of Atlantis.

SUSAN B. MARTINEZ, is a writer, linguist, teacher, paranormal researcher, and recognized authority on the Oahspe Bible with a doctorate in anthropology from Columbia University. The author of *The Psychic Life of Abraham Lincoln* and *The Mysterious Origins of Hybrid Man*, she is the book review editor at the *Journal of Spirituality and Paranormal Studies.* (*earthvortex.com*)

LARRY BRIAN RADKA served in the Army Security Agency for four years and then in the Air Force Communication Service for another four years. He has gained extensive training and experience in electronics, and worked for thirty years in radio and television as a broadcast engineer. He retired in

2005. He is author of *The Electric Mirror on the Pharos Lighthouse and Other Ancient Lighting*, and *Historical Evidence for Unicorns*.

ROBERT M. SCHOCH, a full-time faculty member at Boston University, earned his Ph.D. in geology and geophysics at Yale University. He is best known for his re-dating of the Great Sphinx of Egypt featured in the Emmy-winning NBC production *The Mystery of the Sphinx*. He is a frequent guest on many top-rated talk shows. His latest book is *The Parapsychology Revolution*. (*robertschoch.com*)

LAIRD SCRANTON is an independent researcher of ancient cosmology and language. His studies in comparative cosmology have served help synchronize aspects of ancient African, Egyptian, Vedic, Chinese, Polynesian and other world cosmologies, and have led to an alternate approach to reading Egyptian hieroglyphic words. He became interested in Dogon mythology and symbolism in the early 1990s. He has studied ancient myth, language, and cosmology since 1997 and has been a lecturer at Colgate University. His writings include books and articles published or taught by Colgate University, Temple University, and the University of Chicago. (*lairdscranton.com*)

MARC J. SEIFER, PH.D. is the author of *Wizard: The Life & Times of Nikola Tesla* (Citadel Press) and *Transcending the Speed of Light, Consciousness, Quantum Physics and the 5th Dimension* (Inner Traditions). Dr. Seifer's wide ranging and meticulously researched published articles, novels and books span subjects ranging from metaphysics, behavior analysis to science fiction. Besides his authoring, he is a forensic expert and published master of handwriting analysis. (*marcseifer.com*)

ZECHARIA SITCHIN (deceased 2010) was one of the few scholars able to read and interpret ancient Sumerian and Akkadian clay tablets, Zecharia based his bestselling *The 12th Planet* on texts from the ancient civilizations of the Near East. Drawing both widespread interest and criticism, his controversial theories on the Anunnaki origins of humanity have been translated into more than 25 languages and featured on radio and television programs around the world. His last book, *There Were Giants Upon the Earth*, was published in 2010. (*sitchin.com*)

JERRY E. SMITH (deceased 2010) had a life-long interest in technology and its impact on society. After the publication in 1998 of *HAARP: The Ultimate Weapon of the Conspiracy* by Adventures Unlimited Press, Smith had an exhausting schedule, appearing regularly on TV and radio, as well as speaking at seminars and conferences across the US and around the world. His many years of political and environmental activism and research resulted in the publication of scores of news stories and opinion pieces, and his work appeared in such national publications as *Fate Magazine* and *Paranoia: The Conspiracy Reader*. (jerryesmith.com)

STEVEN SORA lives on Long Island. In 1999, he published the widely read and frequently quoted *Lost Treasure of the Knights Templar*. He is the author of many books dealing with esoteric history and over 100 articles. He is a frequent guest in documentaries dealing with ancient mysteries and lost history.

WILLIAM ("BEN") STOECKER, former Air Force Intelligence Officer, was driven to seek the truth through a lifetime of thought and study. As a result, he can effectively challenge orthodoxy in many fields, including science, history, astronomy and more. He is author of *The Atlantis Conspiracy*. His articles appear regularly on *UnexplainedMysteries.com*.

MICHAEL E. TYMN, a resident of Hawaii, is vice-president of the Academy of Spirituality and Paranormal Studies, Inc., and is editor of the Academy's quarterly magazine, *The Searchlight*. His articles on paranormal subjects have appeared in many publications and he is widely read and referenced on these topics. He is the author of *The Afterlife Revealed*, *The Articulate Dead*, and *Running on Third Wind*. (whitecrowbooks.com/michaeltymn)

JEFF VOLK is a poet, producer, and publisher. In 2001, he reissued Hans Jenny's ground-breaking Cymatics books. He produced a series of videos on Cymatics and recently re-released Dr. Jenny's original films on DVD. His video, *Of Sound Mind and Body: Music and Vibrational Healing*, won the Hartley Film Award. In 2006, he published the English language edition of *Water Sound Images* by Alexander Lauterwasser.

About the Editor

J. DOUGLAS KENYON is the editor and publisher of *Atlantis Rising* magazine. He is also the editor of *Paradigm Busters*, *Forgotten Origins*, *Missing Connections*, *Secret Knowledge*, *Forbidden History*, *Forbidden Science*, and *Forbidden Religion*. (*atlantisrising.com*)